Philadelphia's Wissahickon Valley 1620-2020

METROPOLITAN
paradise
THE STRUGGLE FOR NATURE IN THE CITY

Volume 2 | Park

Philadelphia's Wissahickon Valley 1620-2020

METROPOLITAN paradise

THE STRUGGLE FOR NATURE IN THE CITY

Volume 2 | Park

David Contosta | Carol Franklin

SAINT JOSEPH'S UNIVERSITY PRESS

PHILADELPHIA

This publication was supported by the following foundations:

Drumcliff Foundation

Foundation for Landscape Studies, New York: David R. Coffin Publication Grant

Levittees Foundation

Morris Arboretum of the University of Pennsylvania

Preservation Alliance for Greater Philadelphia

Whitemarsh Foundation

Library of Congress Cataloging-in-Publication Data

Contosta, David R.

Philadelphia's Wissahickon Valley, 1620-2020: metropolitan paradise, the struggle for nature in the city / David Contosta, Carol Franklin. – 1st ed.

    p. cm.

Includes bibliographical references and index.

ISBN 978-0-916101-66-4

1. Wissahickon Creek Valley (Pa.)–History. 2. Wissahickon Creek Valley (Pa.)–Historical geography.
3. Wissahickon Valley Park (Philadelphia, Pa.)–History. 4. Environmentalism–Pennsylvania–Philadelphia Region–History.
5. Environmental policy–Pennsylvania–Philadelphia Region–History. 6. Nature–Effect of human beings on–Pennsylvania–Philadelphia Region. I. Franklin, Carol, 1941- II. Title.

F157.W62C66 2010

974.8'11–dc22

2010024792

Cover photo, Volume 2: Wissahickon Day Parade. The parade, celebrating the banning of automobiles on "Forbidden Drive," was originally an all-equestrian event. Photograph by Carl Klein, c. 1940. Source: Chestnut Hill Historical Society

This volume was designed and typeset at Saint Joseph's University Press, Philadelphia.

Book design: Jonathan Dart and Kori Klyman

Slipcase and cover designs: Jonathan Dart

Image editing: James Brack and Patricia West and Hannah Coale

Index: Joseph Lea

Typeset in Optima, Stone Sans, and Skia

The paper meets the guidelines for permanence and durability of the
Committee on Production Guidelines for Book Longevity of the Council on Library Resources.

Printer: Courier-Kendallville, Kendallville Indiana

Published by
Saint Joseph's University Press
5600 City Avenue, Philadelphia, Pennsylvania 19131-1395
www.sju.edu/sjupress/

Saint Joseph's University Press is a member of the Association of Jesuit University Presses

Table of Contents

Part Two: Park

Metropolitan Paradise
Preface

Sacred to the Lenni-Lenape and to many early Europeans who settled in the area, the Wissahickon Valley has all the elements of "paradise" recognized in many cultures—the dramatic gorge with high cliffs, twisted rocks, dark hemlocks, sparkling water and the bountiful, rolling terrain directly to the north. Ironically, this paradise is part of a large, old North American city and its adjacent suburbs, and suffers from all the troubles of a modern urban area.

In this present era, we are seeing the explosion of cities and their metamorphosis into complex, densely packed, multi-dimensional regional organisms. With six billion people on the planet and a projected nine billion within 50 years, almost everyone will be living in a megalopolis. The 19th century division between nature and the city must be dissolved to make these new conurbations livable. Current scientific insights and technological advances can make a new fusion possible and bring natural systems back into the life of the city.

Philadelphia's Wissahickon Valley provides an unfolding narrative of this struggle to establish and maintain connected natural systems of adequate size, within a densely developed region. The preservation and restoration of this valley is offered as a model for metropolitan regions around the world. As Jaime Lerner, former mayor of the city of Curitiba in Brazil, has said, "The city is not the problem; the city is the solution."[1]

Because we believe, like Salman Rushdie, in the important payoffs of "mongrelism," the authors have combined insights from two different perspectives to create this book.[2] David is a cultural and intellectual historian, and Carol is a landscape architect with a foot in the camps of ecological design and ecological and cultural landscape restoration.

Both of us have a dogged and perverse devotion to Philadelphia, and like so many Philadelphians, we are hopelessly in love with Wissahickon Park and with the rural landscape of the middle valley above it. We have come to see this valley as a microcosm of changes in the American landscape over the past 400 years and believe that the lessons of its history, present treatment and creative future, are both universal and unique. This book is a journey into where we live locally, and by extension, into what we can do to resolve the crises of a natural world that is collapsing all around us.

Left Side
Suggesting that Philadelphia's rivers are vital to the life of the city, the Swann Memorial Fountain is the centerpiece of Logan Square on the Benjamin Franklin Parkway. The fountain looks both towards City Hall and the Philadelphia Museum of Art and to the beginning of the scenic drive along the Schuylkill River that leads to Wissahickon Park. The fountain was designed in 1924 by sculptor Alexander Stirling Calder and architect Wilson Eyre.

Adapting the tradition of "river god" sculpture, Calder created three large Native American figures to symbolize Philadelphia's major waterways: the Delaware River (a man), the Schuylkill River (a woman) and Wissahickon Creek (a girl).

Source: Photograph by Kori Klyman

Sustaining natural lands within the matrix of an increasingly pervasive urban landscape is crucial. These places are our "canary in the mine"—if they cannot succeed, all wildness is imperiled, impoverishing our lives and ultimately threatening our survival. If these wildlands are not connected systems, suffused throughout the fabric of our lives, they will not survive. There is a Quaker saying, "better to light a candle than to curse the darkness." This book is our personal candle in a remarkable and widespread effort to restore the Wissahickon Valley to some semblance of its former glory and to envision a future of bold, imaginative potentials.

How to Read this Book

In this book, the landscape of the Wissahickon Valley is viewed through many lenses—history, ecology, planning, architecture and landscape architecture. It is our hope that by intermingling these different areas of concern, until they fuse and create something new, like the flavors of separate ingredients in a stew, the reader will come away with a better appreciation of the complex and dynamic interaction between people and place.

This study of the Wissahickon Valley is undertaken in the tradition of two classic works: *The Making of the English Landscape* by W. G. Hoskins and *Design with Nature* by Ian L. McHarg. By examining changes in the English landscape over time, and the forces that shaped these changes at certain crucial periods, Hoskins pioneered the idea of the cultural landscape as an evolving entity. He demonstrated that landscapes are the product of the continuous laying down of later patterns of land use over earlier ones, with a surprising amount of the earlier fabric, still present and still germane. Following Hoskins example, each chapter concentrates on a significant period of transformation, highlighting key decisions, fulcrums of change and the physical patterns modified by these changes.[3]

Ian McHarg's *Design with Nature* laid the foundations for design decisions based on a scientific understanding of the natural and social processes that shaped, and continue to shape, each place. This understanding was to be rooted in the latest, best science from ecology to anthropology. Following the McHargian method, the Wissahickon Valley is analyzed and diagnosed. The constraints and opportunities are highlighted, and solutions are suggested that grow from its fundamental qualities. Out of the welter of the rich details of human interaction with the lower and middle valley, during so many generations, instructive patterns should emerge that can lead to better planning and policy decisions.[4]

One of the premises of this book is that complicated places are best understood by exploring the forces that shape them—natural, social, cultural and economic. Following Hoskins and McHarg, changes over time are presented as a series of layers. These overlays have often been compared to a "palimpsest"—sheepskin book pages from the Middle Ages that had been written on and then erased by scraping off the ink. The pages would then be reused, but the old texts were often still faintly visible. All landscapes are palimpsests, whether they are simply an accretion of geological strata and plant and animal life, or have had a long human history.

One of the often-overlooked forces that structure the landscape is human perception of the world (once called "worldviews," and now called "paradigms"). Preserved by a series of decisions, both intentional and accidental, the lower and middle Wissahickon Valley has been shaped and reshaped by the central paradigms of succeeding eras. Recognizing, analyzing and incorporating each accreted layer is the first step in creating solutions that grow out of the best of the past and build new value for a future that is increasingly fluid and refocused on new and different lifestyles.

This book has been written with several audiences in mind. The authors, who live in the valley and are very much part of its larger community, were torn between the desire to explore every detail of interest to local loyalists, and the hope that we will be generic enough to provide insights for other communities with parallel issues. To satisfy both these ends, the more esoteric details of this particular place—vegetation and wildlife, buildings and artifacts and individual movers and shakers—have often been separated from the main narrative and put on individual pages. Accordingly, it is not necessary to read this book straight through, and the reader should feel free to delve into it at any point, moving backwards and forwards to flesh out particular interests.

Wilderness—Park—Valley—Corridor

The Wissahickon Valley is the result of a unique blend of landscape, social and political realities, land management and lifestyle and the consequence of a number of very different proprietors over time. To reflect these proprietors, their choices and the impact of these choices on the landscape, this book is divided into four volumes: Wilderness—Park—Valley—Corridor.

Park

The second volume is called "Park." It concentrates on the creation and elaboration of preserved open space in the lower and middle valley, made possible by the industrial wealth of the region. Philadelphia was one of the first major cities in the United States to establish a municipal park system and the first city to build this system on an interconnected network of stream valleys. Philadelphia's park system stands in contrast to others of the time. These other systems were either islands surrounded by urban development, like Central Park in New York, or a chain of individual parks circling the metropolitan area, like the emerald necklace around Boston. Unlike these other models, preserved valleys along Philadelphia's rivers and their tributaries allowed continuous park spaces to weave through the urban fabric.

In the 1840s, responding to pressure from many prominent citizens, Philadelphia began acquiring land along the Schuylkill River, largely to protect the urban water supply from industrial pollution. The city-county consolidation of 1854 allowed Philadelphia to break out of its two square mile rectangle and to extend its municipal boundaries over 130 square miles. Just after the Civil War, in 1867, the Fairmount Park Commission was established by an act of the state legislature to acquire more land along the Schuylkill and to administer the park. A year later, the Wissahickon Creek corridor was added to this fledgling park system.

Wissahickon Park began as a long, thin corridor that stopped short of the city limits at Northwestern Avenue. Over the years, it has expanded in length, eventually reaching to the edge of the city. A number of creek tributaries have been added to this preserved urban wilderness. In the early 20th century, a group of visionary citizens would try to extend the park, up the creek, into the adjoining suburbs of Montgomery County. The group was only partly successful in realizing this goal, but private estates, semi-private institutions and a small public park system preserved much of the creek corridor in the middle valley.

In preparation for the Centennial of 1876, and as a reflection of the city's growing wealth and power, the Fairmount Park Commission began to "improve" Wissahickon Park in numerous ways. These efforts included condemning and taking land, removing nearly all the mill complexes and all but two of the inns. The few historic buildings that escaped demolition were incorporated into the park fabric. After a 20-year hiatus, at the beginning of the 20th century, there was a second wave of interest in improving the park. The park commission, helped by donations from wealthy, private individuals, added gateways, bridges, roads, trails, lookouts, steps, statues and plantings to a park system that did not have an official master plan. Tensions grew between advocates of an unembellished, scenic experience and those who wanted to improve park access and heighten enjoyment of the park through trails and facilities.

Civic activism, especially the efforts of powerful individuals in the city, was essential to the creation of the Fairmount Park system. This tradition continued to influence the growth and development of Wissahickon Park. Civic groups in Northwest Philadelphia coalesced around the campaign to save Valley Green Inn, a crusade to keep automobiles out of the park and a response to the devastation of the Chestnut blight. The most effective and enduring of these groups was the Friends of the Wissahickon (FOW).

During the Great Depression, another iconic conflict developed over the meaning of "wilderness" and its role in the park. This time advocates of a wilderness park confronted those who wanted to "democratize" the park with enhanced visitor access and organized sports. Local civic groups opposed efforts by New Deal agencies to impose a "recreational model" and build recreation facilities and more popular amenities in Wissahickon Park. Public protests and organized opposition to these pressures, in the 1930s, left a legacy of volunteerism and a well-organized and effective habit of public defense of park values for later generations to augment.

Wealthy residents of Northwest Philadelphia opposing the recreational model saw the park as their personal preserve. Recreational facilities were badly needed in the city, but, ironically, those who favored keeping the park a scenic wilderness ended up preserving "nature in the city" for future generations, when a broad, democratic constituency would flock to this oasis for unimagined recreational activities.

On the eastern side of Wissahickon gorge in the city, the acquisition of major tributaries allowed the park to filter through the neighborhoods. Some of these neighborhoods—Chestnut Hill and Mt. Airy—evolved a particularly sympathetic relationship to the forested valley. From large-scale community organization to the details of architecture and landscape design, there was a remarkable resonance between the built and the natural environments. This "sympathic bond" was expressed as the "Wissahickon Style," which reached its peak between the end of World War I and the middle years of the Great Depression. World War II brought a shift of focus. In the early, postwar period, with the development of the automobile suburbs and the movement of people from the city to the country, Wissahickon Park seemed to lose its public meaning.

Making the Park

1850-1890

Park

6

Making the Park

1850-1890

*No other city in the Union has, within its boundaries,
streams which, in picturesque and romantic beauty,
can compare with the Wissahickon and Schuylkill; and there
are few which can include within their limits landscapes
which, in sylvan grace and beauty, surpass those …
we propose to appropriate. Nature has so adorned them that
little remains for art to do except skillfully … develop the
natural beauties of the ground. The ground we
propose to acquire is peculiarly adapted to Park purposes.*

Annual Report, Fairmount Park Commission, 1868

M any forces came together in the 19th century to create a vast municipal park system in Philadelphia. After the Civil War, pressure grew throughout the country to provide public open space in the densely packed, industrial cities. Victorian notions of civic responsibility and changing attitudes towards nature merged to create a public consensus on the need for recreational areas—a need also reflected in Western Europe, with its growing park movement. Within the city of Philadelphia, particular circumstances fostered this consensus: the merger or consolidation of Philadelphia City and County; a need to safeguard the city's water supply; a Quaker appreciation of the natural world; the scenic beauty of the Schuylkill and Wissahickon valleys and the growing importance of the pleasures of nature to a great city's inhabitants.

The Victorian Park Movement

The Victorian era was an age of expansion and prosperity, especially in Western Europe and the United States. This period was characterized by rapid industrialization, improved transportation systems, the beginnings of consumerism and the dramatic increase in knowledge and wealth. In England and the United States, several social and cultural forces led to widespread private investment in the public domain. These forces included the idea of "noblesse oblige" (the obligation of the privileged to help the less fortunate), a guilty conscience, fears of a revolt by the deprived and downtrodden, a desire for public recognition and a Protestant concern to assist the enterprising poor.

Serving the public good merged with burgeoning civic pride and led to a surge in the development of new institutions—libraries, museums, zoos, large secular universities, improved prisons, asylums for the mentally ill, extensive public school systems and parks. These institutions were to be a bulwark of civic life, to educate the citizenry and foster social order. In the United States, where there was never the same support for government ownership and regulation as in Western Europe, private individuals and groups established many of these institutions. Newly rich industrialists such as Andrew Carnegie funded hundreds of public libraries and supported colleges and universities.[1]

Creating parks to enhance civic pride and to make cities more livable began in earnest in Western Europe in the 19th century, with Birkenhead Park in Liverpool, laid out in 1844, and the Bois de Boulogne in Paris, which was transformed from a royal hunting preserve into a public park during the 1850s. Urban parks were seen as "safety valves," where people could escape from the crowds, noise and stresses of city streets and unwind in attractive, wide-open spaces. Consciously created in the "English style," these parks took their models from the new landscapes designed in the late 18th century by Lancelot "Capability" Brown (1716-83) and Humphrey Repton (1752-1818).

This style had roots in literature, poetry and painting, where a new sensibility had discovered the idealized countryside of ancient Greece and Rome. In these "classical" landscapes nymphs and shepherds disported in meadows and groves. There was an affinity between these "Arcadian" settings and the casualness of the English countryside with its rolling fields and meadows.

New Yorkers of all ages, classes and races gather in North Meadow in Central Park, c. 1900.
Photograph by Robert L. Blacklow
Source: Photograph Collection of Alexander Alland, Sr./CORBIS

Brown and Repton took these images and shaped the landscape into greenswards, dotted with picturesque clumps of trees sweeping down from manor houses. They filled the little stream valleys with lakes and framed the hillsides with belts of woodland. Movement through these landscapes was very much part of the design, with picturesque "walks" and carriage drives and continuously unfolding views.[2] The predominantly "English sensibility" of residents on the East Coast of the United States, coupled with the new "Romantic" appreciation of the natural world (and the corollary rejection of more formal parks and gardens), meant that most American parks were designed in the English landscape style.

In designing their new parks, Americans generally segregated spaces and activities—unlike their European counterparts. In American parks, the typical facilities of a European, urban park—plazas, parade grounds, outdoor pavilions, concessions and varying amusements, such as museums, restaurants and horseracing—were highly controversial and often excluded.[3]

In a country where the cultural tone was set by a radical Protestant heritage, alcohol was almost always forbidden. Liquor of all sorts, and even wine and beer, was thought to stimulate violence and uncouth behavior, so beer gardens and cafes (both staples of The European pleasure park) were strictly forbidden. Extreme purists even opposed organized sports—cricket and baseball—and fought the location of playing fields in the picturesque park. This desire to exclude the temptations of the world from park premises even extended to cultural institutions—museums, concert halls and zoos, no matter how noble their purposes.

Part of the solution to this problem was the segregation of activities into separate park types. Entertainments and concessions, in a garden or park-like setting, were generally found in privately owned amusement parks. In contrast, in the newly established public parks in major American cities, the middle and the "respectable" working classes could only enjoy walking, boating and picnicking in a bucolic or scenic setting.

Love of the Wild

Many factors within the national psyche helped make a wilderness experience part of the American park movement. A deeply embedded love of the wild has been woven into American imagination and culture since early European settlement. The sense of the majesty, beauty and the grand scale of the forests, mountains, prairies and river valleys of this continent is evident in the descriptions of travelers and in the journals and letters of early settlers. Escape from civilization into the healing wilderness is a theme re-enacted repeatedly in American literature, from Cooper and Melville to Twain, and later Faulkner and Hemmingway.[4] These attitudes have been an important sub-text in the growing efforts to provide wilderness recreation in the United States.

In the era when the first great public parks were established, nostalgic memories of Civil War veterans, gathered in campfire reunions with their fellow soldiers, fed the American desire to reconnect to the wilderness. Hunters and fishermen also helped perpetuate the mystique of the wild, evoking the danger, adventure, self-reliance and male bonding of the frontier days.[5]

Wilderness camping in the late 1800s.
Source: Unknown

City—County Consolidation

The creation of the Fairmount Park system in Philadelphia was feasible only with the enlargement of the city through the city-county consolidation act of 1854. This act allowed Philadelphia to break out of Penn's two square mile rectangle and extend its municipal boundaries over 129 square miles.

By the 1850s, Philadelphia had become a large, complex commercial and manufacturing center, producing more textiles and railroad locomotives than any other city in the United States. It was also famous for its saws, shipbuilding, sugar and oil refineries, brooms, umbrellas, surgical instruments, watches, carriages, wheelbarrows, paper boxes, cigars, pharmaceuticals, soaps, ice cream, dentures, and bathroom fixtures. Economic success attracted a steady stream of workers from Europe and from the farms and towns of Eastern Pennsylvania and Southern New Jersey.

Penn's original city of two square miles had been a part of Philadelphia County. Up until the early 1800s, most of the county was rural. With industrialization and population growth, people and industry spread beyond the original municipal boundaries. Philadelphia, however, remained squeezed between the Delaware and Schuylkill Rivers and could not compete with other fast growing East Coast cities. By 1820, Philadelphia, once the largest city in the United States, had slipped behind New York, to second place.[6] Extension of its boundaries was an attractive proposition because it would enlarge the city and keep it from falling further behind in population and importance. Consolidation would also end a wasteful multiplicity of tax districts and allow the city to afford a professional police force to protect its increasingly diverse population from outbreaks of mob violence.[7]

In 1854, without permission from the residents of outlying Philadelphia County, city officials convinced the state legislature to merge the city and county. With this act, Philadelphia could now boast of having the greatest land area of any municipality in the country. Forty outlying towns and villages were swept into the new boundaries, including the townships of Roxborough and Germantown.[8]

Map of the consolidated City of Philadelphia showing the newly established wards. The former Roxborough Township became the 21st Ward and the former Germantown Township became the 22nd Ward.
Map published by R.L. Barnes, 1854.
Source: LCP

Mob violence periodically plagued Philadelphia in the mid-19th century. "The Destruction by Fire of Pennsylvania Hall, the new building of the Abolition Society, on May 17, 1836," shows a group of racists burning down the hall, soon after it opened. Eight years later, in 1844, mob violence directed against Irish Catholics resulted in 15 deaths and the destruction of churches, schools and private residences. Because Philadelphia did not have a police force, the state militia had to be called out to restore order. Consolidation would enable the city to afford a professional police force.
Lithograph, published by J.T. Bowen, 1839. Source: HSP

Creating Fairmount Park

For many years, private citizens and government officials had been urging the city to buy up land and create a park along the Schuylkill River. The consolidation act recommended the acquisition of new parkland for Philadelphia and made the city responsible for its purchase.[9] At the western edge of Penn's original city, the Schuylkill River offered many attractions. In the late 1700s, land on either side of the river had been the site of a string of prosperous country estates. This "villa district" was a largely open landscape on the plateau, interspersed with groves of remnant forest. It gave residents picturesque views of the river. In the 1820s, the municipal waterworks designed by the city engineer, Frederick Graff, was built at "Faire Mount," on the river, just below the present-day Philadelphia Museum of Art. It immediately became a major tourist destination—as visitors flocked to see the machinery, the neo-classical buildings and the gardens.

6:1-2

By the mid-1800s, many of these villas had been sold for industrial sites, with plans for even more factories, warehouses and river wharves. Elizabeth Milroy, an expert on the early years of Fairmount Park, describes the "Ice houses, factories, and warehouses [lining] the river's west banks…. The Belmont Oil Company had started operations on the west side of the river just north of the Columbia Bridge in 1865. Farther upriver the Powers and Weightman chemical company plant extended from the Falls Bridge north almost to the mouth of the Wissahickon."[10]

Lemon Hill, a villa along the Schuylkill River, had been purchased as an industrial site for coal-shipping wharfs. The site was located just above the intake for the Fairmount Waterworks. A report spearheaded by Thomas P. Cope, Quaker merchant and member of Philadelphia's Select Council (the upper chamber of Philadelphia's then bicameral city legislature), called for the purchase of Lemon Hill, urging this purchase "to stave off increased pollution…and to provide the city's working classes with pure air as well as pure water in a retreat…."[11] Combined voices finally spurred the city into acquiring the property the following year.

In 1857, the city, using a combination of public and private funds, also bought the adjoining Sedgeley Estate. This property, with Lemon Hill and the Fairmount Waterworks, created a small park of about 100 acres, and formed the core of the newly designated Fairmount Park System.

These purchases prompted considerable public debate. People objected to the cost and charged that the park would benefit only the rich, at the public's expense. Park supporters stressed the need for parklands for the working classes, who had no time, money or transportation to escape the city.[12] An early Fairmount Park Commission *Annual Report* reiterated this justification, emphasizing that the park would "give to the people the opportunity of breathing the fresh, free air, in the midst of rural surroundings…."[13] Charges that park creation and park expansion benefited mainly the rich would continue to blind people to the value of the park system and its contribution to the quality of life for all Philadelphians.

Villas on the Schuykill

These estates shared a number of similar characteristics:

- Villa sited on the plateau, on a small rise, surrounded by rolling lawns

- Dramatic views of the Schuylkill River

- Villa, lawns and gardens open to cooling breezes

- Each villa intended to be seen from the others—and from the river

Thought to be "Eaglesfield," a villa on the Schuylkill. Oil painting by William Groombridge, 1790s.
Source: Historical Society of Pennsylvania Collection, Atwater Kent Museum of Philadelphia

View of Sweet Brier. Oil painting by Thomas Birch, 1811.
Source: Private Collection

Fairmount Water Works

View of the Fairmount Water Works with the Schuylkill River in the Distance.
Color lithograph by J.T.Bowen, c. 1838.   Source: LCP

Fairmount Water Works

6:2

View of Schuylkill River before the "beautification" of the new aquisitions for Fairmount Park. It shows the increasing industrialization of the river bank. Stereoview by James Cremer c. 1872.
Source: FPC

Another view of Fairmount Water Works. Chromolithograph by Julius Bien after Jacob Keihn, 1867.
Source: S. Robert Teitelman Collection

According to the website of the Fairmount Water Works, "Philadelphia was the first large American city to regard the delivery of safe water as a municipal responsibility. In the late 1700s, yellow fever epidemics—then thought by some to be a water-borne disease—compelled civic leaders to name a Watering Committee (forbearer of the Philadelphia Water Department) to assure a constant supply of uncontaminated drinking water. Committee members eventually chose Frederick Graff to build a water-works on the eastern bank of the Schuylkill where the Philadelphia Museum of Art is today. Graff's initial use of steam engines to lift water from the river eventually gave way to water-wheels in July 1822. Powered by the river, pumps raised water into reservoirs high atop a nearby hill, Faire Mount…. A reliable water supply brought growth to Philadelphia and the entire region. Growth in turn bred pollution as individuals and industry relied on the river as a means of disposing waste…. By 1880, the Schuylkill could barely meet the demands of being both a source of drinking water and a public sewer. Pollution of the river led to the facility's closing in 1909."[1]

1. Website: fairmountwaterworks.org., see also Elizabeth Milroy, "Images of Fairmount Park in Philadelphia," 77-94, in *Thomas Eakins*, ed. Darrel Sewell, (Philadelphia 2001).

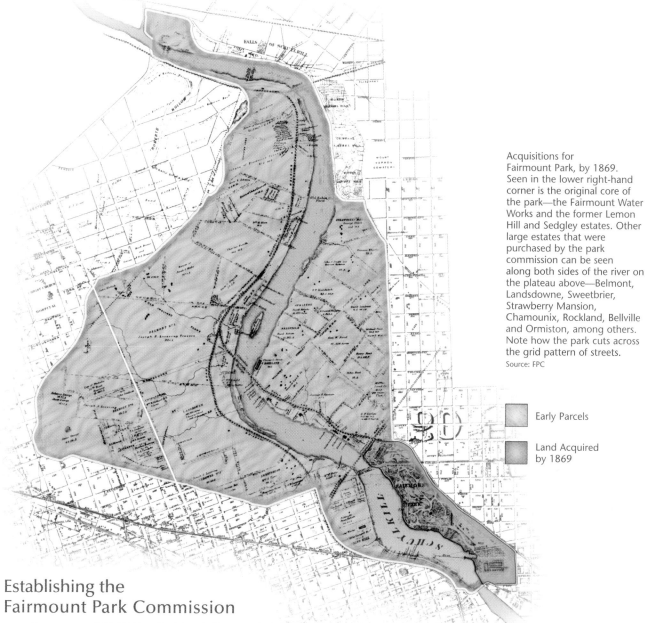

Acquisitions for Fairmount Park, by 1869. Seen in the lower right-hand corner is the original core of the park—the Fairmount Water Works and the former Lemon Hill and Sedgley estates. Other large estates that were purchased by the park commission can be seen along both sides of the river on the plateau above—Belmont, Landsdowne, Sweetbrier, Strawberry Mansion, Chamounix, Rockland, Bellville and Ormiston, among others. Note how the park cuts across the grid pattern of streets.
Source: FPC

Early Parcels

Land Acquired by 1869

Establishing the Fairmount Park Commission

Four years of Civil War (1861-65) distracted Philadelphia's attention from the park movement.[14] When the war was over, attention returned to civic issues. Park supporters proposed a commission to administer and expand the fledging park. Since the city did not have a home rule charter, it could not establish a new governing body without state approval. The creation and empowerment of a separate park commission required an act of state legislature.[15]

In 1867, the state legislature established the Fairmount Park Commission. According to the act, this commission would "maintain [it] forever, as an open public place and park, for the health and enjoyment of the citizens [of Philadelphia], and the

6:3

The Fairmount Park Commission

The Fairmount Park Commission was established by an Act of the Pennsylvania State Legislature in March 1867. The Commission was given responsibility by the city's then bi-cameral legislative body for all Philadelphia's parklands.

Members of the original commission were the mayor of Philadelphia, the presidents of the select and common councils, the commissioner of city property, the chief engineer and surveyor, and the chief engineer of the Water Works (all ex-officio) and 10 unpaid court-appointed citizens. Of these 10 citizens, five were appointed for five years each by the District Court and five were appointed for the same period by the Court of Common Pleas. When the District Court was abolished in 1874, the Common Pleas Court assumed responsibility for appointing the 10 citizen members.[1]

When the Select Council was eliminated in 1920, and Philadelphia went to a unicameral legislative body, the ex-officio seat of the president of the Select Council was eliminated. In 1951, a new Home Rule Charter for Philadelphia added the commissioner of recreation as an ex-officio member of the park commission.[2] With these exceptions, the composition of the commission remained the same.

The first court appointed commissioners were Eli K. Price, John Welsh, William Sellers, Joseph Harrison, Jr., John C. Cresson, N. B. Brown, Theodore Cuyler, Henry M. Phillips, Gustavus Remak, and George G. Meade. The ex-officio members were Morton McMichael, Mayor of the City; Joshua Sperling, President of Select Council; Joseph F. Marcer, President of Common Council; Charles Dixey, Commissioner of City Property; Strickland Kneass, Chief Engineer and Surveyor and Frederick Graff, Chief Engineer of Water Works.[3]

The most famous commissioner was General George Gordon Meade, whose victory at Gettysburg just five years earlier against Robert E. Lee was the turning point of the Civil War. Meade's appointment was probably honorific, but lent stature to the whole park venture. Of the other appointed members, Price, Remak, Phillips, Cuyler and Welsh were lawyers, while Sellers, Harrison, Cresson and Brown were businessmen. Price had been the person most responsible for shaping public opinion in favor of the park and for making it a political and legal reality. People appointed for merit rather than social standing characterized this first commission. Unfortunately, merit selection would not always be the criteria for choosing future commissioners. Some would be appointed only because of political connections and some only because they were members of the Philadelphia WASP establishment.

---

1. Scharf and Westcott, *History of Philadelphia* (Philadelphia, 1884), 3:1855.

2. FPC Fact Sheet.

3. FPC, *Annual Report*, 1868, 14.

Map of Fairmount Park in 1872.
Source: Charles S. Keyser, *Fairmount park. Sketches of its scenery, waters and history.* (Philadelphia, 1872)

preservation of the purity of the water supply to the City of Philadelphia."[16] Almost immediately, the commission began acquiring additional parkland on both sides of the Schuylkill River that included many of the fine old estates lining the top of the bluffs. Commission members were to be appointed by the Philadelphia Common Pleas Court so that they would be independent of the city government.

Unfortunately, the legislation made park funding dependent on general city funds. Without a separate dedicated funding source or independent means of raising money, city government held ultimate control over the Fairmount Park Commission. As a result, its independence was often more symbolic than real. When the city declined economically and lost sight of the park's importance as a key contributor to a vital civic life, the commission lacked the power to get financial support from the city or raise independent funds.

Although not financially independent, when money was available, the commission could and did take the initiative to acquire extensive additions to Fairmount Park. With the coming Centennial, the commissioners bought property and also seized it through the power of "eminent domain." With this power, the commission was able to condemn land, but was required to compensate owners at fair market value.[17] This power remains, but is rarely used because of lack of funds, political will and grand vision.

Two Kinds of Parks

For the new municipal park system, the Fairmount Park Commission initially created two kinds of parks—a "pastoral" park along the Schuylkill River and a "wilderness" park along the Wissahickon Creek. By the early 1870s, East and West Parks along the Schuylkill together had 2,240 acres, which included a relatively broad floodplain. It was flanked on both sides by modest, rocky bluffs. On the tops of these bluffs, the land rolled gently and overlooked the wide river. When the industrial buildings were cleared away, this relatively open land, with ample flat areas, easily accommodated a variety of genteel Victorian recreations—strolling, horseback riding, carriage driving, picnicking, nutting and boating.

To allow the addition of the lower Wissahickon Valley to the Fairmount Park system, the state legislature passed a second park act in April 1868, largely drafted by Eli Kirk Price.[18] In contrast to East and West Parks, the initial 450 acres of parkland along the Wissahickon Creek were confined to a steep, narrow gorge, with considerable forest, despite its industrial history. Charles Keyser's 1872 *Guidebook to Fairmount Park* captured these differences between these two park types: "[The Wissahickon's] unbroken quiet, its dense woodland, its pine-crowned hills, its sunless recesses, and sense of separation from the other world, contrast strongly with the broad lawns, the open flowing river, and the bright sunshine which characterize the banks of the Schuylkill...."[19]

6:4-6

Genteel Recreations

Carriage Path. Engraving by Thomas Moran.
Source: Charles S. Keyser, *Fairmount Park: Sketches of Its Scenery, Waters and History* (Philadelphia, 1872)

Sleigh riding on upper Wissahickon Drive (later Forbidden Drive). Photograph by James B. Rich, c. 1896.
Source: LCP

Boating at Valley Green. Engraving by Smithwick c. 1870.
Source: Charles S. Keyser, *Fairmount Park: Sketches of Its Scenery, Waters and History* (Philadelphia, 1872)

Skating on the creek at Wissahickon Hall, on the pool behind the second Robeson dam. Photograph, c. 1910.
Source: GHS

An outing on the Wissahickon. Photograph, 1903.
Source: GHS

Children seining for minnows in Cresheim Creek. Photograph, c. 1905.
Source: GHS

Eli Kirk Price (1797–1884)

Eli Kirk Price came from a long line of Pennsylvania Quakers. Born in East Bradford, Chester County, Price attended Quaker schools, and at age eighteen took a job with Thomas P. Cope, the prominent Quaker shipping merchant, with whom he would one day work to create Fairmount Park. Price later read law, was admitted to the Philadelphia bar, and quickly became the city's leading legal expert on real estate, writing about it extensively.

He was an outspoken advocate of the merger of Philadelphia City and County, and won election to the Pennsylvania State Senate in 1854 where he became the principal sponsor of the Consolidation Act, passed that same year. During the next dozen years, he was one of the prime movers for the creation of a large municipal park system in Philadelphia. This vision became a reality in 1867 when the state legislature passed an act establishing the Fairmount Park Commission, with Price as its first chairman.[1]

Descendents of Eli Kirk Price have served on the Fairmount Park Commission, including Eli Kirk Price, Jr., and Philip Price, Jr.

1. Elizabeth Milroy, "Assembling Fairmount Park," in *Philadelphia's Cultural Landscape: The Sartain Family Legacy*, edited by Katherine Martinez and Page Talbott (Philadelphia: Temple University Press, 2000), 76, 80-82; *Dictionary of American Biography*, 15:211-12.

Eli Kirk Price. Photograph, c. 1870s.
Source: LCP

Frederick Law Olmsted and Wissahickon Park

At the time Fairmount Park was established, Frederick Law Olmsted, the man who coined the term "landscape architecture," was designing or consulting on almost all of the nation's major park systems. Although Olmsted and his partner Calvin Vaux (Olmsted, Vaux and Company) were not engaged by The Fairmount Park Commission to play a central role in planning Fairmount Park, it did invite these men to come to Philadelphia twice in 1867 to make recommendations. In their report to the commission, they advised the commission to provide the "occasion for the coming together of the poor and the rich on the ground which is common possession and that… produces a feeling which to the poor is a relief from the sense of restriction."[1]

Just around the time the commission was seeking his firm's advice on Wissahickon Park, Olmsted, according to his biographer Witold Rybczynski, was turning away from "the three grand elements of the pastoral landscape—meadows, forest and water." Instead, he was coming to believe that the character of a park should grow out of the intrinsic characteristics of the site itself.[2] Schuylkill East and West were in the tradition of the park that preserved and celebrated the pastoral landscape. The acquisition of Wissahickon Park reflected Olmsted and Vaux's advice to the commission to preserve and capitalize on areas with wild and scenic qualities.

They also urged the commissioners to extend a carriage drive, later known as East River Drive (and still later as Kelly Drive) along the banks of the Schuylkill River as far upstream as East Falls, where it could connect with the Wissahickon Turnpike. During one of his two visits to Philadelphia, he remarked on the Wissahickon's "unparalleled attractions" for carriages and horseback riding, and suggested that the commission appropriate the Wissahickon gorge.

---

1. A very thorough account of this early park development was given by the Fairmount Park Commission in its first *Annual Report* in 1868. See 5-13 of this *Annual Report*.

2. Witold Rybczynski, *A Clearing in the Distance* (New York, 1999) 93-94.

Painting of Frederick Law Olmsted by John Singer Sargent,1895.
Source: Used with permission from The Biltmore Company, Asheville, North Carolina

By the early 1870s, the park commission had acquired most of the corridor along the main stem of the Wissahickon Creek, within the expanded city limits. The combined parks (on the west and east sides of the Schuylkill River and along Wissahickon Creek) extended for over thirteen miles—seven of them along the Schuylkill and a little over six miles along the Wissahickon. With a total of nearly 3,000 acres, this new, public open space was one of the largest metropolitan parks in the United States, and was, at the time, the largest river valley park in the nation.[20]

Sewers and Stream Valleys

Stream valleys in Penn's original city had served both as sanitary sewers and as storm drains. Combining sewage and rainwater in a single pipe was characteristic of most cities at the time. In Philadelphia, where the original city was located in the relatively flat Coastal Plain, this drainage system required some engineering, but was not prohibitively difficult or expensive. As the city expanded outward, it took increasing time, money and effort to bury the steeply incised stream valleys. In the newly consolidated city, turning stream valleys into parks was ultimately cheaper than using these valleys as a part of Philadelphia's sewage disposal system.

In the 1880s, when the city engineers drew up their preliminary drainage maps for the consolidated city, they showed many smaller streams converted into sewers. As described by Adam Levine in his "History of Philadelphia's Watersheds and Sewers," "Culverting the streams before they became polluted was seen as a positive step to protect the public health. In undertaking these projects, the engineers also hoped to reduce the cost of the city's infrastructure in a number of ways. Sewage, being mostly liquid, flows most cheaply by gravity —pumping it up a slope is expensive in terms of fuel costs, and is only as reliable as the pumping equipment. By placing sewers in the natural stream valleys, the engineers got the gravity flow they needed, and in the process they managed to avoid the high cost of making extensive excavations. Once the valleys were filled in over the newly built pipes—in some stream valleys in Philadelphia, more than 40 feet of fill was used—the cost of building a bridge each time a main street crossed the stream was avoided as well.

"Building sewers in advance of development also gave engineers more freedom in their designs. Since most of the land the sewers traversed was open farmland or woodland, the cost of paying out land damages to property owners was less. Often, building a sewer in a creek bed was to the advantage of private landholders, especially in areas of the city where the rectangular grid system of streets prevailed.

"A piece of land with a creek cutting through it was impossible to subdivide into regular slices, but with the creek in a sewer, and the grid laid over the valley, real estate speculators could divide their property into the tightly fitted rectangular lots so common throughout Philadelphia. Since the streets were built on top of the new sewers, with water and gas lines put in as well, the developers had a ready-made infrastructure that tended to speed up the sales of these lots. The City, in return, could count on a quick return on its investment in infrastructure from the resulting increase in tax revenues from the new buildings. In some watersheds, it took many years to completely obliterate the main stream and its tributaries. The Mill Creek conversion from creek to sewer took more than 25 years, and the city's largest such project, the burying of both branches of Wingohocking Creek, took about 40 years."[1]

---

1. *"History of Philadelphia's Watersheds and Sewers,"* Philadelphia Water Department Website: phillyh2o.org; and "From Creek to Sewer: A Brief Overview of Topographical Change in Philadelphia," 2005; also, Adam Levine, interview by authors, May 6, 2003.

Purchase of the Wissahickon Valley set a precedent for Fairmount Park's eventual acquisition of four other tributary streams within the city—Cobbs, Tacony, Pennypack and Poquessing Creeks—all tributaries of the Delaware River. By doing so, the park system preserved at least the key riparian corridors. Even more important, the Wissahickon Creek and its tributaries ultimately created a network that reached into the urban fabric, and allowed both water and forest to become an integral part of many neighborhoods, connecting them intimately to a large, natural system.

6:7

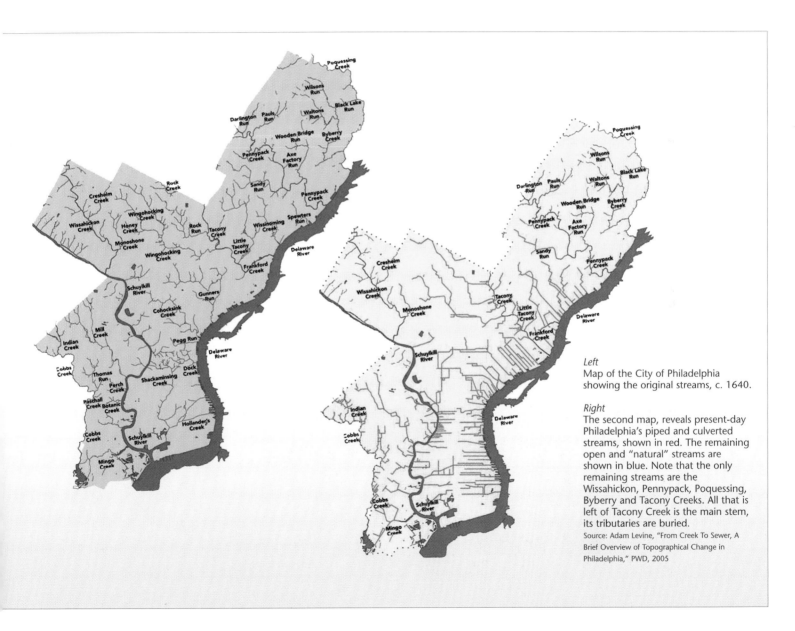

Left
Map of the City of Philadelphia showing the original streams, c. 1640.

Right
The second map, reveals present-day Philadelphia's piped and culverted streams, shown in red. The remaining open and "natural" streams are shown in blue. Note that the only remaining streams are the Wissahickon, Pennypack, Poquessing, Byberry and Tacony Creeks. All that is left of Tacony Creek is the main stem, its tributaries are buried.
Source: Adam Levine, "From Creek To Sewer, A Brief Overview of Topographical Change in Philadelphia," PWD, 2005

Defining Park Boundaries

After receiving permission from the legislature to acquire land along Wissahickon Creek, one of the park commission's first tasks was to delineate park boundaries. Its twin goal was to protect the valley from further development and to maintain the special sense of separation that visitors felt within the gorge. The commission began with a careful survey of the valley. It appears (although this cannot be verified) that the surveyors were directed to project "sight lines" from the valley bottom up the enclosing slopes to ensure that no buildings would be seen from along the creek. These sight lines helped to determine the boundaries of the park and suggested that the initial park include the confluences of the main tributaries.

Despite the best intentions, Wissahickon Park was initially only a slender corridor that included the creek and a thin ribbon of land on either side. This ribbon averaged about 600 feet in width, with the narrowest portion, at the mouth of the Schuylkill River, measuring only 100 feet across.[21] The park began at Ridge Avenue and extended to Thorp's Mill Road (later Bell's Mill Road) in Chestnut Hill. Public land would not reach the city limits at Northwestern Avenue until the 1890s, and then only on the eastern side, in upper Chestnut Hill.

Original survey of Wissahickon Park. The map shows the early boundaries, the forest areas and the locations of the mills, inns, roads and bridges in the valley at the time. Map, 1868.
Source: FPC

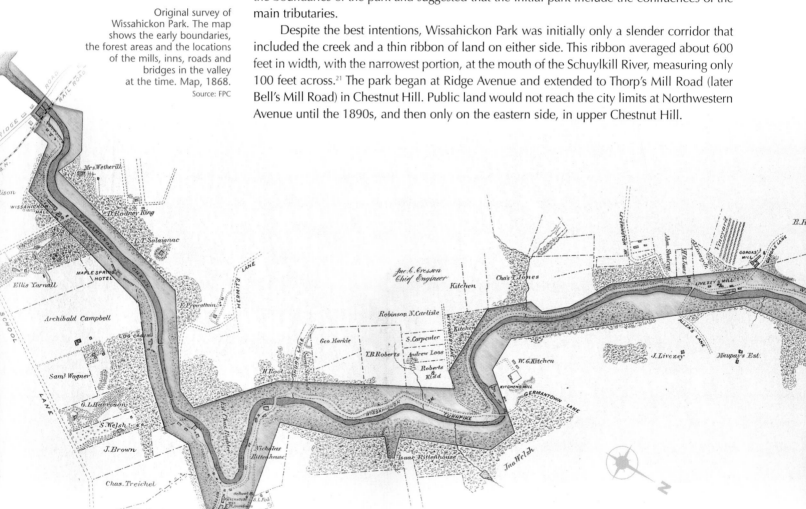

The commissioners considered enlarging the park on the Roxborough side, beyond the top of the valley. According to the 1870 *Annual Report*, "A line was run for two miles along the western crest to ascertain the practicability of locating a ride or drive along the boundary."[22] The commission abandoned this idea, "When it became apparent that this additional area included within such lines would be greater than was thought admissible, being nearly equal to that of the large park [along the Schuylkill River]."[23] These wider boundaries would have included the land paralleling the edge of the park in Roxborough, where Henry Avenue would be built eight decades later. This plan would have added about 2,000 acres to Wissahickon Park.[24]

The Roxborough plateau was then largely farmland and country estates, including Richard Wister's "Andorra." Acquisition of this land would have been relatively easy. Failure to make Wissahickon Park wider on the western side meant that most of the parkland would remain a long, narrow corridor, constricted over time by development, as farmland metamorphosed into houses, apartment buildings and shopping centers.

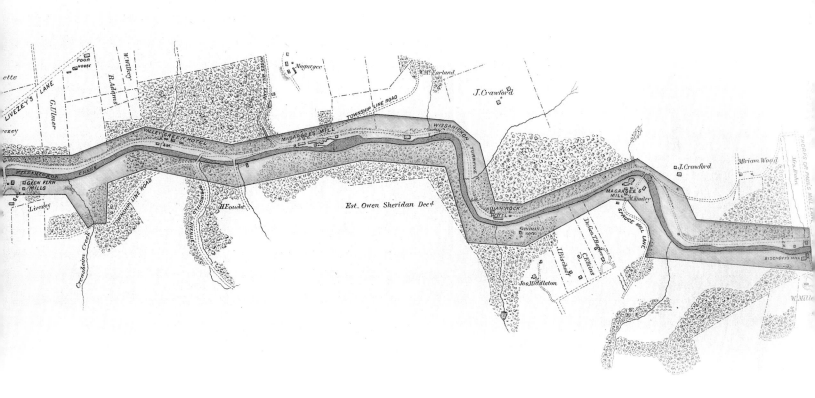

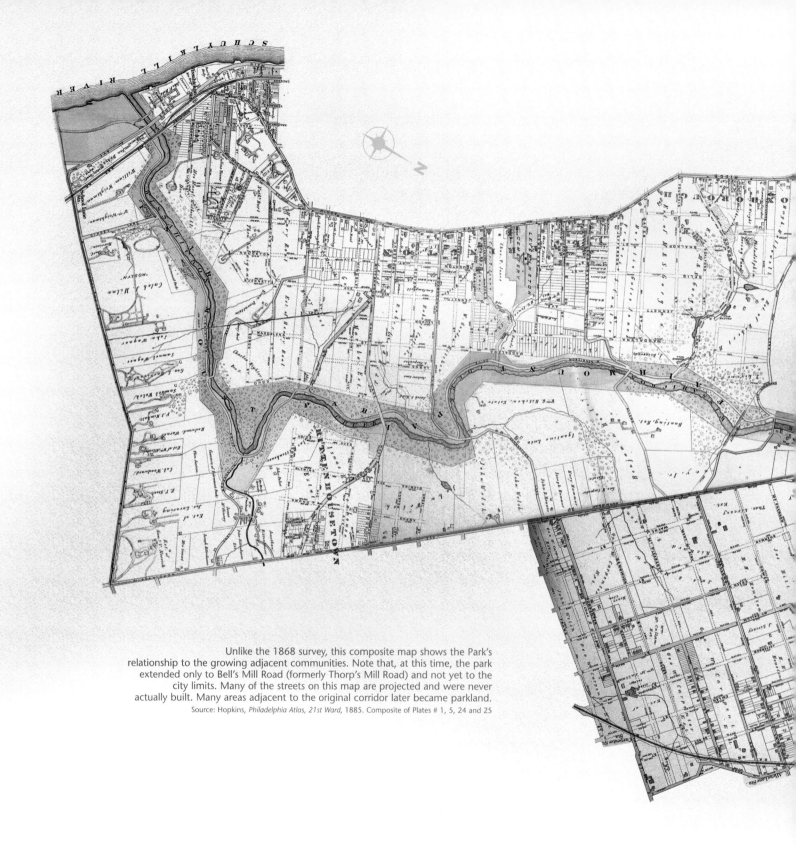

Unlike the 1868 survey, this composite map shows the Park's relationship to the growing adjacent communities. Note that, at this time, the park extended only to Bell's Mill Road (formerly Thorp's Mill Road) and not yet to the city limits. Many of the streets on this map are projected and were never actually built. Many areas adjacent to the original corridor later became parkland.

Source: Hopkins, *Philadelphia Atlas, 21st Ward*, 1885. Composite of Plates # 1, 5, 24 and 25

Improvement and Expansion

The land purchased along the creek included an existing toll road—the Wissahickon Turnpike. When this road became a part of the park in 1870, it was made "toll free," with the commission undertaking extensive repairs. "The hill side drains have been reconstructed along the whole line [of roadway]; numerous cross drains are laid beneath the road and silt basins set where needed; guard rails on all precipitous ledges have been erected along the whole length of the road. Wooden bridges were replanked, and roofs and weather boarding removed [from the bridges] or repaired; ... culverts and retaining walls in some places repaired and in others rebuilt...."[25]

Driven by a desire to make Fairmount Park a showpiece of the Centennial celebration in 1876, the commission continued to make "improvements." Park staff demolished most of the remaining mills and their associated buildings, and blasted away more of the huge rock that had once completely blocked access to the valley from Ridge Avenue.[26]

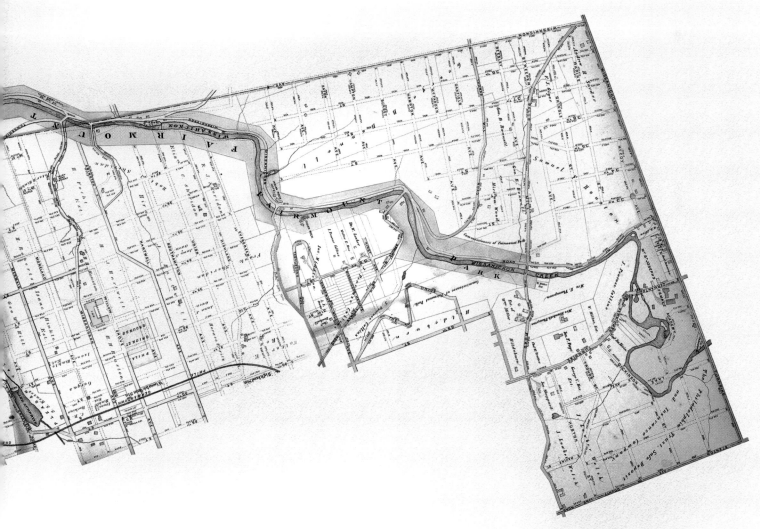

The commission's 1878 *Annual Report* also set out a plan to replant denuded areas, and to open vistas to heighten the scenic effect of the forested gorge to "develop and render this portion of the park accessible, and....open to view [the] most beautiful and romantic scenery."[27]

At this time, the first official park trail—a walking and bridle path (later known as the "yellow trail") was constructed on the west bank of the creek. The trail began at Ridge Avenue and ran along the Roxborough side, ending at the Wissahickon Turnpike (later called Forbidden Drive) where the creek makes a sharp bend to the northwest.

Along with these improvements, the commission continued to acquire more land to widen and flesh out a band of park that was far too constricted to be viable for public use, purchasing approximately 84 more acres at the edges of the new park. These additions brought the total size of Wissahickon Park to just over 530 acres.[28] Eli Kirk Price, in charge of land purchases, was still not satisfied and urged the city to appropriate funds and acquire even more land: "The outside lands up the Wissahickon are mostly wooded, which, if sold, would cause the hill sides to be stripped of their timber, and make the scenery of that part of the Park very unsightly." Estimating that the additions would cost only $300 to $600 per acre, he added, "It would be a great dereliction of duty not thus to secure them to the public, both for ornament and the protection of the purity of the water supply to the city."[29] However, once the Centennial was over, almost nothing was done for two decades to improve the park or acquire more land. The commission did not even issue another annual report until 1899.[30]

6:8

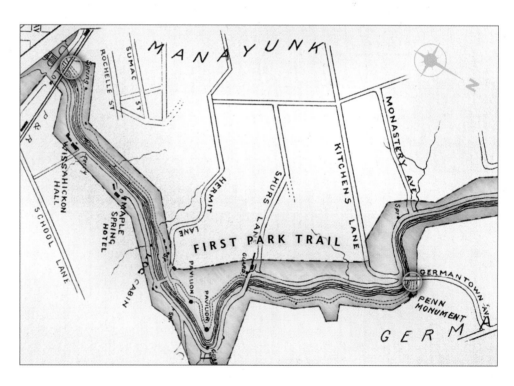

The first "park" trail ran along the west bank of the creek from Ridge Avenue to the confluence of the Wissahickon with its tributary, the Monoshone Creek. Map, c.1870s.
Source: GHS

Facing Page
The first park trail.
Photograph, 1901.
Source: HSP

Metropolitan Paradise: The Struggle for Nature in the City

Early Fairmount Park Guard

In 1868, the year after the creation of the Fairmount Park Commission, the state legislature authorized the establishment of a special park guard, whose responsibility was to enforce park rules, keep order and assist visitors. The guards could arrest violators without warrants, but they were urged to enforce regulations by "quiet words" whenever possible.[1]

According to Marion Rivinus, who published a history of the Fairmount Park Guard in 1976, these guardians of public welfare rescued skaters who fell through the ice, extracted fish hooks from many parts of fishermen's anatomies, talked people out of committing suicide, and retrieved and returned an astounding variety of items lost by park visitors. They often served as unofficial guides to the park, answering questions about its history and special features. Park guard presence did a great deal to curb dumping and vandalism and give the public a strong sense of safety and security.[2]

The first Fairmount Park Guard consisted of one captain, four sergeants and 35 guards. They patrolled 28 acres of parkland. Formal instructions to the park guard directed them to "render all possible aid and assistance in case of accident to pedestrians, horsemen or carriages, and particularly to protect females and children against every kind of annoyance, rudeness or insult from evil-disposed and disorderly persons…. Great indulgence is recommended towards children, but discreet, dignified, yet firm and decisive action towards gangs of unruly boys."[4]

---

1. FPC, *Annual Report*, 1868, 14

2. Marion W. Rivinus, *The History of the Fairmount Park Guard, 1868-1972* (Philadelphia, 1976), 12.

3. Website: http://hometown.aol.com/simudave/indexhtmlpfppolice.html

4. FPC, *Annual Report*, 1878, 44.

Above
The original Fairmount Park Guard. Photograph, c. 1868.
Source: FPC

Facing Page
A Fairmount Park Guard on the upper Wissahickon Drive (now Forbidden Drive), outside an early guardhouse built into the rocky hillside. Photograph, c. 1880s.
Source: CHHS

Making the Park

In linking the valley of the Schuykill River to the Wissahickon gorge, the Fairmount Park Commission created an extraordinary demonstration of what a city could be. Fairmount Park brought nature's patterns into Penn's rational grid, and gave the promise of gracious urbanity—allowing Philadelphians to live simultaneously within the city, the countryside and the natural world. This bold model should inspire creative action to sustain an asset that distinguishes Philadelphia from many other large, bleak and formerly industrial cities.

While park authorities made a groundbreaking start in setting aside the land along the Schuykill River and connecting it to a second park within the Wissahickon gorge, the middle and upper valley remained outside municipal boundaries and unprotected. Far-sighted actions of several individuals would set the stage during the early 20th century to safeguard portions of the Wissahickon corridor within the middle valley.

Preserving the Middle Valley

1900-1935

7

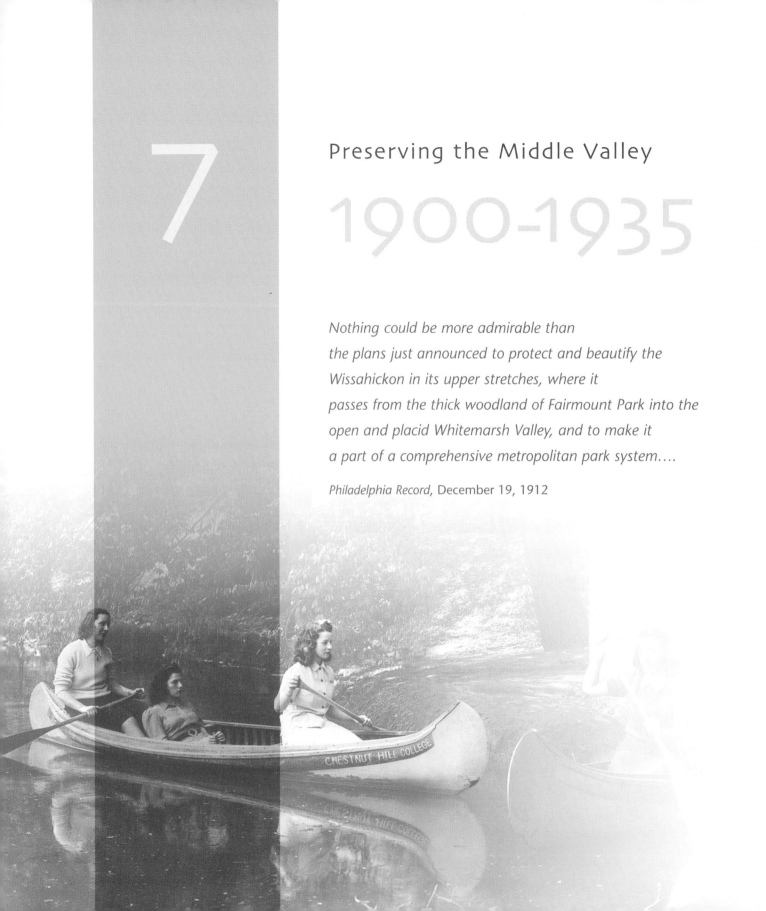

7

Preserving the Middle Valley

1900-1935

*Nothing could be more admirable than
the plans just announced to protect and beautify the
Wissahickon in its upper stretches, where it
passes from the thick woodland of Fairmount Park into the
open and placid Whitemarsh Valley, and to make it
a part of a comprehensive metropolitan park system....*

Philadelphia Record, December 19, 1912

oing up the watershed, the Wissahickon Creek breaks through a steep ridge and expands out of the gorge into the very different landscape of the middle valley. The broader lowlands here are known locally as the Whitemarsh Valley. The creek runs through this valley for a distance of about four miles between the edge of Northwest Philadelphia and the village of Fort Washington in adjoining Montgomery County.

Thick bands of sedimentary, carbonate rocks—limestones and dolomites of varying hardness—underlie the middle valley and have eroded into gentle landforms. The soft carbonate rocks wear away more easily than the harder schist formations. The name "Whitemarsh Valley" is possibly a corruption of "wide marsh." It may also derive from the white mists that hovered over the valley in the early mornings, or from exposed areas of white limestone bedrock.

Two prominent east-west Chickies quartzite ridges frame the Middle Valley at the northern and southern ends. They form a continuous line of hills broken by gaps of varying sizes. The lower ridge extends through the top of Chestnut Hill, and the upper ridge runs just below the village of Fort Washington and the route of the later Pennsylvania Turnpike.

The middle valley from the top of Chestnut Hill in the City of Philadelphia to Fort Washington in upper Whitemarsh Township. The two Chickies quartzite ridges that frame the Whitemarsh Valley and the Wissahickon Creek corridor are called out in orange. Historic USGS Map, 1928.
Source: USGS Map, 1928, Author's collection

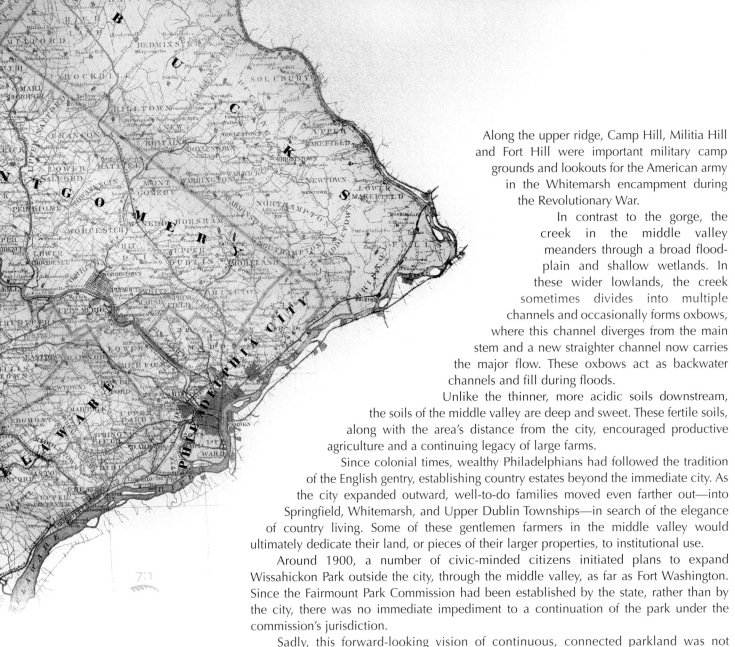

Southeastern Pennsylvania showing
Philadelphia and the surrounding
counties—Bucks, Montgomery, Chester
and Delaware. The contrast between the
built-up center of Philadelphia and the
surrounding rural counties is clearly visible.
Source: G.M. Hopkins, *Atlas of the County of
Montgomery and the State of Pennsylvania*
(Philadelphia, 1871). Courtesy of Joseph B. Timoney

Along the upper ridge, Camp Hill, Militia Hill and Fort Hill were important military camp grounds and lookouts for the American army in the Whitemarsh encampment during the Revolutionary War.

In contrast to the gorge, the creek in the middle valley meanders through a broad flood-plain and shallow wetlands. In these wider lowlands, the creek sometimes divides into multiple channels and occasionally forms oxbows, where this channel diverges from the main stem and a new straighter channel now carries the major flow. These oxbows act as backwater channels and fill during floods.

Unlike the thinner, more acidic soils downstream, the soils of the middle valley are deep and sweet. These fertile soils, along with the area's distance from the city, encouraged productive agriculture and a continuing legacy of large farms.

Since colonial times, wealthy Philadelphians had followed the tradition of the English gentry, establishing country estates beyond the immediate city. As the city expanded outward, well-to-do families moved even farther out—into Springfield, Whitemarsh, and Upper Dublin Townships—in search of the elegance of country living. Some of these gentlemen farmers in the middle valley would ultimately dedicate their land, or pieces of their larger properties, to institutional use.

Around 1900, a number of civic-minded citizens initiated plans to expand Wissahickon Park outside the city, through the middle valley, as far as Fort Washington. Since the Fairmount Park Commission had been established by the state, rather than by the city, there was no immediate impediment to a continuation of the park under the commission's jurisdiction.

Sadly, this forward-looking vision of continuous, connected parkland was not achieved, but by the late 1920s, a combination of public, semi-public and large, private properties had preserved much of the creek in the middle valley by keeping a large portion of the landscape in open space. The largest and most critical of these properties were the Andorra Nurseries, Mount St. Joseph's Academy (later Chestnut Hill College), John and Lydia Morrises' Estate (later the Morris Arboretum of the University of Pennsylvania), Erdenheim Farms (later Erdenheim Farm), Carson College for Orphan Girls (later the Carson Valley School), Fort Washington State Park, and three golf courses (Whitemarsh Valley, Sunnybrook and the Philadelphia Cricket Club).

Middle Valley—late 1920s

View of the beginning of the middle valley, with Mount St. Joseph's Academy (later Chestnut Hill College) in the foreground. The buildings are located on the Chickies quartzite ridge with the limestone valley spreading out in the background. The Dewees millpond and mill race can be seen in the lower right-hand corner. Behind the academy are the lower portions of the Morris Estate (later the Morris Arboretum) and the Whitemarsh Valley Country Club's golf course.

In the middle distance, Erdenheim Farms and the Carson College for Orphaned Girls (later the Carson Valley School) are part of the landscape of fields and hedgerows. At the upper edge of the photo-graph, in the far distance, the second Chickies quartzite ridge is just visible. This ridge was the site of a revolutionary war encampment, called Militia Hill. The Wissahickon Creek can be traced by a thin, forested riparian corridor that runs through this open landscape.

Source: LCP

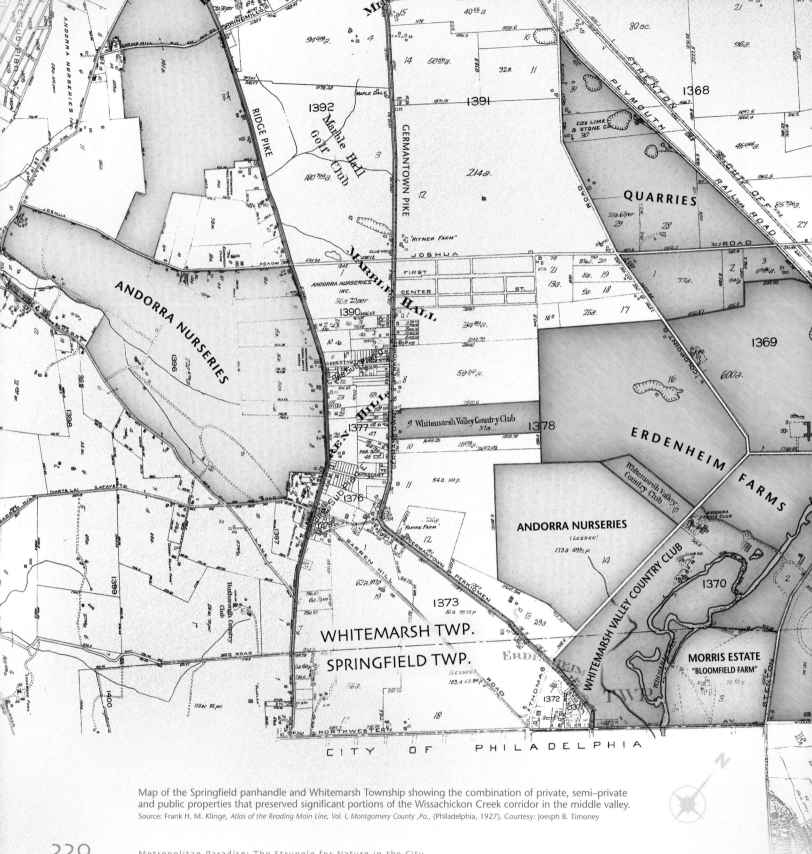

Map of the Springfield panhandle and Whitemarsh Township showing the combination of private, semi–private and public properties that preserved significant portions of the Wissachickon Creek corridor in the middle valley.

Source: Frank H. M. Klinge, *Atlas of the Reading Main Line, Vol. I, Montgomery County ,Pa.*, (Philadelphia, 1927). Courtesy: Joesph B. Timoney

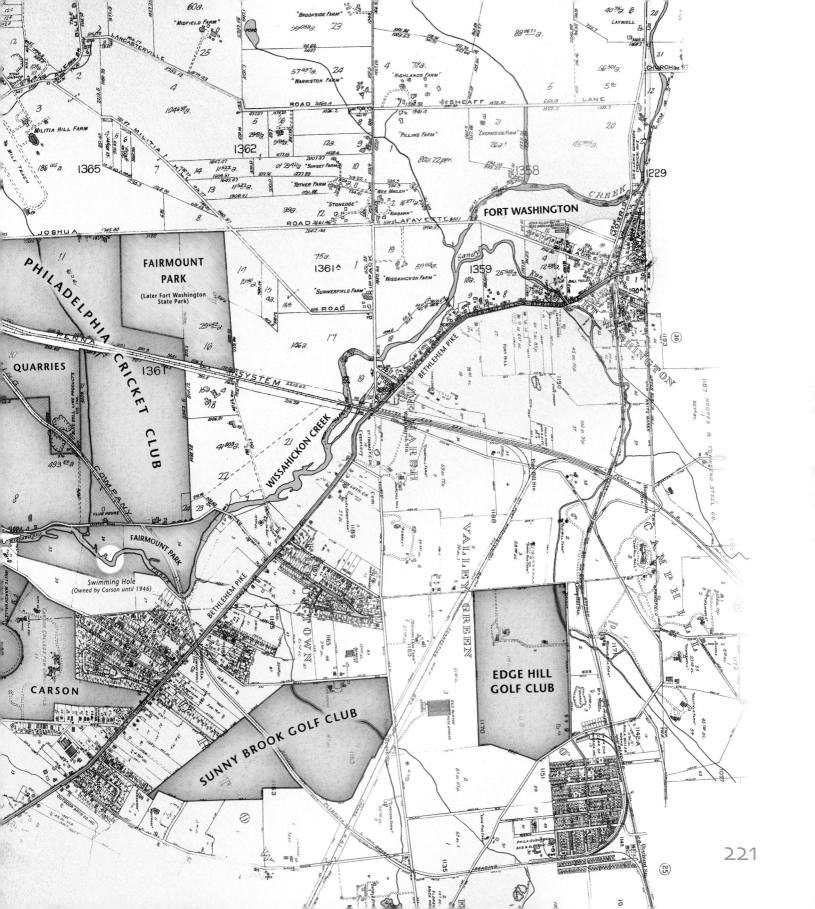

Swimming Hole
(Owned by Carson until 1946)

FAIRMOUNT PARK
(Later Fort Washington State Park)

PHILADELPHIA CRICKET CLUB

QUARRIES

PENNA RAILWAY SYSTEM

WISSAHICKON CREEK

FORT WASHINGTON

CARSON

BETHLEHEM PIKE

SUNNY BROOK GOLF CLUB

EDGE HILL GOLF CLUB

Andorra Nurseries

Three large properties sat along the lower ridge in the transitional area—between the city and the suburbs, between two geologic formations and between the dramatic, forested gorge and the open, cultivated countryside. These properties were Andorra Nurseries, Mount St. Joseph's Academy and the Morris Estate. All three eventually stretched into the Whitemarsh Valley beyond their primary sites on the ridge. Andorra Nurseries used the good agricultural land for the bulk of its nursery operation, while the academy and the Morrises used it to raise food.

The Andorra Nurseries were established in 1886 by Henry Howard Houston, a multi-faceted entrepreneur and owner of much of Upper Roxborough and the west side of Chestnut Hill. He named it "Andorra" after Richard Wister's mid-19th century estate and deer park on the property. The initial 60 acres of the nurseries were located on the steep slopes and on the thin, acidic soils of the Chickies quartzite ridge.[1]

In 1891, Houston hired William Warner Harper as the business manager for the nurseries, and when Houston died in 1895, Harper took a 99-year lease from the Houston Estate. An expert horticulturalist with a genius for merchandizing, Harper offered his customers landscape design services along with his large and varied nursery inventory. These skills led to the phenomenal success of the business and in the early 1920s, Harper began buying adjacent farms in Springfield and Whitemarsh Townships, eventually bringing together over 1,400 acres. The nurseries ultimately extended as far as Ridge and Butler Pikes in upper Whitemarsh Township, and kept this land open and undeveloped until the suburbanizing pressures of the early 1960s.[2]

Detail of the 1928 USGS Map showing the lower ridge at the southern edge of the middle valley site of the Andorra Nurseries, Mount St. Joseph's Academy and the Morris Estate.
Source: USGS Maps 1928, author's collection

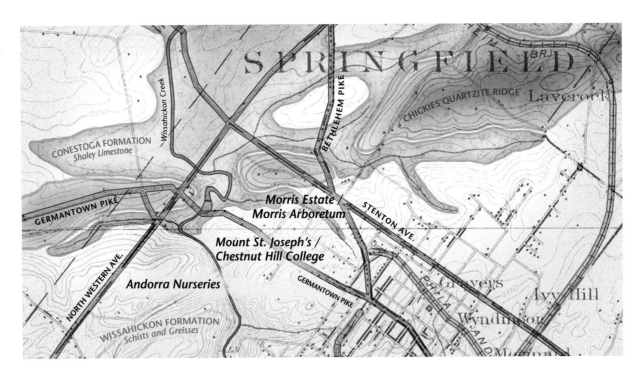

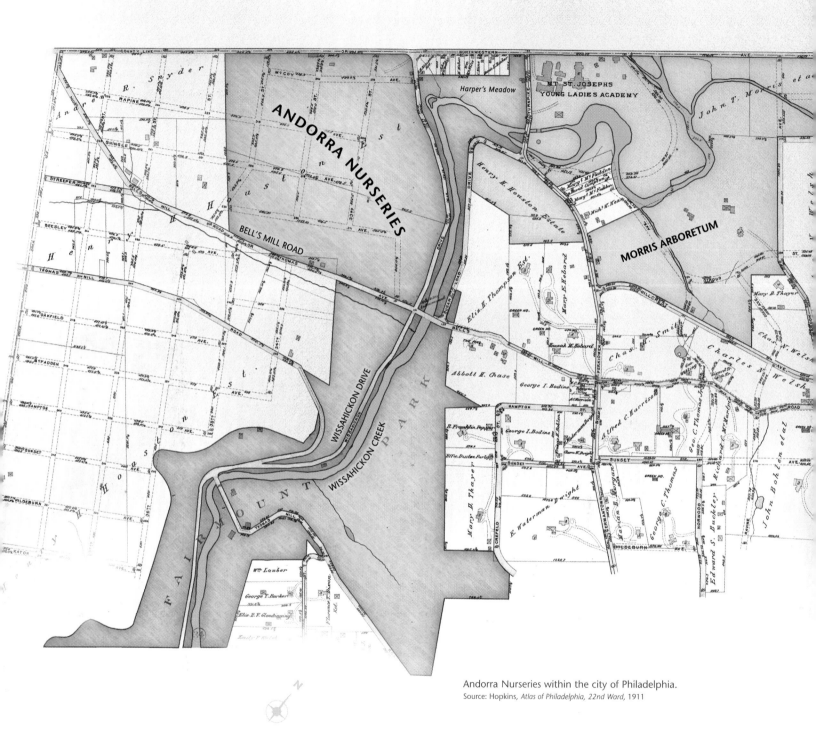

Andorra Nurseries within the city of Philadelphia.
Source: Hopkins, *Atlas of Philadelphia, 22nd Ward*, 1911

Andorra Nurseries in Whitemarsh Township. The Wissahickon Creek is not shown but would wind through the lower right hand corner beyond the borders of the photograph. Germantown Pike, an extension of Germantown Avenue out of the city and the route to Reading, runs along the lower part of the photograph. Thomas Road crosses Germantown Pike and marks the boundary between the nurseries and the golf course of the Whitemarsh Valley Country Club. "Andorra House," where William Harper lived, is the large mansion in the lower right, below Germantown Pike. Aerial photograph, 1929. Source: LCP

Andorra Nurseries

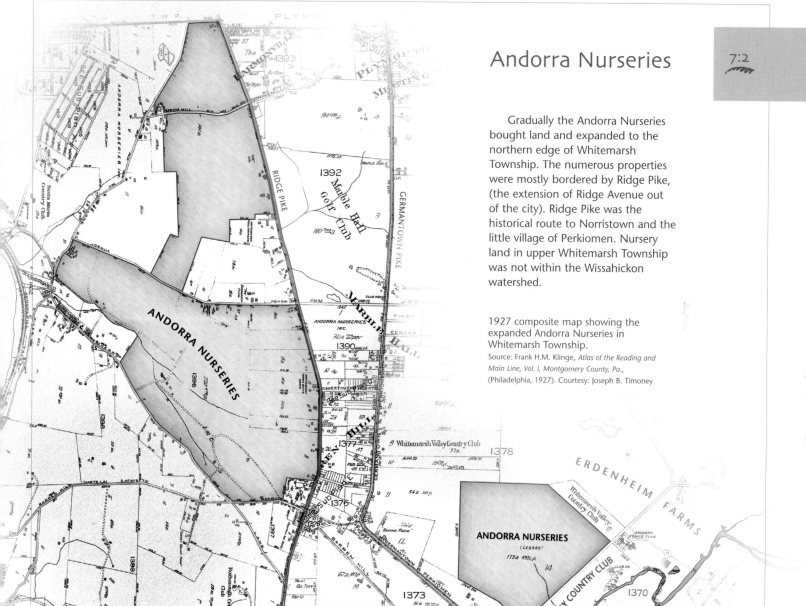

Gradually the Andorra Nurseries bought land and expanded to the northern edge of Whitemarsh Township. The numerous properties were mostly bordered by Ridge Pike, (the extension of Ridge Avenue out of the city). Ridge Pike was the historical route to Norristown and the little village of Perkiomen. Nursery land in upper Whitemarsh Township was not within the Wissahickon watershed.

1927 composite map showing the expanded Andorra Nurseries in Whitemarsh Township.
Source: Frank H.M. Klinge, *Atlas of the Reading and Main Line, Vol. I, Montgomery County, Pa.,* (Philadelphia, 1927). Courtesy: Joseph B. Timoney

Mount St. Joseph's Academy (later Chestnut Hill College) showing the college on the ridge with the campus stepping down to Wissahickon Creek. The Dewees mill, mill race and pond (which backed water up into an old oxbow) can clearly be seen on the right. At this time, electric trolleys ran on Germantown Avenue, with the end of the line and trolley turnaround just north of the academy. Drawing, c. 1910.
Source: GHS

Mount St. Joseph's Academy (later Chestnut Hill College)

Moving east along the ridge, the second large property in this transitional area was Mount St. Joseph's Academy, a Catholic boarding school for girls.[1] In the early 18th century, the property was part of some 93 acres belonging to William Dewees, who, about 1708, built the second paper mill in North America. Later, members of the Dewees family built two additional mills, both across Germantown Avenue in Harper's Meadow. The three mills, along with William Dewees's house and a scattering of workers' cottages, created a small village.[2] After the Dewees mills were abandoned and the site became a sleepy spot on the outskirts of Chestnut Hill, Joseph Middleton built a modest country house in the early 1850s, on the ridge overlooking the creek, which he grandly named Monticello, in honor of Thomas Jefferson.[3]

The Sisters of St. Joseph, who bought the Middleton property in 1858, came to this site as shelter from the increasing violence and anti-Catholicism in Philadelphia, which lingered for decades after the "nativist riots" of the 1840s. The creek and the millpond helped to create a psychological moat against the outside world.[4]

The academy site was directly across Wissahickon Creek from what would become the Morris Estate, the third major landholding along the lower ridge. Between these two large properties, the creek flows through a narrow gap in the ridge and opens into a broad flood plain. The long, sharp ridge with the relatively wide, flat land below, provided an isolated and protected site—an ideal location for training nuns and operating a series of schools for young, Catholic women. Mount St. Joseph's Academy, opening in 1871, was the first of these.

The sisters also owned a substantial piece of property in adjoining Montgomery County and farmed this area until the early post-World War II period. The neighboring Morris Estate shared this pattern of using the ridge to site buildings, the creek for recreation and the fields in the limestone valley for food.

In 1924, the sisters established a separate institution, Mount St. Joseph's College, on the same site, which changed its name to Chestnut Hill College in 1938. When the academy moved east to the corner of Stenton and Wissahickon Avenues (the site of the old convent farm), the college took over the academy buildings.

Composite map showing the site of Mount St. Joseph's Academy. The broad flood plain, the bend in the creek, the Dewees millpond and millrace can be clearly seen. The map also shows the farm of the Sisters of St. Joseph at Stenton and Wissahickon Avenues in Springfield Township. Later this property became the site of the relocated Mount St. Joseph's Academy and the St. Joseph's Villa.
Source: Hopkins, *Atlas of Philadelphia, 22d ward*, 1911. and A.H. Mueller, *Atlas of the North Penn Section of Montgomery County, Pa.*, 1916

7:3

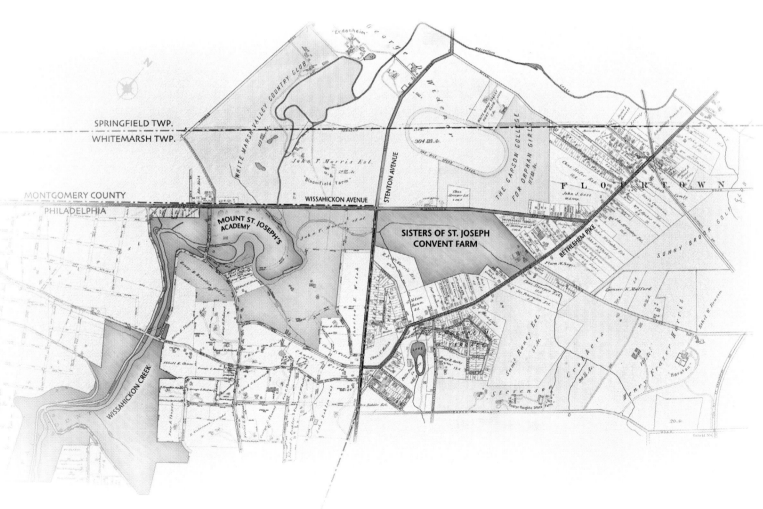

Early Chestnut Hill College | 1924–1935

In 1924, the Sisters of St. Joseph opened what was originally called Mount St. Joseph's College, a four-year liberal arts college, renamed Chestnut Hill College in 1938. Co-existing with the academy on the same grounds, the college grew rapidly. In 1928, the Sisters put up a separate college building, a combination dormitory and classrooms.

The newly constructed college was designed in the "Lombard Romanesque" style, complete with bell tower, arcade and red tiled roof. This style projected the image of a safe and cloistered place for young, Catholic women living away from home.

View of the Dewees milldam and pond, with the academy and college buildings in the background. Photograph, c. 1930. Source: Chestnut Hill College

Aerial view of the Mount St. Joseph's Academy and the early Chestnut Hill College, coexisting on the same site. Looking northwest, the Mother House (with the chapel behind it), the academy building and the new college building form a complex on the ridge.

The old Dewees millpond and millrace were kept and incorporated into the campus experience. The waterfall at the dam can be seen in the center left. The Wissahickon Creek follows the Chickies quartzite ridge, bending close to the foot of the slope below the college building. Photograph, c. 1930.
Source: Chestnut Hill College

Above
College students paddling on the old Dewees millpond.
Photograph, c. 1940. Source: Chestnut Hill College

The Wissahickon Creek and the old millpond also created rich recreational possibilities for the students on the lower campus. The women could canoe on the creek and pond, and walk along an extensive path system that led down from the college buildings, followed the creek and circled the pond. Several rustic bridges carried these paths across the millrace. There were multiple places for student life—gathering places of many different scales—outdoor rooms, alcoves and passageways.

This integration of buildings on the ridge and the wooded creek corridor in the floodplain made the campus one of the most attractive in the area. In the first year of the college, the catalogue called it "Mount St. Joseph's on the Wissahickon."

After World War II, to create more usable land, the college drained and filled the millpond and millrace and straightened the creek. With this decision, the college lost its special relationship to the natural part of the campus. Just a few years later, environmental regulations—floodplain zoning and wetland protection—would prohibit such planning decisions.

Rustic bridge over the old Dewees millrace. Photograph, c. 1930.
Source: Chestnut Hill College

The Morris Estate (Later the Morris Arboretum)

In 1887, three and a half decades after the Sisters of St. Joseph moved to their ridge overlooking the Wissahickon Creek, Quaker industrialist John Morris (1847-1915) and his sister Lydia Morris (1849-1932) began assembling a series of contiguous parcels to create a summer residence on what would ultimately be an estate of 166 acres.[5]

The Morris money came from John and Lydia's father, Isaac P. Morris, who founded and ran I.P. Morris and Company, Ironmongers (later known as the Port Richmond Iron Works, a firm that manufactured gears and shafts for ship engines). John and Lydia, who remained unmarried and lived together all their lives, planned from the beginning to make their property a public resource. They agreed, in John's words, to make "an exhibit as may have an educational value to the young people and those who will be helped to understand their surroundings intelligently."[6]

On his death, John left the property to Lydia and she, in turn, willed it to the University of Pennsylvania in 1932, directing that the property—renamed the Morris Arboretum in their honor—be used as a botanical garden, horticultural museum, and educational facility. She envisioned a "laboratory … disseminating….knowledge to the world," with major lectures hosted by the institution "for students and the public generally, [and given] by eminent scientists."[7] When the arboretum officially opened to the public in June 1933, *The Philadelphia Ledger* wrote that it rivaled "the Arnold Gardens in Boston, the Kew Gardens of London or the Jardin d'Acclimation of Paris."[8]

The estate in its final form was assembled in two big pieces, with the Wissahickon Creek running along the western boundary of both parcels. The first piece, brought together through a number of purchases over the years, was called "Compton." Located

The early Morris Estate was almost entirely farmfields with only a few large trees forming hedgerows and small remnants of woodland on the steepest slopes leading down to the Wissahickon. Photograph, c. 1880s.
Source: Morris Arboretum of the University of Pennsylvania

entirely within the boundaries of Philadelphia the topography of this land was complex and sharply dissected, reflecting the underlying schist and quartzite bedrock.

In 1913, John Morris acquired "Bloomfield" in Springfield Township across Northwestern Avenue. Separated from Compton by Northwestern Avenue, the landforms of this second piece of property were simpler and gentler, expressing a different geology. The harder dolomite at Bloomfield had formed a shallow ridge, and the softer limestones had worn down into undulating slopes. This land provided good soils for a working farm and allowed the estate to become relatively self-sufficient.

When the Morrises made their initial purchases in the late 1880s, the land had been cut over and farmed for generations. Like Mount St. Joseph's Academy across the creek, buildings at Compton were grouped along the ridge. At the academy, these were institutional in scale and grouped tightly together. At the Morris Estate, smaller, individual structures dotted the ridge. The Morrises' large, late Victorian mansion, designed by the well-known Philadelphia architect Theophilus P. Chandler, Jr., commanded a view in all directions. It was the orienting feature for the gardens in this complex landscape, and both a visual and symbolic anchor for the surrounding grounds.

With Bloomfield, the Morrises acquired the remaining elements necessary for a "picturesque" gentleman's country estate. From the mansion, the view to the north swept down into the misty bottomlands of the Whitemarsh Valley. From there, the eye was carried up to the farm in the distance, and to the mill and barn on the ridge beyond.

The Morris properties not only protected the main stem of the Wissahickon Creek, but also a portion of two tributaries. Paper Mill Run, the larger of the two, originates in a spring near the Chestnut Hill-East railroad station, flowing from there into Springfield Township and then circling back again into Chestnut Hill, where it winds through broad, swampy bottomland on the north side of the Morris Estate, before joining the Wissahickon.

The Morrises' mansion—like the property—was called "Compton." It was designed by the prominent Philadelphia architect, Theophilus P. Chandler, and built in 1888. On the top of the hill, it commanded views in all directions and anchored a complex landscape. Photograph, 1937.
Source: Morris Arboretum of the University of Pennsylvania

Lydia and John Morris
on the steps of the
"Love Temple" at the edge
of the Swan Pond.
Photograph, c. 1909.
Source: Morris Arboretum of the
University of Pennsylvania

John Morris, an enlightened farmer and engineer who practiced the progressive land reclamation ideas of his day, straightened Paper Mill Run, filled the wetlands where this stream emptied into the Wissahickon and built an extensive network of perforated clay pipes to drain the floodplain and marshy lowlands.

The estate also included a smaller tributary, preserved and elaborated as part of the gardens. The "Swan Pond" stream originated as a spring in the hillside of a neighboring property on Hillcrest Avenue. It emerged from this spring into marshy ground on a small terrace in the hillside. Later, when the house was remodeled, a grotto was built into the hill to capture the spring. Water flowed out of the grotto into small pools joined by a formal channel and down the hillside into the Morris Estate. The Morrises took advantage of this small, clear, rocky stream to create the many different water features that ultimately tied the garden together—damming it to form the "Swan Pond."

The Swan Pond Stream continues through the property, meeting the Wissahickon Creek at a dramatic bend, where it flows into the narrow gap between Mount St. Joseph's Academy (now Chestnut Hill College) and the Morris Estate. Here, the ridge drops abruptly down and encloses the creek with high cliffs, forming one of the most theatrical and romantic spots along the gorge. Just upstream from this meeting of tributary and creek, the Morrises built a rustic boathouse, with a porch and small dining area above it, as the symbolic "river entrance" to their estate.

As Quakers, the Morrises had a deep commitment to the public good. John was a life-long champion of playgrounds and parks throughout the Philadelphia region. Both John and Lydia shared an interest in preserving historic architecture. As individuals, they were in many ways typical, wealthy Victorians—well-educated and avidly curious about newly available knowledge and an increasingly accessible world. They had the time and the money, and they traveled widely, satisfying their curiosity and collecting plants.[9]

Collecting plants combined the Morrises' love of travel with their deeply felt Quaker respect for the sacredness of the earth. They brought back to their Philadelphia estate not only individual plant species, but also the historical garden styles of Europe and Asia. Travel to Northeast China, Korea and Japan in the 1890s led to a collection of plants from the temperate, deciduous forests of Asia, where plant families (genera) were parallel to the plant families of the temperate, deciduous forests of Northeastern United States.

Lydia and John Morris and their traveling companion Louise Kellner in India, riding on an elephant. Kellner's diaries recording this trip and other world travels with the Morrises are available at the Historical Society of Pennsylvania. Photograph, c. 1889–90.

Source: Hagley Museum and Library

The Morrises also established long-term professional friendships with the major horticulturalists and collectors of the time—Charles Sargeant, then director of the Arnold Arboretum (outside Boston, Massachusetts); writer and plant explorer David Fairchild; Thomas Meehan, a local nurseryman; and E. H. "Chinese" Wilson, the famous plant collector.[10]

There are several important Morris legacies. Their estate became a public institution and preserved a portion of the main stem of Wissahickon Creek and two tributaries. Their commitment to providing educational facilities and programs about temperate, deciduous plants has evolved into a significant national and international resource, with widespread partnerships with Asian botanical institutions. At the beginning of the 21st century, the arboretum, continuing a key concern of John Morris, has taken a major role mediating between city and suburbs. They have also become a leader in the restoration of the ecosystems of the Wissahickon Valley.

7:4–8

7:4 The Temperate Deciduous Forest Zones

The Morris Estate was located in the Northeastern Deciduous Forest zone, and The Morrises appropriately collected plants from the Deciduous Forest Regions of the world. As a result, many of the original trees, understory and shrubs brought back to the site have survived and flourished on their property.

Within these parallel zones, the individual species are distinct, but the genera of both woody and herbaceous plants are the same. The Temperate, Deciduous Forests of Asia were particularly captivating to the Morrises because of the great richness of species found there. By contrast, the variety of plants in northern Europe were greatly diminished by the effects of glaciation. There, the mountain ranges ran east to west (rather than north to south as

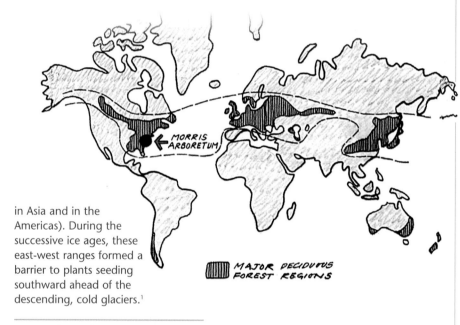

in Asia and in the Americas). During the successive ice ages, these east-west ranges formed a barrier to plants seeding southward ahead of the descending, cold glaciers.[1]

1. Hui-Lin Li, *Floristic Relationships between Eastern Asia and Eastern North America* (Philadelphia, 1971), 371-77.

Map of the Deciduous forests of the world.
Source: Andropogon, drawing by Colin Franklin

Morris Estate

Wissahickon Creek remains in open space on both sides of the city boundary. Within the city, the Morris Estate protected the creek on the east side, while Mount St. Joesph's Academy protected it on the west. Beyond the city, in Springfield Township, the Morrises' Bloomfield Farm kept the land surrounding the creek open on the east, while the Whitemarsh Valley Country Club kept it open on the west.

Two tributaries—the Swan Pond Stream and Paper Mill Run— passed through the Morris Estate. Like Cresheim Creek and Sandy Run, Paper Mill Run is one of the most extensive stream networks to flow into the Wissahickon. One of the branches of Paper Mill Run was dammed just below Bethlehem Pike, probably as a millpond. This pond became the water feature and paddling pond at White City, an early amusement park.

Composite map showing the two pieces of the Morris Estate— Compton, within city boundaries, and Bloomfield across Northwestern Avenue in Springfield Township.
Source: Hopkins *Atlas of Philadelphia, 22d Ward,* 1911 and A H. Mueller, *Atlas of the North Penn section of Montgomery County, Pa.,* 1916

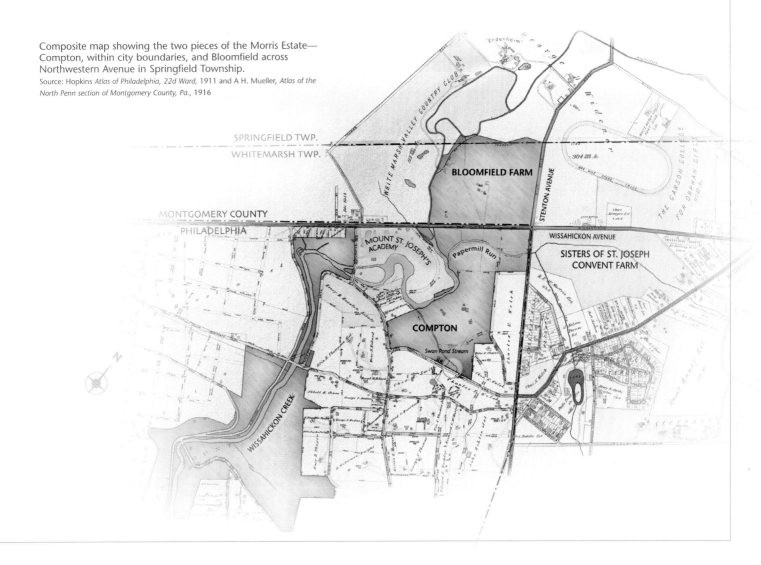

Morris Estate *(Continued)*

The mansion, sited on the nose of the ridge, commands 180-degree views. The Morrises entered the estate from Germantown Avenue at a secondary high point, which gave them a view of the house and the sweep of the Swan Pond Valley. The Rose Garden, formerly a vegetable plot, was located on a terrace in the hillside, below the house and overlooking the valley.

An "English Park," complete with picturesque pond, copies of Greek and Roman temples and an Italian Renaissance water stairs, was created in the open valley of the Swan Pond Stream.

Following the dictums of "Capability" Brown, the famous 18th-century garden designer who transformed the English landscape, the Morrises planted the hillsides and elaborated the stream in the valley. Brown believed that planting the hillsides obscured the property boundaries and made the estates look larger and grander. Damming the streams to make lakes brought continual interest to the landscape, with reflections and changing views.[1] In the Morrises' garden, water features acted like miniature tributaries bringing water from both real and imaginary springs in the hillside down to the Swan Pond Stream.

1. See Thomas Hinde, *Capability Brown: The Story of a Master Gardener,* (New York, 1978); and Roger Turner, *Capability Brown and the Eighteenth-Century Landscape* (New York, 1985).

Workers excavating the Swan Pond. Photograph, c. 1908.
Source: Morris Arboretum of the University of Pennsylvania

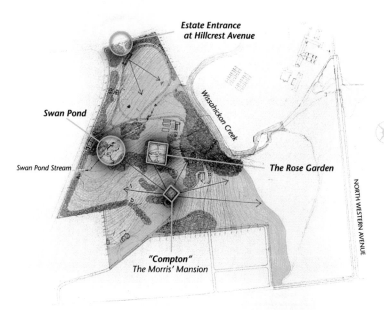

Estate Entrance
at Hillcrest Avenue

Wissahickon Creek

Swan Pond

Swan Pond Stream

The Rose Garden

NORTH WESTERN AVENUE

"Compton"
The Morris' Mansion

A plan showing the initial structure of the Morrises'
garden at Compton c.1890s. Source: Andropogon,1976.
Drawing by Rolf Sauer

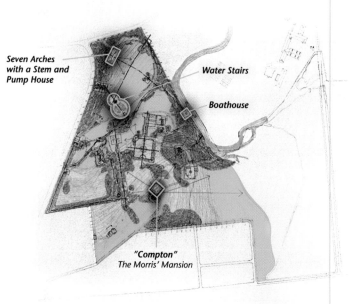

Seven Arches
with a Stem and
Pump House

Water Stairs

Boathouse

"Compton"
The Morris' Mansion

A plan showing the elaboration of the gardens
at Compton. Source: Andropogon,1976.
Drawing by Rolf Sauer

The Mercury Temple and
fern rivulet which flowed
from its basement grotto—
under construction.
Photograph, c. 1913.
Source: Morris Arboretum
of the University of Pennsylvania

E. H. "Chinese" Wilson | (1876-1930)

At the height of Western imperialism, commanding the botanical resources of the world was a way of demonstrating wealth and power. This impetus to collect was also driven by a consuming curiosity about the world and late Victorian ideas of civic responsibility and public education.

The botanist known as "Chinese" Wilson brought more than 1000 new species of plants to North America, primarily from Northeastern Asia. He collected for both wealthy private estate owners and for botanical institutions.

Many of the plants Wilson collected have remained relatively docile and have simply enriched the plant palette of the Wissahickon Valley.

On the other hand, a number have escaped from gardens to become invasive exotics—spreading rapidly in the park and other parts of the valley. These plants include ailanthus (*Ailanthus altissima)*, barberry (*Berberis*), Russian olive (*Pawlownia torientosa*), euonymus (*Euonymus alatus*), honeysuckle (*Lonicera, spp.*), pawlownia (*Pawlownia tomentosa*), amur cork tree (*Phellodendron amurense*), rugosa rose (*Rosa rugosa*), dewberry (*Rubus almus*), viburnum, and wisteria.

Born in Gloucestershire, England, Wilson trained as a gardener at the Birmingham Botanic Gardens and later worked at the Royal Botanic Gardens at Kew. He also studied at the Royal College of Science in South Kensington, London. He took the first of his many collecting trips to China in 1899 to bring back plants and seeds for James Veitch and Sons, a well-known private English nursery business.

In 1907, Charles Sprague Sargent, then director of Harvard University's Arnold Arboretum, sent Wilson on a two-year expedition to China to collect trees and shrubs. He made three more trips for the Arnold—to Japan in 1914-15; to Formosa (Taiwan), Korea, and Japan in 1917-19; and to India, Australia, New Zealand and Africa in 1920-22. Many of the plants that he brought back from Northeastern Asia were shared among the Morris Estate, the Arnold Arboretum in Boston and the Biltmore Estate in North Carolina.

New England winters at the Arnold Arboretum proved too cold, and summers in North Carolina at the Baltimore Estate too hot for the plants Wilson brought back to survive. By the 1970s, it was only the Morris Arboretum, located in the more temperate climate of the middle Atlantic states, that could proudly display 100 trees collected in Northeastern Asia by E.H. Wilson.

In 1919, Wilson was made assistant director of the Arnold Arboretum and in 1927 given the odd title of "keeper." His important and impressive career was cut short in 1930, when at the age of fifty-four, Wilson and his wife were killed in an automobile accident near Worcester, Massachusetts.[1]

Ernest Henry Wilson (second on the left) with a group of men, sitting among the trees on a collecting expedition in Korea. A species of Korean maple (*Acer pseudosieboldianum*) can be seen in the foreground. Photograph, 1917.
Source: Copyright President and Fellows of Harvard College, Archives of the Arnold Arboretum

1. DAB, 20:321-22.

The cabin of Lydia Morris, along
the Swan Pond Stream, built 1908.
Source: Morris Arboretum of the University of Pennsylvania

Lydia's Cabin and the "American Wilderness"

Lydia's cabin sits in a little woodland along the Swan Pond Stream. This piece of the English Park was not designed in the English Romantic style, but rather was an evocation of the American frontier. In some respects, this little cabin served the same emotional purpose as Marie Antoinette's country dairy at Versailles. It was both a rustic and elegant place where Lydia could retreat to entertain friends. It also has parallels to the Japanese teahouses which Lydia probably saw on her travels to the Far East. Although the banks of the stream are partially formalized, the artistic aim was to create a little mountain stream. The woodland was kept largely natural and planted with the trees, under-story, shrubs, ferns and wildflowers of the Wissahickon Valley.

Pavilions and Boathouses in the Middle Valley

In the flatter topography of the middle valley, private estate owners built small boathouses and pavilions along the creek that had counterparts in the "club" boathouses along the Schuylkill River and the public pavilions that were sited high on promontories and steep rock outcrops, both above the Schuylkill River and in the Wissahickon gorge.

Below
A rustic summer house at Erdenheim Farms, built by then owner Robert N. Carson. The description of this pavilion as a "summer house" comes from the photographer, Thomas Shoemaker. Photograph c. 1910. Source: HSP, Shoemaker Collection

Morris boathouse along the Wissahickon Creek in the middle Valley. Photograph, 1909.
Source: Morris Arboretum of the University of Pennsylvania

In contrast to the gorge, the landscape of the shallow, low lying Whitemarsh Valley is open and flat. Beyond the "summer house" seen in the photograph are the typical open fields of the middle valley, with a country road in the background. The creek bank has been cut over and looks scruffy, with only a few trees that have been allowed to regrow on the banks. The braided channel, characteristic of this landscape, can be seen in the foreground. None of these pavilions and boathouses in the middle valley have survived to enrich the experience of this portion of the creek with a layer of cultural artifacts.

The summer House at the confluence of Sandy Run and Wissahickon Creek, just below Fort Washington. The Wissahickon Creek can be seen in the foreground and the mouth of Sandy Run behind. Photograph, c. 1910.
Source: HSP, Shoemaker Collection

Erdenheim Farms (Later Erdenheim Farm)

In the heart of the Whitemarsh Valley, several large properties remained mostly fields and remnant forest. Carson Valley School and the three golf courses had once been working farms. Erdenheim Farms continued as a gentleman's estate, raising race horses, sheep and angus cattle.

In colonial times, "Erdenheim" had been a fragment of the large tract owned by Edward Farmer, one of the original grantees of William Penn. The property was later inherited by his two sons-in-law, Peter and Jonathan Robeson, who owned the Robeson Mills at the mouth of the Wissahickon. After passing through several owners, 200 acres of this land were sold to Johann Georg Hocker, a German immigrant who settled there in 1761 and named his new property "Erdenheim," meaning Earthly Home.[11] Hocker's sons sold the land to a mill owner, Henry Scheetz. The property became a stock farm during the Civil War, when it was bought by Aristides Welsh, who began a long tradition of breeding race horses at Erdenheim. Welsh added substantially to the acreage and to the value of the farm. His racehorses were renowned for their first-place showings at famous racecourses such as Ascot and the Kentucky Derby.[12] Just before the turn of the century, the land was purchased by Robert N. Carson, who would later give part of this land and a large endowment to the Carson College for Orphan Girls.

George Widener, Jr., whose grandfather, Peter Arrell Widener, made a fortune in the streetcar and railroad industries, bought the land from Carson's widow in 1915. Widener, a young man of 24 that year, had recently lost his father and his brother when the Titanic sank. Influenced by his uncle, Joseph E. Widener, who bred and raced championship horses, and who would transform Hialeah Park in Miami, Florida, into a first class racetrack, Widener returned Erdenheim Farms to the stud farm tradition established by Welsh.

An important Philadelphia philanthropist, Widener was a director of the Land Title Bank and Trust Company, the Philadelphia Traction Company, and the Electric Storage Battery Company, but his first love was horse breeding and one of his horses, Jaipur, won the Belmont Stakes in 1962. His ownership of Erdenheim Farms was distinguished by exceptional stewardship of the property, which included maintaining its agricultural operations, as well as breeding and training thoroughbred race horses. Widener would enlarge the farm to approximately 500 acres and shape the landscape into an ideal English country estate, creating scenic views and building elegant barns. Before his death, he donated 113 acres of the farm to the Natural Lands Trust, with a life-interest for his nephew and heir, Fitz Eugene Dixon.[13]

Erdenheim, undiminished by time, is still a vision of a 19th-century gentleman's farm. It is a composed landscape with an arched stone bridge crossing the Wissahickon. The creek winds through a gentle, grassy valley, framed by the house and barns. Woodlands line the ridges, enclosing the pastures on the slopes that are bordered by split rail fences, where cows and sheep graze picturesquely.

7:9–11

View of Sheep Barn at Erdenheim Farms.
Source: Photograph by Paul Meyer

Erdenheim Farms | The English Romantic Landscape

Unlike the dramatic Wissahickon gorge, which romantics associated with the awesome and sometimes frightening powers of nature, the landscape of the middle valley, preserved at Erdenheim Farms, resembles the benign English countryside painted by Constable with sheep grazing in wide meadows and cows wading in the creek, or lying under great, old trees left along the banks.

The Wideners owned this painting for many years before donating it to the National Gallery in Washington D.C. It hung over the fireplace in the Widener house and is believed to be the inspiration for the Erdenheim Farms landscape.

Below
Wivenhoe Park, Essex, England, oil on canvas. Painting by John Constable, 1816.
Source: Widener Collection, Image copyright Board of Trustees, National Gallery of Art, Washington, D.C.

Inset
The pastoral landscape of Erdenheim Farms with Wissahickon Creek running through.
Source: Photograph by CLF

Erdenheim Farms | The Architecture

George Widener built several extraordinarily attractive barns at Erdenheim Farms. These barns were not treated as functional necessities, but were designed to complement the landscape and to be a part of the public view. According to historian Tom Williamson, in his book on

18th-century English country estates, placing attractive farm buildings in full view announced the ownership of fine livestock (especially horses) and proclaimed the owner's status.[1]

1. Tom Williamson, *Polite Landscapes: Gardens and Society in 18th Century England* (Phoenix Mill, UK, 1995), 124.

Sheep Barn at
Erdenheim Farms, built c. 1915.
Source: Photograph by CLF

Horse Barn at Erdenheim Farms, built c. 1920s. Source: Photograph by CLF

The Whitemarsh Hunt

The landscape of the Whitemarsh Valley had many of the qualities of the English countryside in Buckinghamshire and other parts of Southern England. The gently rolling terrain provided an ideal setting for an autumn foxhunt. In this era of gentlemen farmers, East Coast landowners imitated the English aristocracy in many of their recreational pursuits and "riding to the hounds" had been one of the favorite pastimes since the 18th century.[1]

The headquarters of the Whitemarsh Hunt was located on a small piece of Erdenheim Farms. In October 1925, hunt participants were described by a local newspaper as "Throngs of men and women prominently identified in social, club, financial, and professional circles, augmented by many of the hunting set, from New York, Long Island, Washington and Baltimore… met on horseback, in their pink riding coats."[2]

---

1. E. Digby Baltzell, *Philadelphia Gentlemen: The Making of a National Upper Class* (New York, 1958: reprint, 1979), 362-63.

2. *Chestnut Hill and Mount Airy Herald*, October 23, 1925.

The Whitemarsh Hunt Headquarters between Erdenheim Farms and the Carson College for Orphan Girls. Source: Frank H.M. Klinge, *Atlas of the Reading and Main Line, Vol. I*, Montgomery County, Pa. (Philadelphia, 1927). Courtesy of Joseph B. Timoney.

The Whitemarsh Hunt. Photograph, c. 1940. Source: Highlands Historical Society

Carson College for Orphan Girls (Later Carson Valley School)

Robert N. Carson, who owned Erdenheim in the late 19th and early 20th centuries, willed 87 acres of the farm (subsequently augmented to 98 acres) and virtually all his $5 million estate to endow the Carson College for Orphan Girls (later known as the Carson Valley School).[14] Carson left the money, the land and the moral imperatives, but had nothing to do with the physical design of this institution. The Carson board—largely men from Germantown, Mt. Airy and Chestnut Hill—held an architectural competition for the design of the school and set aside one million dollars for its construction.

The competition was won by the Philadelphia architect Albert Kelsey (1870-1950) who designed what he called a "children's fantasy village." Kelsey had graduated from the University of Pennsylvania School of Architecture and had apprenticed with the well-known firm of T. P. Chandler and with Cope and Stewardson. Later he formed his own firm, Kennedy, Hays & Kelsey. When this firm dissolved, he collaborated on a number of competitions with Paul Cret and worked with him on the Benjamin Franklin Parkway.

To create the village, Kelsey worked closely with landscape designer Arthur Paul, who was the chief designer at the Andorra Nurseries; J.H.Dulles Allen, the owner of Enfield Pottery and Tile Works; and a sculptor, Otto Schweizer, one of the best-known artists of the period. The arts and crafts movement encouraged the idea that visual richness was therapeutic. Otto Mallery, an influential member of the board, and Elsa Ueland, the brilliant headmistress at Carson, firmly believed that the integration of architecture, landscape design and arts and crafts, would stimulate the impoverished imaginations of the orphaned girls. It was Mallery and his connection to the Enfield Pottery, as investor and close friend of Dulles Allen, who fostered this collaboration.

Arthur Paul, the landscape designer, created an English romantic landscape out of a piece of Carson's farm. He planted copses of oak, ash, and other native trees to give shade and create focal points in the "middle distance," and large groves of hemlocks at the Wissahickon Avenue entrance to create a strong, visual transition between the outside world and the sheltered "village" within. With Kelsey, he laid out a drive that meandered along the natural contours of the land, aligning and grading it to give broad, picturesque views at curves and overlooks. The drive was kept narrow by allowing cars to pull over into occasional lay-bys (widened sections of the road), which allowed oncoming vehicles to pass.[15]

At the center of the site, this drive brought people to a tight group of school buildings and dormitories, set in the open countryside—a village along a country road. It was a widespread belief at the time that the countryside was therapeutic— taking children away from the ugly, polluted city.

Beyond the northwestern boundary, the orphanage had a small, six-acre plot on Wissahickon Creek. At a big bend in the creek, there was a swimming hole, a favorite spot for the orphans and residents of neighboring Flourtown to swim on hot summer days. Hikes and picnics along the Wissahickon were a favorite outing for the children. As part of their progressive education program, teachers used the Wissahickon as a laboratory for "Nature study" classes. In these classes, they followed the creek to its source near Montgomeryville, and to its mouth where it joined the Schuylkill River.[16]

The Carson College swimming hole on Wissahickon Creek. Photograph, c. 1920.
Source: Carson Valley School

Carson College for Orphan Girls

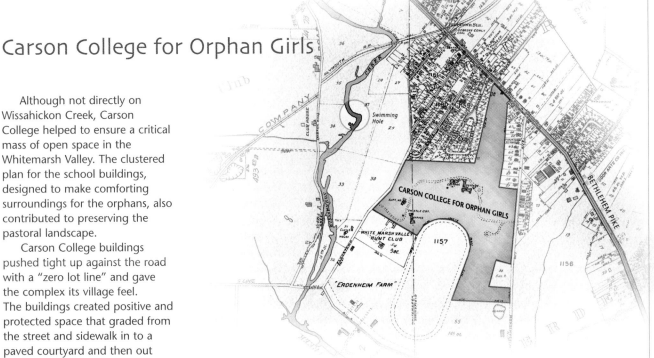

Although not directly on Wissahickon Creek, Carson College helped to ensure a critical mass of open space in the Whitemarsh Valley. The clustered plan for the school buildings, designed to make comforting surroundings for the orphans, also contributed to preserving the pastoral landscape.

Carson College buildings pushed tight up against the road with a "zero lot line" and gave the complex its village feel. The buildings created positive and protected space that graded from the street and sidewalk in to a paved courtyard and then out into a lawn defined on three sides by the walls of the cottages and on the fourth by an oak grove. Through the screen of oak trunks, a meadow beyond the property terminates in a hedgerow along the creek.

1927 Map showing Carson College for Orphan Girls in the center, with Flourtown directly to the east and a portion of Erdenheim Farms directly to the west. Wissahickon Creek is north of the site. The general area of the swimming hole on the Wissahickon is shown by the small circle. The winding road through the property and the little "village" along it can be seen in the center of the map.
Source: Frank H.M. Klinge, *Atlas of the Reading and Main Line, Vol. I,* Montgomery County, Pa. (Philadelphia, 1927). Courtesy of Joseph B. Timoney

Below
View of Carson College from the fields at the edge of the property adjacent to larger fields bordering Wissahickon Creek.
Source: *Architectural Record,* July 1921

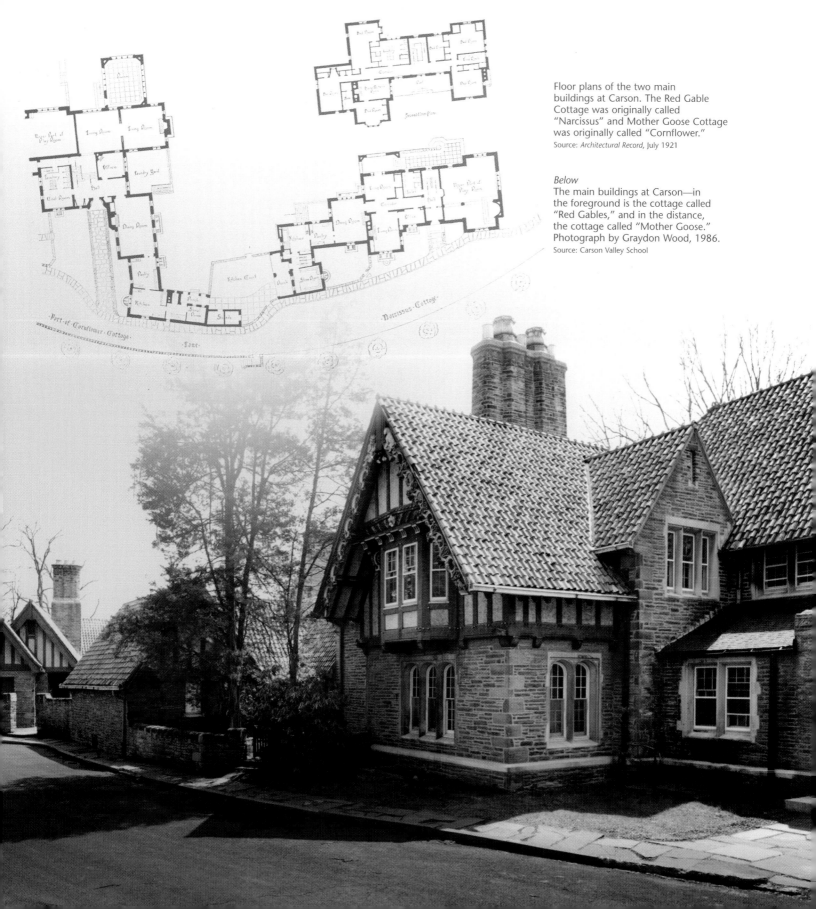

Floor plans of the two main
buildings at Carson. The Red Gable
Cottage was originally called
"Narcissus" and Mother Goose Cottage
was originally called "Cornflower."
Source: *Architectural Record*, July 1921

Below
The main buildings at Carson—in
the foreground is the cottage called
"Red Gables," and in the distance,
the cottage called "Mother Goose."
Photograph by Graydon Wood, 1986.
Source: Carson Valley School

Carson College for Orphan Girls

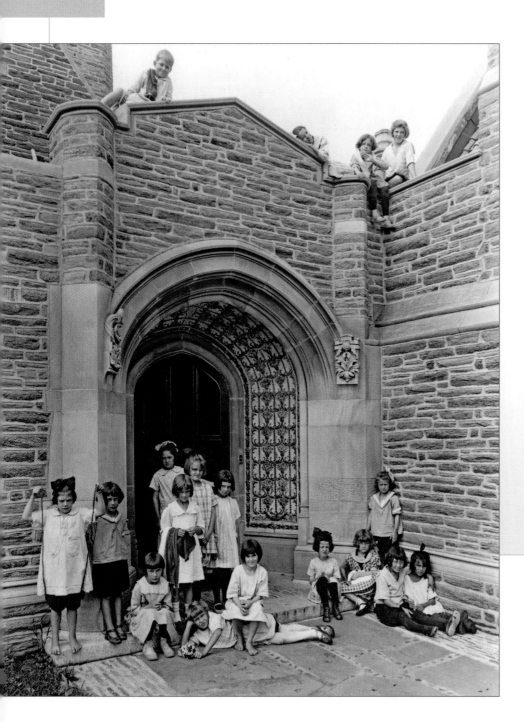

All the buildings at the orphanage were constructed of Wissahickon schist in the Tudor-Jacobean style, with steep, gabled polychrome tile roofs and low Gothic arches forming their entrances. The roofs themselves were a fantasy of color and detail. Covered with multi-hued, rounded pentiles, the red tiles prevailed toward the roof peak and gradually shifted to greens and blues towards the eaves. Kelsey worked with the Enfield Pottery and Tile Works in nearby Oreland at Paper Mill and Church Roads. All the arched doorways at Carson are decorated with Enfield tiles. The verge boards along the gable ends are elaborately carved with brightly painted flowers and animals, and the triangular areas between the gables are decorated in bas-reliefs illustrating nursery rhymes—with Mother Goose herself in the entrance forecourt to the main building. The huge walk-in fireplaces inside, resembling those in a medieval banquet hall, are lined with tiles that tell the story of Cinderella and Alice in Wonderland.[1]

---

1. For a fuller account and description of the archetecture and decoration, see David R. Contasta, *Philadelphia's Progressive Orphanage* (University Park, Pa., 1997).

Children looking like little gargoyles on the roof, at the elaborately tiled and carved entrance to Mother Goose Cottage. Photograph, c. 1903.
Source: Carson Valley School

The Golf Courses

Several golf courses, of a 100 acres or more each, also preserved open space along the main stem of Wissahickon Creek and two of its tributaries—Lorraine Run and Sunny Brook. Until the mid-19th century, this fertile landscape had been working farms. When farmers in this area could no longer compete with the large-scale grain production in the Midwest and the Plains States, many of these properties became gentlemen's country estates. Before the automobile suburbs emerged, and as the older generation of wealthy property owners died and the remaining working farms were less and less profitable, gently rolling land was available for a new use at a reasonable price. Close and accessible to the growing city, golf courses offered recreation in a bucolic setting for Philadelphia's prosperous residents. The ridge roads, which had become major arteries leading out of the city, made these courses easy to reach. All three of the major golf courses established in the middle valley were developed on or near one of these roads: Whitemarsh Valley Country Club along Germantown Pike, Philadelphia Cricket Club's golf course close to Stenton Avenue, and Sunnybrook Golf Club near Bethlehem Pike. These three courses formed a triangle (separated by other landholdings) that protected two main tributaries and a significant part of the main stem of Wissahickon creek.

Representation of Mother Goose on the gable end of Cornflower Cottage (later nicknamed Mother Goose Cottage). This bas-relief was part of a series of nursery rhyme figures by sculptor Otto Schweitzer. Source: Photograph by CLF

Despite preserving the land in open space, the golf courses also had a negative impact on the creek—warming the water, increasing runoff and depositing sediment. Developed on farmland, these golf courses were almost entirely open, with only a few trees clustered around the farm buildings.

To maximize space for fields and pastures, the farmers had cleared all the land, including the stream banks. This loss of forest increased runoff and, over time, the denuded banks were ripped and gouged by the increased volume and velocity of stormwater in the developing middle valley. These open stream banks suited golfers—allowing them to see over the "water hazards"—and the riparian corridors were not replanted or left to grow back into forest. On the other hand, the ideal of perfectly manicured turf had not yet captured the national imagination, and there were no organophosphates (developed after World War II) for use as fungicides and herbicides. This meant that toxic chemicals and nutrients did not run off the fairways into the stream.

The 122-acre Whitemarsh Valley Country Club was established in 1908 and laid out on a piece of the property called Bloomfield Farm. In 1913. John Morris bought the remaining piece of this land for his estate and retained the earlier name "Bloomfield Farm."[17] It was the only golf course sited along the main stem of the Wissahickon. Here, the creek meanders through a wide bottomland where the main channel splits twice to form side channels. One of these channels was cut off from the main stem and created a small oxbow, later made into several ornamental ponds.

View of the Wissahickon Creek in the Whitemarsh Valley Country Club. In the flat flood plain, the stream often divided into multiple channels. These channels continously shifted, forming and obliterating small islands, as seen here. Previously farmed, the stream banks had lost their tree and shrub cover and were badly eroded. Photograph, c. 1910. Source: GHS

Composite Map showing the golf courses along the Wissahickon in the Middle Valley.

Source: Frank H.M. Klinge, *Atlas of the Reading and Main Line, Vol. I*, Montgomery County, Pa. (Philadelphia, 1927).

Courtesy of Joseph B. Timoney

Whitemarsh Valley Country Club golf course was designed by George C. Thomas, Jr., the previous owner of Bloomfield, who not only designed this course on his own property, but also went on to create a number of famous courses on the West Coast.[18] The design preserved the stream channel, but did not capitalize on the pastoral qualities of the site. In contrast to the drama and simplicity of Erdenheim Farms, the golf course design did not express the structure of this landscape—a broad, open flood plain enclosed on two sides by hills. This lack of response to the landforms has encouraged random tree planting and undifferentiated fairways. The wetlands, probably eliminated during the agricultural period, was not restored by the country club and incorporated into a richer golfing experience.

A second course, Sunnybrook Golf Club, originally located in lower Flourtown, preserved a portion of Sunny Brook, a small tributary of the Wissahickon. Six men, defecting from the Philadelphia Cricket Club in Chestnut Hill, bought land for a new club in 1913, to provide an alternative to the full-fledged country clubs with activities other than golf. The course was designed by Donald Ross, the preeminent golf course designer of his day.

This land had been a farm located between Mill Road and Haws Lane. The old farmhouse north of the 13th green served as the original clubhouse. By the late 1950s, development pressures and the proposed construction of Route 309 (which would take a part of the course) forced the club to move farther out into Whitemarsh Township.

The old Sunnybrook property was divided roughly in half, with one piece becoming typical suburban development. The remaining nine holes were acquired by Springfield Township as the publicly owned Flourtown Country Club.

A third golf course was established by the Philadelphia Cricket Club, which had already built a course in Chestnut Hill in the 1890s. One of the earliest golf courses in the United States, it was relatively small and undistinguished. The Houston Estate, which owned the Chestnut Hill site, was considering ending the lease and developing the property. Eventually, the estate did take back half the course, reducing it to just nine holes.

With an uncertain future, and to get out from under the control of the Houston family, the club bought 376 acres of agricultural land in Whitemarsh Township.[19] Just outside Flourtown and north of Erdenheim Farms, they built an 18-hole course, opened in 1922, designed by A.W. Tillinghast, another well-known golf course designer. Lorraine Run, a tributary of the Wissahickon, flows through the property and joins the creek in a piece of Fort Washington State Park.[20]

Aerial view of the Philadelphia Cricket Club golf course near Flourtown, in Whitemarsh Township. Wissahickon Creek can be seen in the lower right-hand corner. A part of the extensive Corson Quarries can be seen left center.

To help pay for the course, the club set aside the southeast corner of the property for a high-end residential development along Cricket and Valley Green Roads. This development can be seen in the lower right.
Photograph, c. 1960s.
Source: CHHS

7:13–14

Fort Washington State Park

Not quite half a century after the Fairmount Park Commission began acquiring land along the Wissahickon in Philadelphia, a group of civic-minded individuals pressed for the extension of public open space along the creek outside city boundaries. According to the *Philadelphia Record*, "The plan for making [this] section into a public park is due to the City Parks Association, although for the past 20 years there has been talk of such an undertaking. During the summer of 1912 the matter was taken up by John T. Morris, who is at the head of the association, and Andrew Wright Crawford, its secretary." The following year, as part of this vision, the Wissahickon Park Extension Committee was formed as a lobbying group, to implement the project by raising money for a survey of the proposed park lands and to galvanize the state legislature into passing the necessary laws. This committee was chaired during its first two years (1913-14) by John Morris.

The committee set out its goals in a fundraising letter: "To secure a parkway to extend from the northern end of Fairmount Park… along the Wissahickon to Gwynedd, expanding at Fort Washington so as to include as part of the park the forest-covered Fort Hill and Militia Hill…."[21] This extension would have created continuous parkland along both sides of the

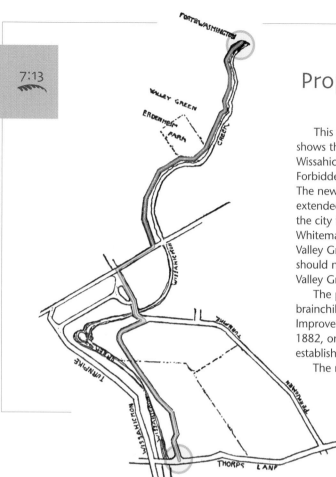

Proposed Middle Valley Parkway | 1899

This rather crude newspaper map shows the proposed extension of Wissahickon Turnpike (later renamed Forbidden Drive) to Fort Washington. The new parkway would have extended the park experience outside the city through Springfield and into Whitemarsh Township. (The village of Valley Green shown on this map should not be confused with the Valley Green Inn in Wissahickon Park.)

The parkway extension was the brainchild of the Chestnut Hill Improvement Association, founded in 1882, one of several early civic groups established in Northwest Philadelphia. The route would have begun

within the park at Bell's Mill Road (shown as Thorp's lane on the map) and continued along the east side of the creek. The proposed alignment would have required extensive cutting and filling on the steeper side of the valley in the city.

The middle valley parkway would then have crossed the Germantown Avenue Bridge and continued up Germantown Avenue to Northwestern Avenue following the stream corridor, on the northern side, to Fort Washington.

Source: GHS

Approximate Park and Open Land in the Middle Wissahickon Watershed, c. 1930

Property	Acres
Carson Valley School	87
Chestnut Hill College	47
Erdenheim Farms	503
Fort Washington State Park	350
Morris Arboretum	166
Philadelphia Cricket Club Golf Course	376
Total Acreage	**1,529**

Wissahickon Creek—from the edge of the city to the village of Fort Washington—a distance of about four miles.

Responding to petitions from the Extension Committee, the Pennsylvania legislature, in 1917, passed an act authorizing the purchase of 1,100 acres along the Wissahickon in Montgomery County. Lawmakers appropriated $100,000 for the purpose, but Governor Martin G. Brumbaugh insisted that it be cut in half to just $50,000. With properties ranging in price from $415 to $800 per acre, these funds allowed only a purchase of 114 acres—about 10 percent of the original authorization.[22] Initially, just a small piece of land opposite the Philadelphia Cricket Club golf course was purchased along the creek. The other purchases were two small farms at Militia Hill— a Revolutionary War site. This hill was used as a temporary look out when Washington's troops,

Proposed Middle Valley Parkway | 1925

A 1925 version of a similar proposal for a parkway from the northwestern boundary of Philadelphia to Fort Washington. When automobiles were banned from Wissahickon Drive in 1921, this parkway extension (which would have belonged to Fairmount Park) could have become a pedestrian promenade linking the middle valley suburbs to the city.

This connection would have strengthened arguments for creating a broad riparian corridor extending from Fairmount Park into Montgomery County. A public park along Wissahickon Creek in Montgomery County, combined with Wissahickon Park in the city, would have included nearly one-half of the total Wissahickon watershed.

The extension would also have given a continuous park experience that would have begun with the Benjamin Franklin Parkway, traveled through East and West Parks along the Schuykill River, continued along Wissahickon gorge and ended on the proposed middle valley parkway.

Note that the map is incorrect, since it does not show Wissahickon Drive (later Forbidden Drive), crossing the creek to the west side, on the Bluestone bridge.

Source: GHS

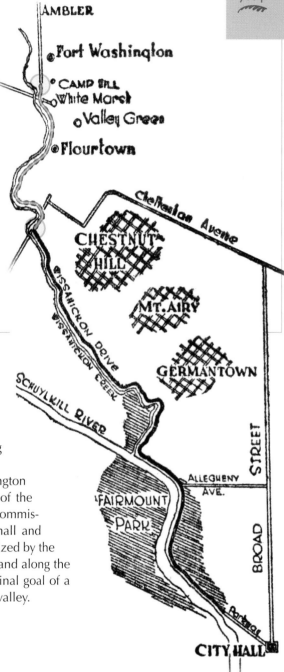

defeated at Germantown, retreated to Whitemarsh in the fall of 1777, before moving on to Valley Forge. The place took its name from the Pennsylvania Militia who occupied the hill.[23] These sites were purchased entirely for their historic value and did little to preserve land along the creek corridor.

In 1927, on the 150th anniversary of this historic event, Fort Washington State Park officially came into being. It was placed under the jurisdiction of the Fairmount Park Commission, whose members simultaneously served as commissioners of the Fort Washington portion.[24] State appropriations remained small and sporadic. By 1935 the park was only 350 acres of the 1,100 originally authorized by the state, with nearly all of it at Revolutionary War sites and only a thin strip of land along the creek. The single parcel acquired along the creek did little to fulfill the original goal of a park and parkway extending from the city through the length of the middle valley.

Preserving the Middle Valley

By the late 1920s, the Wissahickon Valley between Chestnut Hill and Fort Washington was partially preserved in open space—in a combination of private, semi-private and public properties. However, the dream of an entirely public "park" corridor was not realized in the middle valley for several reasons.

From the beginning, Wissahickon Park was generally seen by those living outside the city as a purely municipal institution. Economic realities also played a part in the failure to extend the park beyond city limits. Land along the Wissahickon, within the city, with its steep slopes and acidic soils, was essentially worthless for agriculture, while the fertile soils of the middle valley and its gently rolling terrain made agriculture viable for a longer period. New aesthetic sensibilities focused attention on preserving the forested gorge, a landscape inherently more dramatic than the broad tracts of open farmland in the middle valley. The advent of steam power and better transportation along the Schuylkill and Delaware River corridors made the lower valley less attractive to industry. It could then be considered for public parkland.

By the early 1900s, American cities, influenced by movements in Europe, turned to urban planning to tame the chaos of the burgeoning industrial city. In a time of civic pride, the Fairmount Park Commission obtained the funds and political support needed to add more park land and to make a series of impressive improvements to the Philadelphia park system.

Coming of Age in a New Century

1890-1910

8

Coming of Age in a New Century

1890-1910

*Almost every resident … benefits in some
measure by the pleasant features of that part
of [Wissahickon] Park along Lincoln Drive.
A delightful bit of nature is there preserved as a
readily accessible breathing spot for the people.
This has been possible largely through the
generosity of the Houston family.…
Few better ways of conferring a lasting blessing
upon the people who live in cities can be
attempted than this conserving and fostering the
woods and streams and the greenswards and
the other fast disappearing traces of nature.*

Germantown Independent-Gazette, June 11, 1909, on the
qualities of the "Houston Ramble" along Lincoln Drive

At the turn of the 20th century there was a new sense of wealth, power, and confidence in the United States. In its recent war with Spain, the nation had won an overseas empire with little expenditure in blood and treasure, and had outstripped all its rivals in industrial production, making it the wealthiest country the world had ever known. Returning from Europe early in 1900, Henry Adams, descendent of a founding father and two presidents, was struck with the change in atmosphere, prompting him to write to his brother, " I was conscious of a change of scale. Our people seemed to sling at least twice the weight, twice as rapidly, and with only half the effort."[1]

In Philadelphia, still an industrial powerhouse, new confidence and new wealth spilled out into the city's first tall buildings, in banks designed to look like Greek and Roman temples, in large houses and country estates, in the completion of a massive city hall that looked like a huge Mansard wedding cake and in greater leisure time for many citizens. Despite a notoriously corrupt political system, the flourishing economy and rising tax revenues allowed a tremendous expansion of Fairmount Park, another manifestation of the city's pride. Total park acreage more than tripled, largely the result of enlarging the original boundaries of Wissahickon Park and of acquiring parkland along other stream valleys in the city.

The City Beautiful Movement was in full swing. These ideas had been demonstrated spectacularly in the Chicago World's Fair and the re-design of the nation's capitol in Washington D.C. The efforts of these cities spurred Philadelphia to improve its presentation. The Benjamin Franklin Parkway was on the drawing boards as the new century began. This parkway would lead from the heart of the city to a proposed new art museum at "Fairemount." From there it would connect to East River Drive (now Kelly Drive) and lead into a great urban park along both sides of the Schuykill River. These connecting park drives would continue as a parkway up the Wissahickon gorge as the present day Lincoln Drive (the earlier Wissahickon Drive).

Parallel to the improvements to the city, the Fairmount Park Commission, after two decades of relative inactivity, resumed land acquisitions and demolition of industrial remains in the Wissahickon Valley.[2] To enhance the park, the commission and private individuals created new amenities and better public access—adding or upgrading roads, bridges, gateways, paths, steps, lookouts, leaps and statues.

Prosperity and Growth

Between 1901 and 1915, Philadelphia's success resulted in explosive growth, with its population increasing from 1,293,000 to 1,684,000, or by almost a third—the largest percentage increase in the city's history. Philadelphia's industries ranked third in the nation in the number of wage earners and in the value of its manufactured products. Fueled by many factors, government corruption in the United States took hold after the Civil War at every level. Corruption was particularly rampant in Philadelphia, provoking muckraker Lincoln Steffens to write in a 1903 article for *McClure's Magazine*, "Other cities, no matter how bad their own condition may be, all point to Philadelphia as worse—the worst governed city in the country."[3] However, with new industries starting up and people pouring into Philadelphia, employment was high and tax revenues were plentiful. With city coffers full, corrupt politicians realized that building new parks and parkways would create extensive opportunities for patronage and kickbacks, while allowing them to take credit for improving and beautifying the city.

Wealthy Philadelphia movers and shakers, continuing a tradition of civic activism, formed the City Parks Association (established in 1888) and pushed for the creation of additional parkland. By the early 1900s, Andrew Wright Crawford, a new activist secretary of the City Parks Association (also assistant city solicitor and an early urban planner), led the association's efforts to add parkways and boulevards to the Fairmount Park system. The campaign for park improvements included other key figures—architect Frank Miles Day and Eli Kirk Price, Jr., president of the City Parks Association and Vice President of the Fairmount Park Commission, namesake and grandson of one of the original founders of Fairmount Park.[4]

The City Beautiful

The years around 1900 were a turning point in American society. Mass immigration, rural migration to the cities and rapid industrialization had brought social upheaval and economic dislocations. Increasingly, social thinkers, reformers and philanthropists were preoccupied with the problems of the ugly, crowded and chaotic city, and with controlling the behavior of the potentially dangerous urban poor.

The "City Beautiful" movement grew out of these concerns. Although it might appear, by its name, to be a superficial campaign for "beautification," it was, in fact, a comprehensive planning initiative. This initiative sought to cure social ills and to inspire civic loyalty and moral rectitude through rational planning and design. The design idiom borrowed heavily from a number of sources, primarily the French "Beaux-Arts" style (which included French and Italian Renaissance and Neoclassical Revival architecture), as well as the English Garden City movement. Above all, this movement reintroduced to a nation, which was coming of age, a holistic view of the city. In this view, all design improvements—from minor civic embellishments to grand boulevards lined with monumental public buildings—contributed to the whole.[5]

City Beautiful advocates hoped that with comprehensive planning and design, American cities could equal the cosmopolitan and charming urban centers of Europe. The layout and design of the 1893 World's Columbian Exposition in Chicago was the first large

From the Heart of the City to the Wissahickon Wilderness

The Benjamin Franklin Parkway, originally the Fairmount Parkway, was designed largely by two French architects—Paul Cret and Jacques Greber. Modeled after the Champs Elyseés in Paris, it was a tree-lined boulevard that connected City Hall to the pleasure drives along both sides of the river. This grand parkway was envisioned as a place for pedestrians to promenade up and down shaded sidewalks and a place for city residents to see and be seen by passing carriages (and later automobiles). Its latter-day Baroque design, slicing dynamically across Penn's original grid, brought Fairmount Park from the heart of downtown to the wilderness of the Wissahickon Valley.

The idea for such a parkway went back to 1871, when an anonymous pamphlet prophetically declared, "If the great park, with which we have undertaken to adorn the city, is to be a place of general resort and to benefit all of our citizens, it must be brought within the reach of all. It must be connected with Broad Street and with the centre of the city by as short a route as possible; and the avenues which lead to it must be made elegant and attractive; in short, must be made part of the park."[1]

It would take another 36 years to begin construction and several more decades to complete this vision. Framed by museums and civic institutions, the parkway ran from City Hall to "Faire Mount" on the Schuylkill River, the site of the old waterworks and later the Philadelphia Museum of Art. From the waterworks, it joined the river drive that followed the Schuylkill out to Manayunk—East River Drive, later Kelly Drive—and joined Wissahickon Drive, the northwest parkway at Ridge Avenue.

View of Philadelphia before demolition for the parkway. Photograph, 1909.
Source: Philadelphia City Archives

Proposed parkway design. Drawing by Paul P. Cret, 1907.
Source: Philadelphia Museum of Art

---

1. Quoted in David Browlee, *Building the City Beautiful: the Benjamin Franklin Parkway and the Philadelphia Museum of Art* (Philadelphia, 1989), 15.

and impressive demonstration of these ideas. In 1901, the McMillian Commission magnified and expanded L'enfant's original plan for the heart of Washington, D.C.. The revised plan called for reclaiming land for waterfront parks, parkways, an improved Mall and new monuments and vistas. This project provided the county with a second convincing demonstration of the power of a coherent plan.

Philadelphia, the Parkway and the Park Associations

During this period, Philadelphia also adopted the goals and strategies of the City Beautiful movement. Planning the city rationally—largely dormant in Philadelphia since Penn's original "Greene Country Towne"—again became a city-wide concern. Hampered by decades of corruption and one of the most entrenched political machines, the private groups rather than city goverment took the initative in planning. This was in direct contrast to Washington D.C., where Congress spearheaded the McMillian Plan, and Chicago and Cleveland where the mayors took leadership in the physical renewal of the city fabric.

In Philadelphia, physical renewal focused on creating parkways in all sections of the city. There was to be a northwestern boulevard, which became Wissahickon and Lincoln Drives, various radiating boulevards in South Philadelphia, which were never realized, and a northeastern parkway, which became Roosevelt Boulevard. The jewel of this system was to be a grand boulevard punctuated by outdoor sculpture that would connect City Hall to East and West Parks.

In 1900, two private activist groups—the City Parks Association, and the Fairmount Park Art Association, founded in 1872 as the nation's first private, nonprofit organization dedicated to integrating public art and urban planning—both appointed new activist directors. The City Parks Association turned their attention to the broader concerns of the role of parks in the city. In 1902, these two groups collaborated to publish "A Special Report on the City Plan." This report protested against the city extending the rectangular street grid of the flat coastal plain into the steep topography of the surrounding piedmont. They suggested instead the creation of broad, diagonal parkways.[6]

By 1904, they established Organizations Allied for the Acquisition of a Comprehensive Park System." This consortium "campaigned tirelessly for the conversion of virtually all of the regions creek and river valleys into parkland."[7] In an age of greater mobility and leisure, these acquisitions and the other city-wide improvements expressed Philadelphia's economic impor-tance, provided spaces for a burgeoning public life and promoted the important role that art plays in the creation and enhancement of civic spaces.

Enlarging the Park

Between 1888 and 1938 the total acreage in the entire Fairmount Park system increased from approximately 2,250 acres to 7,500 acres, the greatest expansion of any equivalent time in the park's history.[8] The bulk of these land acquisitions were along major stream valleys in the city: 786 acres in Cobb's Creek Park, beginning in 1904; 1,618 acres in Pennypack Park, beginning in 1905; and 255 acres in Tacony Creek Park, beginning in 1915.[9]

Local residents in Northwest Philadelphia actively campaigned for broadening and lengthening the Wissahickon Park. One group in particular, the Chestnut Hill Improvement Association, headed by Colonel Samuel Goodman, pushed to acquire additional parkland on both sides of the creek—25 acres in Chestnut Hill and 390 acres in Roxborough.[10]

This association's vision included a parkway to Fort Washington that would begin at Bell's Mill Road, where the park stopped at that time, and continue for approximately four miles along the creek to the village of Fort Washington.[11] This parkway would be built through private subscription, with property owners donating land for the cartway and for an extension of Wissahickon Park on either side. Heavy wagons would be banned, and the road reserved for "carriage driving, horseback riding and bicycle riding only."[12] The parkway to Fort Washington was never built, but these proposals would launch discussions about extending Fairmount Park up through the middle valley—an idea for a continuous park corridor connecting the lower and middle valley that would have increasing meaning after World War II.

By the early 1900s, Wissahickon Park had grown to slightly over 1,100 acres from the 450 acres originally acquired. These additions were primarily a number of small tributary streams. The largest and most important of these tributaries were the Cresheim and Monoshone Creeks. Up to this time, the narrow ribbon of parkland along the Wissahickon Creek had only included the confluences of these tributaries and a small area above them. These new acquisitions brought the forest and the natural drainage system into the heart of the neighborhoods of a major city. Many more houses were now located adjacent to parkland—greatly increasing the residential area with park frontage. In contrast, New York's Central Park, at only 850 acres, along with many other American city parks, were magnified versions of an English square, defined by the grid of city streets. This configuration kept any but the immediately adjacent neighborhoods from direct contact with the park.

8:2-7

Additions to Wissahickon Park 1888-1917

8:2

1888: 7.263 acres— part of Rittenhouse Town, through purchase.

1889: 20 acres— part of Rittenhouse Town, through purchase.

1891: 10.905 acres— at Wissahickon Avenue and Lincoln Drive, later known as the Houston Ramble, gift of Henry Howard Houston.

1895: 25.274 acres—east side of Wissahickon Creek, between Bell's Mill Road and Northwestern Avenue, through purchase.

1895: 17.16 acres—near Hermit Lane, through purchase.

1896: 390.187 acres—from Bell's Mill Road to Andorra Nurseries, by eminent domain.

1897: 3.571 acres—along Lincoln Drive, added to Houston Ramble, gift of George C. Thomas.

1902: approx. 35 acres—Wise's Mill Run, through purchase.

1903: 4.112 acres—Walnut Lane and Lincoln Drive, in exchange for "outlying lots."

1906: 2.067 acres—Lincoln Drive near Harvey Street, gift of Sallie Houston Henry.

1906: 12.242 acres—in Cresheim Valley, west of Germantown Avenue, gift of Gertrude Houston Woodward and Sallie Houston Henry.

1908: 75 acres—Livezey Mill property and surrounding land, through eminent domain.

1909: 0.233 acre—near Harvey Street and Lincoln Drive, gift of Bayard Henry.

1912: 26 acres—along Gorgas Lane, through purchase.

1914: 8.43 acres—along Cresheim Creek, east of Germantown Avenue, gift of George Woodward.

1914: 6 acres—along Cresheim Creek, east of Germantown Avenue, gift of Randall Morgan.

1915: 41.925 acres—a combination of five unspecified parcels on both the Roxborough and Chestnut Hill sides of creek, by eminent domain.

1916: 6.17 acres—at Wissahickon Avenue and Hermit Lane, site of the Lotus Inn, by eminent domain.

1916: 2.5 acres—at Monastery Avenue and Wissahickon Drive, the site of the Second Indian Rock Hotel, by eminent domain.

1916: 37 acres—Carpenter's Meadow (later Carpenter's Woods), through purchase.

1917: 28 acres—southwest side of Walnut Lane, from park boundary to Daniel Street, partly through purchase and partly by eminent domain.

Source: FPC, *Annual Reports*

Additions to the Park | Monoshone Creek: 1880s – 1910s

27 Plus Acres by Purchase
17 Acres by Donation

The first of the Wissahickon tributary extensions was the upper part of Monoshone Creek. The lower part was already parkland as far as Rittenhouse Town. In 1888-1889, the park commission acquired Rittenhouse Town itself, amounting to just over 27 acres. Across Wissahickon Avenue from this former industrial village, the multi-millionaire and well-known philanthropist Henry Howard Houston donated nearly 11 acres in 1891, with six more contiguous acres added during the next two decades by the Houston family and by other landowners in the neighborhood.[1] Together with the land at Rittenhouse Town, this made a total of 44 new park acres along the Monoshone.

---

1. FPC, *Annual Report*, 1899, 10; 1912, 15; GHS, Edwin C. Jellett Scrapbooks, 3:127.

 Original Boundaries   Land Acquired

Above
Map showing land acquired from Rittenhouse heirs for Wissahickon Park.
Source: Hopkins, *Philadelphia Atlas*, 21st Ward, 1885

View of Monoshone Creek looking north at Rittenhouse Town. When the land was acquired by Fairmount Park, it was a bustling mill town of over 40 buildings. As with the other industrial sites, the park began to demolish all the mills and most of the other structures. The Rittenhouse family intervened to save five of the houses. Source: GHS

Additions to the Park | Carpenter's Meadow: 1916

37 Acres by Purchase

Proposed housing developments in the early 1920s threatened a twelve-acre forest bounded by Wissahickon Avenue, Sedgwick, Sherman and Mount Pleasant Streets. This tract, called Carpenter's Woods, was the headwaters of an important and very beautiful little stream that flowed into the Wissahickon in the valley between Kitchen's Lane and the Monastery. Beyond protecting the stream corridor, Carpenter's Woods bulges out to include the broad hillsides, which form a natural amphitheater. As late as the 1940s, this area, designated as a bird sanctuary, was a damp bowl filled with wetland wildflowers.

A much-loved community resource, a favorite picnic area and later the site of Boy Scout outings, the park commission saved Carpenter's Woods, purchasing 37 acres in the 1916 for nearly $122,000. The commission gave as a reason for this acquisition the need "to preserve the watershed free from contamination," because "this stream empties into the Wissahickon and the Wissahickon[,] in turn[,] into the Schuylkill."[1]

---

1. Newspaper clipping in Jane Campbell, Scrapbooks 47:141.

Above
Map showing Carpenter's Meadow addition to Wissahickon Park.
Source: Hopkins, *Philadelphia Atlas, 21st Ward*, 1885

View of Carpenter's Meadow, the central open space in the valley of the little tributary that runs through the site. The meadow was framed by a thin fringe of woods on the surrounding hillsides. Photograph, c. 1900.
Source: GHS

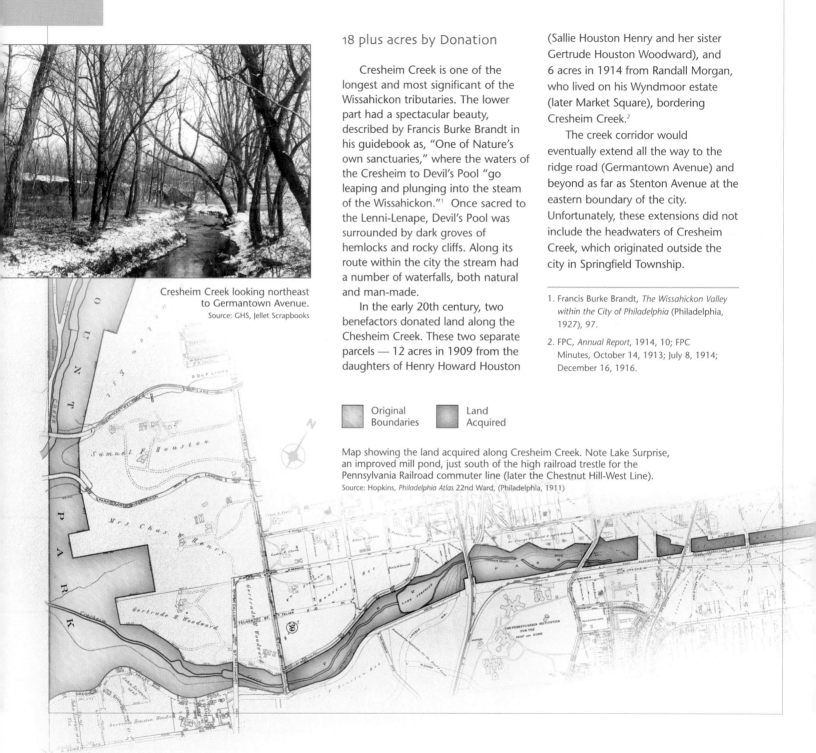

Cresheim Creek looking northeast
to Germantown Avenue.
Source: GHS, Jellet Scrapbooks

18 plus acres by Donation

Cresheim Creek is one of the longest and most significant of the Wissahickon tributaries. The lower part had a spectacular beauty, described by Francis Burke Brandt in his guidebook as, "One of Nature's own sanctuaries," where the waters of the Cresheim to Devil's Pool "go leaping and plunging into the steam of the Wissahickon."[1] Once sacred to the Lenni-Lenape, Devil's Pool was surrounded by dark groves of hemlocks and rocky cliffs. Along its route within the city the stream had a number of waterfalls, both natural and man-made.

In the early 20th century, two benefactors donated land along the Chesheim Creek. These two separate parcels — 12 acres in 1909 from the daughters of Henry Howard Houston (Sallie Houston Henry and her sister Gertrude Houston Woodward), and 6 acres in 1914 from Randall Morgan, who lived on his Wyndmoor estate (later Market Square), bordering Cresheim Creek.[2]

The creek corridor would eventually extend all the way to the ridge road (Germantown Avenue) and beyond as far as Stenton Avenue at the eastern boundary of the city. Unfortunately, these extensions did not include the headwaters of Cresheim Creek, which originated outside the city in Springfield Township.

1. Francis Burke Brandt, *The Wissahickon Valley within the City of Philadelphia* (Philadelphia, 1927), 97.

2. FPC, *Annual Report*, 1914, 10; FPC Minutes, October 14, 1913; July 8, 1914; December 16, 1916.

Original Boundaries

Land Acquired

Map showing the land acquired along Cresheim Creek. Note Lake Surprise, an improved mill pond, just south of the high railroad trestle for the Pennsylvania Railroad commuter line (later the Chestnut Hill-West Line).
Source: Hopkins, *Philadelphia Atlas* 22nd Ward, (Philadelphia, 1911)

Lake Surprise looking northeast. Photograph, 1912.
Source: GHS

Additions to the Park | Wise's Mill Run: 1902

Approx. 35 Acres by Purchase

Wise's Mill Run, a small tributary on the Roxborough side of Wissahickon Creek, was purchased in its entirety by the Fairmount Park Commission in 1902. *The Philadelphia Bulletin* described this creek and the corridor along it as "a wooded valley, which has a beauty and completeness peculiar to itself."[1] Early 20th-century photographs show it as a small stream cascading down a steep hillside over rock ledges, filled with shrubs, ferns, and wildflowers, and framed by tall overarching trees.[2]

---

1. *Philadelphia Evening Bulletin*, January 2, 1902.
2. Edwin C. Jellett, Scrapbooks, 8:7.

Gorgas Mill Run: 1912

26 Acres by Purchase

Gorgas Lane was intended as a widened and improved road, but instead this unimproved track became a park trail to Forbidden Drive (formerly Wissahickon Drive and earlier, Wissahickon Turnpike).

 Original Boundaries   Land Acquired

Map showing Wise's Mill Run and Gorgas Mill Run additions to Wissahickon Park.
Source: Frank H.M. Klinge, *Philadelphia Atlas*, Lansdale, Pa., 1929, Courtesy Joseph B. Timoney

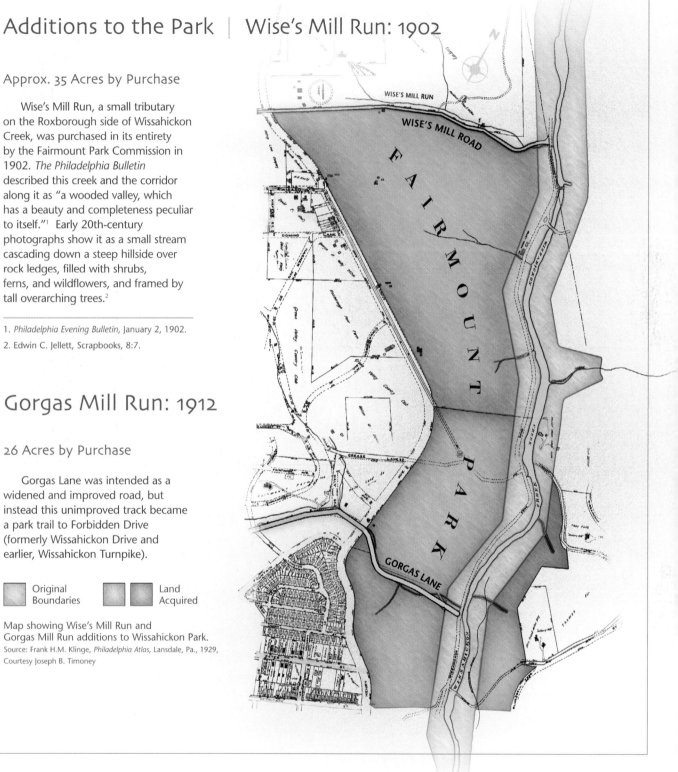

Park Embellishments | Parkways

At the turn of the century, parallel to the plans for Philadelphia and inspired by the City Beautiful Movement, Wissahickon Drive was improved and extended as Lincoln Drive. These roads were conceived as the parkway for the Northwestern section of the city. The Northeastern parkway became the Roosevelt Boulevard.

In 1900, Russell Vodges, Chief Engineer of Fairmount Park, recommended widening and paving the lower end of Wissahickon Drive, east of Ridge Avenue, to remedy a dangerous traffic problem resulting from a sharp curve near the entrance, long known as "dead mans curve"[13] At this place, drivers could see no more than 100 yards ahead because of the large rock formation that came down to the road. The initial proposal called for blasting away more of this scenic rock, described in the local press as a "beautiful natural entrance," prompting residents in Northwest Philadelphia to begin an intense newspaper campaign against removing any more of the obstruction. Park commissioners compromised and went to great expense to preserve the remaining rock by building a wall out into the east side of the creek, and filling in behind it to allow the roadway to be widened. While this construction narrowed the creek and increased the flow, it also raised the road, helping to alleviate the frequent flooding and washouts that had plagued this lower stretch of the drive.

Lincoln Drive, the proposed extension to Wissahickon Drive, was begun in 1900 and completed seven years later.[14] The alignment of this new road followed the Monoshone Creek Valley from Rittenhouse Street all the way up to Allen's Lane, three miles away. It became the main carriage and then the main automobile route into the community of Mt. Airy.

The Germantown *Independent-Gazette* described the new road as a splendid way to experience the park, and explained the importance of its alignment in providing views that stirred the imagination: "Where the new drive meets the Wissahickon Drive, the fine broad curves of the two roads make one of the most imposing prospects, from a horseman's point of view, that the Park contains."[15] These two roads together fulfilled Olmsted's idea of a carriage drive that extended the park experience into residential neighborhoods and that linked parks to a city's downtown.[16]

Wissahickon Drive (later Lincoln Drive), at the curve just below Wissahickon Hall. The road is crushed stone, the traffic is leisurely—bicycles and carriages—and the framing forest is short and young. Photograph c. 1890s.
Source: The Free Library of Philadelphia

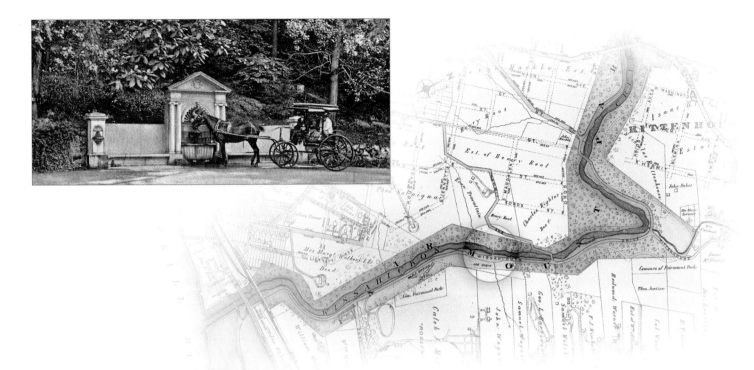

The Leonidas Fountain was one of a number of embellishments along the newly improved Wissahickon Drive. In 1899, Jeanette Springs donated money for this fountain in memory of her father, William Leonidas. The fountain was built on the east side of the creek, at the site of the former Old Log Cabin Inn. Like the Pro Bono Publico fountain, built half a century earlier along the Wissahickon Turnpike (later Forbidden Drive), it marked one of the many springs that flowed out of the cracks in the crystalline bedrock of the lower valley. At a time when horses required frequent watering places and when people in the area prized this still pure drinking water, such fountains offered an important public service while beautifying the park.

Leonidas Fountain along Wissahickon Drive (Lincoln Drive) just below the Hermit Lane Bridge. Photograph, 1916.
Source: David Bower, postcard collection

Map showing Wissahickon Drive. This road began at the junction with the old Wissahickon Turnpike (later Forbidden Drive). This junction was located at the big bend in the creek, where the Monoshone entered the Wissahickon. This drive then traveled along the lowest portion of the creek, meeting Ridge Avenue near the confluence with the Schuykill River. The map also shows the location of the Leonidas Fountain. A small tributary stream fed by two springs, flowing out of the steep slopes below East Falls, supplied the fountain. Source: Hopkins *Philadelphia Atlas*, 21st Ward, 1885

Leonidas Fountain. Photograph, 1908.
Source: GHS

Park Embellishments | Bridges

There have been four generations of ways to cross the creek and its tributaries: fords, planks and crude wooden bridges over the breasts of mill dams, covered bridges, and stone and iron bridges. Each generation made crossing easier and safer with more extensive and more permanent structures. As late as 1900, rotting wooden bridges, frequently knocked over and washed away in floods, continued to inconvenience the communities surrounding the valley. Even the small, low stone bridges that had already been built over the stream meant that people had to go down a steep hill on muddy roads and then climb back up another steep hill to reach the other side.[17]

Stone bridges had already been built at Bell's Mill Road (1820), Springfield Avenue (1832), Rex Avenue (1882), and Ridge Avenue (1888). In 1897, the park replaced "the Old Red Covered Bridge" at the foot of Shurs' Lane with the new "Blue Stone Bridge."[18] New permanent stone bridges were then built at Hermit's Lane in 1903 and at Allen's Lane in 1905.[19] All these improved bridges still crossed the creek at the bottom of the valley, rather than taking the traveler across the valley at the level of the plateau and eliminating the problem of traveling up and down precipitous slopes. Walnut Lane and Henry Avenue Bridges built in the early 20th century, were massive construction projects and required remarkable feats of engineering. The construction of these new bridges (and also the sewer aqueduct over Cresheim Creek at Devil Pool) severely damaged the steep slopes of the gorge and, in many cases, removed ancient stands of trees.

Stone Bridge at Hermit Lane. The first official park drive can be seen on the left, and Wissahickon Drive on the right. Photograph, c. 1905.
Source: David Bower, postcard collection

8:8–10

Walnut Lane Bridge

The new bridge at Walnut Lane, completed in 1908, provided a direct, level crossing between Roxborough and Germantown. This bridge was designed by George S. Webster. According to *Scientific American*, it included as part of its structure the longest concrete arch in the world at the time. Its construction required 19,000 cubic yards of concrete weighing 50,000 tons, all of which had to be hauled one and a quarter miles in horse drawn wagons. The bridge was 585 feet long, with a 60-foot wide roadway, and the large central arch, spanning 233 feet, soared 120 feet above the valley floor.[1]

This park improvement did not come without a cost to the wilderness fabric. Building the bridge destroyed part of "Hemlock Glen," described as containing "the largest hemlocks in the valley"—and a strip of forest up the slopes on both sides.[2] A century later, the bridge continues to carry traffic between Roxborough and Germantown, and the land scarred by its construction has regrown into deciduous forest.

1. GHS, Jane Campbell, Scrapbooks, 1:39; 2:47, 79; 7:24; 10:56; *Philadelphia Press*, April 27, 1907; *Philadelphia Public Ledger*, December 17, 1908; *Independent-Gazette*, January 19, 1906; *Scientific American*, November 30, 1907, 392-93.

2. GHS, Edwin Jellett, Scrapbooks, 2:76; Sarah West, *Rediscovering the Wissahickon*, (Philadelphia, 1993) 61-62.

Walnut Lane Bridge under construction.
Photograph, c. 1907.
Source: Philadelphia City Archives

Future site of the Walnut Lane Bridge.
Photograph, c. 1907.
Source: Philadelphia City Archives

Excavation for the new bridge abutment.
Photograph, c. 1907.
Source: Philadelphia City Archives

The completed Walnut Lane Bridge arching over the Wissahickon and Forbidden Drive. Photograph, c. 1910. Source: GHS

Henry Avenue Bridge

Carrying traffic high above the park, the Henry Avenue Bridge, designed by Paul Cret and built in 1930-32, seemed to leap across the valley. It was 905 feet long and 180 feet wide. With this high bridge, the forested valley walls flowed unimpeded beneath it. Before the construction of the high bridge, the Hermit Lane Bridge (nestled below the new bridge) had been the main route over the creek between Roxborough and East Falls—a difficult and time-consuming journey, requiring a torturous descent and ascent.

The new bridge was part of a larger traffic plan that included carrying Henry Avenue into Upper Roxborough, where it would intersect with a proposed "Chestnut Hill—Bryn Mawr Bypass" at Andorra. This by-pass would connect Chestnut Hill directly to the Main Line and open Upper Roxborough (then in large farms owned mainly by the Houston Estate) to residential development. This by-pass was never built, since the Henry Avenue Bridge was finished just as the Great Depression was setting in. Henry Avenue remained a short stretch of road leading southeast from the bridge through East Falls into

North Philadelphia. There would be no northward extension of Henry Avenue until after World War II—delaying the development of Upper Roxborough for another generation.

The small Hermit Lane Bridge, seen below the Henry Avenue Bridge, was built in stone in 1903 to replace an earlier wooden bridge. It had been part of Charles Miller's plans to upgrade the infrastructure and beautify the park. In the 1990s, this dramatic location, with its juxtaposition of the two bridges—Henry Avenue and Hermit Lane—was the location for a scene in the movie *Blow Up*.

The Henry Avenue Bridge under construction. This work destroyed a swathe of large, old hemlocks on the steep slopes. Hermit Lane Bridge and the road to Roxborough can be seen in the left hand side. Photograph, 1930.
Source: Philadelphia City Archives

The Henry Avenue Bridge under construction. The bridge is seen from Wissahickon Drive (later Lincoln Drive) and the small, stone Hermit Lane Bridge can be seen below and in front of the new bridge. Photograph, 1931.
Source: Philadelphia City Archives

Aerial view of the Henry Avenue
Bridge nearing completion
On the plateau, the community
of East Falls and the later site
of Philadelphia University are to
the right. Lower Roxborough
is on the left of the photograph.
Hermit Lane, still open and
now a park trail, can be seen on
the Roxborough side, winding
up a partially denuded hillside.
Photograph, 1932.
Source: Free Library of Philadelphia

Henry Avenue Bridge, after completion, seen from Wissahickon
Drive (later Lincoln Drive). Photograph, c. 1932.
Source: Philadelphia City Archives

The Henry Avenue Bridge in the 21st century showing the
Hermit Lane Bridge below, now for pedestrians, bicycles and
horses only. Over time, the trees on the steep valley walls have
regrown, so that the bridge seems to leap out of the forest.
Source: Photograph by CLF

The Pipe Bridge

"Its light ironwork bore aloft the two great mains that carried water from the reservoir at Shawmont, above Flat Rock Dam on the Schuylkill, to Germantown.... It wasn't much of a success.... for the pipes froze in winter and split, even when great clasps were bolted around them. In the end it had to be abandoned and underground pipes relied on."[1]

One the most curious pieces of infrastructure in the Wissahickon was the "pipe bridge," an iron, cage-like aqueduct, that spanned the creek just below Glen Fern and the old Livezey mills. This pipe bridge was built in 1870 to carry water to Germantown from the reservoir at the Shawmont section of Roxborough on the Schuylkill River. The engineers had not anticipated that 20-inch iron water mains along a bridge suspended 197 feet above the gorge would freeze in winter, resulting in burst pipes and an interruption of service for the people in Germantown. To solve the problem, in the late 1880s, the Philadelphia Water Department buried the water mains well beneath the creek bed, where they would not freeze. The pipe bridge was demolished in 1891.[2]

---

1. Cornelius Wegandt, *The Wissahickon Hills. Memories of Leisure Hours Out of Doors in an Old Countryside* (Philadelphia, 1930), 292.

2. George W. Schultz, "Hazardous Business," *Germantown Crier* (December, 1954), 7-9; Edwin C. Jellett, 5:134; Edward W. Hocker, Abstracts, 117; Campbell, Scrapbooks, 1:36; *The Suburban Press of Roxborough,* October 22, 1931.

The pipe bridge taken from the plateau, crossing Wissahickon Valley. Photograph, c. 1890. Source: FPC

The pipe bridge seen from below as it crosses Wissahickon Drive (later Forbidden Drive) just below Glen Fern. Photograph, c. 1890. Source: FPC

Park Embellishments | Gateways

Access to the park, along with new and improved trails within the park, called for embellishments—new park pathways with gateways, journeys, lookouts, and destinations—to frame and punctuate the visitor's experience. In 1899, Charles Miller, landscape gardener for Fairmount Park, chief horticulturist for the Centennial and a prominent Philadelphia nurseryman, proposed a series of park improvements. According to historian Galen Cranz, gateways convey "the message that the parks should be taken seriously as an expression of a high level of cultural achievement."[20] Miller's first park improvement was to be a gateway at the entrance to the park at Ridge Aveune. This site, where Wissahickon Creek meets the Schuylkill River, was a place of great drama, the transition between the relatively pastoral and open valley of the Schuylkill River, and the deep, narrow forested gorge of the Wissahickon Valley. An article in the *Philadelphia Record* described Miller's plan to, "Construct a fine, bold entrance to the drive by making an artistic use of the Reading [Railroad] stone bridge, which, with its three fine arches, affords a splendid opportunity for scenic effects...." [21]

8:11-15

8:11

Charles H. Miller | 1829-1902

Like Thomas Meehan, another prominent nurseryman in northwest Philadelphia, Miller was born in England and studied at Kew Gardens. He came to the United States in 1858, and later moved to Philadelphia to work for Fairmount Park as Consulting Landscape Engineer.

He was best known as the "Chief of the Bureau of Horticulture" for Philadelphia's Centennial Exposition in 1876. The sunken plaza in front of Horticultural Hall was his work.[1]

Miller was also a seasoned and well-respected landscape designer. In the 1880s. He designed the original landscape for what would become the Morris Arboretum in Chestnut Hill,[2] and was a co-proprietor of the Miller and Yates Nurseries (also known as the Mount Airy Nurseries), at the southwestern corner of Gowen and Germantown Avenues.[3]

1. Miller's Obituary, *The Germantown Guide*, Nov. 8, 1902

2. *Firmly Planted*, The story of the Morris Arboretum, (Philadelphia, 2001) 7.

3. Bromley, *Philadelphia Atlas, 22nd Ward*, (Philadelphia, 1889).

Charles H. Miller.
Source: GHS

Ridge Avenue Gateway | Confluence

By the late 1800s, the confluence of the Wissahickon Creek with the Schuylkill River was a nexus of railroads, roads, and waterways. Both Ridge Avenue and East River Drive led out from center city to Manayunk and Wissahickon Park. At East Falls and Manayunk, trains, flat bottomed steamboats, coaches, private carriages and later trolley cars brought a variety of travelers needing rest and refreshment at hotels and inns.

The peninsula at the base of Manyunk had a boat landing and pleasure garden and the Riverside Hotel. A century later this landscape has been replaced by boxy commercial buildings and their parking lots, along with a dingy electric power sub station and a bus turnaround.

By the early 1900s, the former Robeson mills had disappeared—burned down or demolished—except for the late 17th-century sawmill sitting at the edge of the little peninsula where the Wissahickon Creek empties into the Schuylkill River. From 1876 to 1905, this building was the headquarters of the "State in Schuylkill," an exclusive men's club founded in 1732, for fishing, hunting and dining.[1] Beginning in 1905, after the club had moved to a new location, it became the headquarters of the Philadelphia Canoe Club, not to be confused with the Valley Green Canoe Club farther up the creek.[2]

1. Edward W. Hocker, *Along the Wissahickon*, "At the Mouth of the Stream." *Independent-Gazette*, 1911.

2. Sarah West, *Rediscovering the Wissahickon*, (Philadelphia, 1993), 55, 61-62.

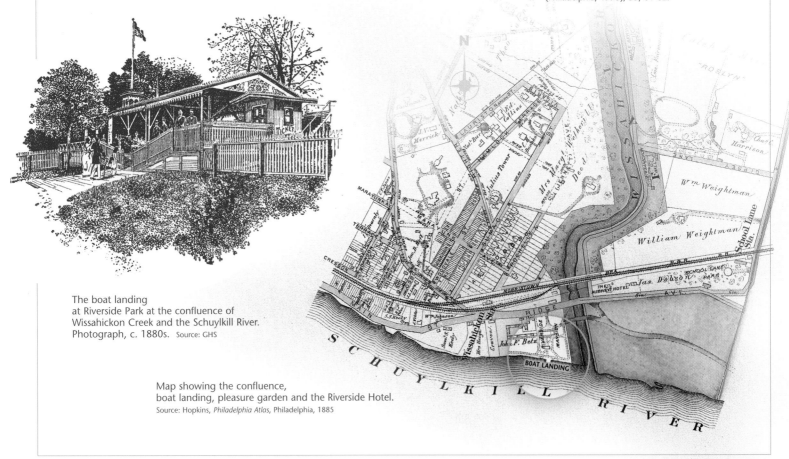

The boat landing at Riverside Park at the confluence of Wissahickon Creek and the Schuylkill River. Photograph, c. 1880s. Source: GHS

Map showing the confluence, boat landing, pleasure garden and the Riverside Hotel.
Source: Hopkins, *Philadelphia Atlas*, Philadelphia, 1885

Ridge Avenue Gateway | Improvements

Accompanying a critical newspaper editorial was a caricacture of Charles Miller's proposed improvements, showing a new entrance with hideously elaborated gothic towers, crenellations along the walls and a row of formal planting along the creek edge.

Miller's desire to enhance the scenery alarmed some park users who thought he planned to make elaborate changes to the park along Wissahickon Creek which would diminish its natural beauty. One of these critics was the editor of the *Germantown Independent-Gazette*, who wrote: "Mr. Miller's 'report' sent a chill of horror down everyone's back. A brand-new, artificial,

pretentious 'entrance' to the Wissahickon, with the beautiful and characteristic spur of rock that now masks the debouching stream blasted away and a retaining wall set in its place; the whole drive, as far as the red bridge [replaced by the Blue Stone Bridge], transformed into a smug, spick and span, Central Park variety of parade ground, with heaven knows what trimmings of stone walls, bastard gothic entrances, comic opera terraces and flower beds, and spirit level speedways; the woods cut down to make vistas and thinned out to suit the demands of 'scientific forestry.' And the willows along the edge of the stream uprooted because they are

not sufficiently dignified for their prominent station...."[1]

Miller did remove considerable vegetation, including trees, from around the bridge to make the lower portions more visible. This work increased the sense of entrance into the park through one of the archways of the stone railroad bridge. The results were generally pleasing to the public. This park entrance—along with the wide cobbled street, the railroad bridge, the falls of the Wissahickon, and the hotels and restaurants—came together to create a very special place.

1. Edwin C. Jellett, Scrapbooks, 1:103

Illustration that appeared with an editorial in the *Germantown Independent-Gazette*, c. 1900, showing the newspaper's conception of Charles Miller's gateway to Wissahickon Park. This caricature bore no resemblance to Miller's proposed improvements for the Ridge Avenue gateway.
Source: GHS, Jellett Scrapbooks

Entrance to
Wissahickon Park at Ridge Avenue
after Miller's improvements.
Photograph, c.1920.
Source: FPC

Ridge Avenue Gateway | Highbridge

Visitors from the city entered Wissahickon Park at Ridge Avenue near the mouth of the creek, where two new dams with their spillways had replaced the old Robeson Mill dams. On the avenue itself, a stone bridge, built in 1888, accommodated first carriages, then automobiles and electric trolleys.

At this time, Wissahickon Drive connected directly to the drive along the Schuylkill River and entered the park through the arch of the railroad bridge, making an uninterrupted roadway along the river and creek. With the construction of the Schuylkill Expressway and the Roosevelt Boulevard extension (in the 1950s), this connection was broken and this graceful entrance was badly compromised.

According to an article in the *Philadelphia Record*, in the spring of 1900, Fairmount Park's chief landscape gardener, Charles H. Miller, saw the railroad bridge as a crucial part of the visual composition of the entrance. Miller told the newspaper that he "would first construct a fine, bold entrance to the drive by making an artistic use of the Reading [Railroad] stone bridge, which, with its… fine arches, affords a splendid opportunity for scenic effects," adding, "the sight of the setting sun through the arches of this bridge is one of the finest in the world…." To show off the bridge to its fullest, Miller had "the heavy growth [of trees and shrubs] along the road cleared away."[1]

By July 1914, the *Germantown Independent-Gazette* was full of praise, rejecting earlier complaints about the gateway improvements: "The handsome stone structure known as the 'High Bridge,' with its gracefully sweeping arches and symmetry of design forms a fitting gateway to the Wissahickon Valley, one of the most romantic and beautiful valleys in the county, if not the world…. Looked at from every viewpoint, it harmonizes most beautifully with the remarkable scenery and the creeping ivy that covers most of the masonry renders it all the more charming."[2]

1. *The Germantown Telegraph*, May 2, 1900; Edwin C. Jellett, Scrapbooks, 1:28.

2. GHS, Jane Campbell, Scrapbooks, 7:181.

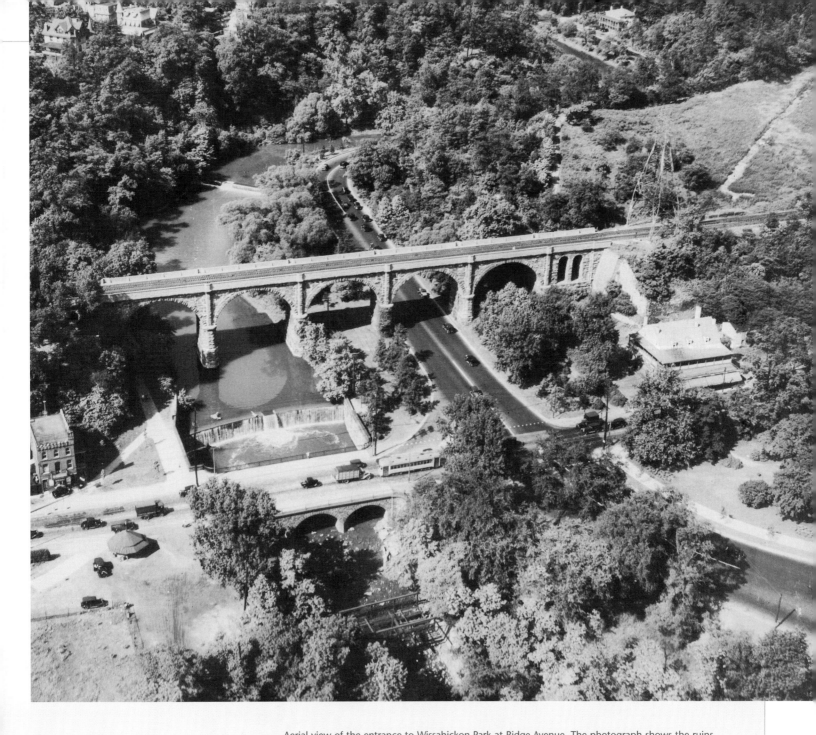

Aerial view of the entrance to Wissahickon Park at Ridge Avenue. The photograph shows the ruins of an old footbridge, the Ridge Avenue Bridge, the Reading Railroad Bridge and two dams. The Wagonette Café flanks the left side of the creek and the Robeson Mansion flanks the right. A small octagonal snack pavilion can be seen just to the left of the Ridge Avenue Bridge, on the site of the later SEPTA bus stop and PECO Electric substation. Photograph, c. 1931.

Source: The Free Library of Philadelphia, *Airplane Photographic Studies of Philadelphia*, June, 1931

Ridge Avenue Gateway | Visitor Amenities

One of the lodgings at the Ridge Avenue gateway was the Highbridge Hotel, established in the old Robeson Mansion at the southeast corner of Ridge Avenue and the creek. This hostelry operated into the late 19th-century.

Also at the entrance was the Wagonette Café at the northwest corner of Ridge Avenue, and across Ridge Avenue there was the small Centennial Hotel. A century later these travelers' facilities are gone, replaced by the off-ramp of the Schuylkill expressway and by a small fast food restaurant.

Highbridge Hotel. Photograph, c. 1890s.
Source: GHS

Wagonnette Café. On the right hand side, the stable for the Highbridge Hotel is visible. Postcard, c. 1890s. Source: GHS

In this period, several other gateways were built. At Johnson Street, the park commission erected two large piers that flanked Lincoln Drive and marked the beginning of Wissahickon Park along Monoshone Creek. Adding to the elonagated and elaborated sense of entry to the park, the Houston Ramble, located between Walnut Lane and Wissahickon Avenue, included a pond, a statue of Henry Houston, a series of trails and a waterfall topped by a small pergola. This landscape was a gift of the Houston heirs who also donated parkland along Cresheim Creek, the other major tributary. Cresheim Creek had two gateways, one an entrance to the park from the commercial spine on Germantown Avenue, the other, an entrance from the mouth of this tributary at Devil's Pool. At this time, no gateway was conceived or built between the lower and middle valley—or into the community of Upper Roxborough.

8:16-20

Mt. Airy Gateway to the Park at Johnson Street

8:16

Where the park ended in Mt. Airy at Johnson Street, the commission built a set of gates made of carved wooden beams mounted on stone pillars. This structure announced that vehicles were entering or leaving the park. Within the park and just below these gates, an extended garden called the Houston Ramble was begun in 1900. This garden, which ran from the foot of Harvey Street to Wissahickon Avenue, was made possible by a gift of $30,000 from the Houston family, on land they had already donated to the park.

Johnson Street entrance to Wissahickon Park. Two giant piers form a pergola on both sides of the road and mark the entrance to the park from the residential community of Mt. Airy, Photograph, c. 1910.
Source: GHS

Mt. Airy Gateway from the Park | Houston Ramble

The Germantown Independent-Gazette described the completed Ramble: "There are two charming little lakes, crossed by rustic bridges, with shrubbery planted on their banks. Waterfalls, winding pathways, thick forests and graceful seats add to the beauty of the scene. The lakes have picturesque shapes; the lower one is precisely like a drop–stem bulldog pipe. Papermill Run [later renamed the Monoshone] supplies the water for the lakes. The stream has been shut in between thick walls of bluestone, topped with mica sandstone, and where it winds from one fall to another. Rocks have been set to give a picturesque and wild effect."[1]

A century later, the statue, the walls and the stone piers of the gates remain, but the pools are gone and the pergolas and footbridges have long rotted away. The Ramble itself has almost disappeared in a tangle of highly disturbed woodland.

1. *Germantown Independent-Gazette*, August 10, 1900.

Detail of pergola over the dam on the pond south of Lincoln Lake, looking north towards Mt. Airy. Source: Courtesy Richard Wood Snowden

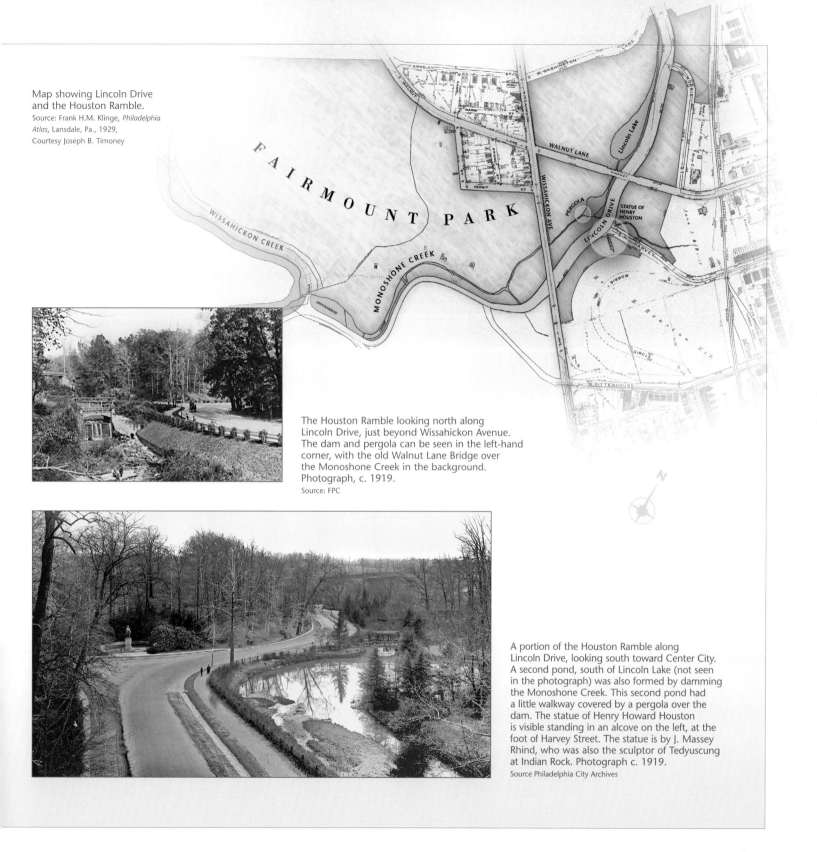

Map showing Lincoln Drive
and the Houston Ramble.
Source: Frank H.M. Klinge, *Philadelphia
Atlas*, Lansdale, Pa., 1929,
Courtesy Joseph B. Timoney

The Houston Ramble looking north along
Lincoln Drive, just beyond Wissahickon Avenue.
The dam and pergola can be seen in the left-hand
corner, with the old Walnut Lane Bridge over
the Monoshone Creek in the background.
Photograph, c. 1919.
Source: FPC

A portion of the Houston Ramble along
Lincoln Drive, looking south toward Center City.
A second pond, south of Lincoln Lake (not seen
in the photograph) was also formed by damming
the Monoshone Creek. This second pond had
a little walkway covered by a pergola over the
dam. The statue of Henry Howard Houston
is visible standing in an alcove on the left, at the
foot of Harvey Street. The statue is by J. Massey
Rhind, who was also the sculptor of Tedyuscung
at Indian Rock. Photograph c. 1919.
Source Philadelphia City Archives

This gateway, with pergola and horse-watering trough, marks the entrance to Cresheim Valley from Germantown Avenue. Photograph, c. 1919. The smokestack and building roofs of the former Pennsylvania School for the Deaf can be seen in the upper left.
Source: HSP, Shoemaker Collection

8:18

Cresheim Creek Gateway at Germantown Avenue

Where Cresheim Creek crosses Germantown Avenue, a gateway was built at the southwest corner of this main thoroughfare. This gateway was a small pergola on an elevated plaza. Its architecture of walls and piers of Wissahickon schist and a trellis of heavy wood echoed the vocabulary of the Houston Ramble. A gift from members of the Houston family, who had donated land along the Cresheim, this structure was intended to be an entrance to the park along the creek.

Restored several times over the decades, the pergola remains a century later.[1] It still marks the transition from one neighborhood to another—between Chestnut Hill and Mt. Airy—and from these neighborhoods into the park.

1. Jane Campbell, Scrapbooks, 8:10, 12:126

Cresheim Creek Gateway at Confluence | Devil's Pool

In 1900, a rustic bridge and gazebo were built in the Adirondack style, where Cresheim Creek meets the Wissahickon at Devil's Pool. This footbridge over a precipitous valley allowed park users to cross from one side to the other without damaging the vegetation on the rocky slopes or having to wade across the creek.

Just beyond, a single-span stone aqueduct, built in the same year, carried a new intercepting sewer line over Cresheim Valley above the pool.[1] Although not intended as a formal gateway, the bridge and pavilion, together with the aqueduct, marked the arrival at the mouth of Cresheim Creek and at

Devils Pool, a place that had been special to the Lenni-Lenape and to the earliest settlers. From both the pavilion and the bridge there were shifting views into a dense grove of dark hemlocks and wet shining rocks.

1. Francis Burke Brandt, *The Wissahickon Valley within the City of Philadelphia* (Philadelphia, 1927), 97-99.

Rustic footbridge and pavilion over Devil's Pool at the mouth of Cresheim Creek. The aquaduct carrying the intercepting sewer can be seen in the background. Postcard, c. 1905. Source: Author's postcard collection; GHS

Cresheim Creek Gateway at Confluence | Devil's Pool

An outing at Devil's Pool. Photograph, c. 1890
Source: LCP, Doering Collection

Park Embellishments | Steps, Leaps, and Lookouts

Miller also wanted to "erect substantial lookouts on the knolls, which abound in that vicinity, and all along the drive, where the views are particularly charming, he would open broad vistas, which would look out on the [creek]."[22] Steps, leaps, and overlooks were added to the park to take advantage of the drama of the steep rocky gorge.

In 1901, just above the second of the newly reconstructed Robeson dams, on the northwest bank of the creek, the park commision constructed a zigzag flight of "One Hundred Steps"—103 of them to be exact. They led up from the bridal and walking path along the creek, then known as "Lovers' Lane," to a lookout at the top.[23] Ornate iron railings bordered granite steps and cement landings, which were lighted by electric lanterns, shaped as glass globes, on metal posts.[24] The new steps gave park users a dramatic view of the valley, and created one of many smaller side entrances to the park from the surrounding neighborhoods. For residents of lower Roxborough/Manayunk, the steps were a convenient access to the trolleys (and later buses) on nearby Ridge Avenue.

At about the same time, just a few hundred yards up the creek and on the same side as the One Hundred Steps, the commision built a hexagonal "summer house" at the top of Lovers' Leap. This small wooden platform eventually decayed and was removed. The pond directly below, created by the water backed up from the rebuilt Robeson dams, had long been a favorite spot for boating, picnicking, and illicit swimming. Here the floodplain was wider than at many places along the creek. A "cable ferry" took people from one bank to the opposite. On the other side, Wisssahickon Hall, the park guard headquarters (that had earlier been an inn) enhanced the romance of this spot by throwing a shimmering reflection into the creek.[25]

Over the years, many guidebooks of the Wissahickon highlighted these promontories, which were "points of focus in the landscape as well as observatories and gathering [spots]."[26] In a forested landscape, overlooks were the places where hikers could come out of the blanket of trees and get a broad sense of the sweep and scale of the valley. In Wissahickon Park these outlooks gave visitors a feeling of anticipation and arrival, of exploring and discovering special places, which were isolated and slightly dangerous.

8:21-22

This photograph by James B. Rich, c.1896, is called "cavern of faces." It demonstrates that from the beginning the park provided spaces for both large, noisy parties and for a single person in solitary contemplation.
Source: LCP

A picnic party on the first park trail. In 1901, the 100 Steps were completed, connecting lower Roxborough to this trail. At this time, the pavilion and overlook at Lover's Leap were also built. A small path from this main trail led park visitors to this overlook. Photograph, c. 1890. Source GHS

View of steps from below the second Robeson Dam looking up toward the houses along Freeland Avenue in Roxborough. Photograph, 1906.
Source: GHS

The 100 Steps

In 1901, just above the second of the rebuilt Robeson dams, on the northwest bank of Wissahickon Creek, Fairmount Park constructed a zigzag flight of "One Hundred Steps" They led up from the bridal and walking path along the creek, then known as "Lovers' Lane," to a lookout at the top.[1] The new steps gave a dramatic view of the valley, and created one of many smaller side entrances to the park from the surrounding neighborhoods.

1. *The Philadelphia Evening Bulletin*, November 23, 1901; Edwin C. Jellett, Scrapbooks, 1:28, 2:85.

Left
The 100 steps under construction. The steps lead up from the park into Roxborough at Freeland Avenue. Photograph, c. 1901.
Source: GHS

Right
The 100 steps showing the ornate iron railings that bordered the granite steps and the cement landings, which were lighted by electric lanterns on metal posts. These steps were allowed to deteriorate badly and in 2004, a renovation designed by Menke and Menke, Landscape Architects, was completed by the park. Photograph, c. 1901. Source: GHS

Lover's Leap

A few hundred yards from the hundred steps, and on the same side of the creek, the park built a hexagonal "summer house" at the top of Lovers' Leap. This small wooden platform eventually decayed and was removed. The pond directly below, created by the water backed up from second Robeson dam, had long been a favorite spot for boating, picnicking and illicit swimming.

This area was another of the many "wides" along the creek where the flood plain in the gorge broadened slightly. A "cable ferry" took people from one bank to the other. Wissahickon Hall, on the south side of the creek, now the park guard headquarters, enhanced the romance of this spot by throwing a shimmering reflection into the creek.[1]

---

1. Edwin C. Jellet Scrapbooks, 2:91; Sarah West, *Rediscovering the Wissahickon*, (Philadelphia, 1993) 60.

The summer house on top of a steep rock outcrop called Lovers' Leap. Photograph, c. 1910.
Source: GHS, A.C. Chadwick Collection, Wissahickon Valley #1

First park path and boating area below Lovers' Leap. Photograph, c. 1910.
Source: GHS, A.C. Chadwick Collection, Wissahickon Valley #1

Park Embellishments | Statues

Two statues were placed within the gorge on the tops of the steepest rocky outcrops overlooking the east side of the creek. The first, a statue of William Penn, with the word "Toleration" carved on its base, was placed on a huge rock outcropping that rises 200 feet above the creek. The ridge and steep slopes were once covered in ancient gnarled hemlocks (*Tsuga canadensis*) growing out of the rock crevices. It was long known as "Mom Rinker's Rock" after Revolutionary War spy Molly Rinker. who according to legend had dropped sensitive information off the cliff to runners below. John Welsh, a member of the Fairmount Park Commission from its inception in 1867 until his death in 1886, and a former U.S. minister to Great Britain, donated this statue, along with 12 acres around it.[27]

In 1902, at the foot of Rex Avenue, Mr. and Mrs. Charles W. Henry installed an Indian statue—actually a generic Indian figure supposed to represent a Lenni-Lenape chief named Tedyuscung. This statue was designed by J. Massey Rhind, the New York sculptor who also created the statue of Henry Howard Houston at the Houston Ramble. Tedyuscung symbolized a lost era before industrialization and rapid change. The statue stands on Indian Rock, the highest point along the valley, also once known for its solid, dark clusters of hemlocks, where the Lenape had held their tribal councils. Just after the third big bend in the creek, the site offers a commanding view of the Roxborough Hills on the opposite side of and of the stream far below.[28] The top of this massive rock forms a small clearing in the woods and was once covered with mosses, ferns, wild flowers, and soft, low-growing grass-like sedges.

Commemorative sculptures were common at the time, especially at battlefields such as Gettysburg. In the Wissahickon these sculptures seem part of an elegiac vision of the past, when the proud and free Lenni-Lenape once hunted in the valley, or of the time when William Penn's Holy Experiment seemed to hold such promise for toleration and peace. Historian Michael Kammen, in his *Mystic Chords of Memory*, captures the spirit of that era, when men and women used sculpture to feel more at ease with an unsettling time: "It is precisely because so much that genuinely mattered was new that people needed notions of the past that would help to define their … identities in positive ways…. Our enduring legacies of that nostalgic surge take several forms. The most visible are great public monuments of various sorts: statues, memorials, obelisks, fountains, … and other structures."[29]

In the Wissahickon the two mythic men on the tops of the steepest and highest rock outcrops—William Penn and Teduyscung—also brought a human presence from an idealized past into the natural world. In many ways they represented the enduring American tension between the progress that generated wealth and new creature comforts, and the progress that also despoiled the wilderness and drove the American Indian from the forest.

Statues in the Park | Toleration

The statue of William Penn was placed on the top of what was called Mom Rinker's Rock (after the mythical revolutionary spy Molly Rinker). This statue was a gift of John Welsh, one of the original Fairmount Park Commissioners. In addition to the statue of William Penn, Welsh gave the park 12 acres of surrounding land. Called "Toleration," the statue celebrates William Penn's extraordinary policies of toleration, which led to a recruitment of people from a wide variety of ethnic and religious backgrounds and to generally fair dealings with the local Indian tribes. This limestone statute by the sculptor Moses Jacob Ezekial was erected in 1883.[1]

---

1. Sarah West, *Rediscovering the Wissahickon* (Philadelphia, 1993), 68; Edwin C. Jellett Scrapbooks, 4:125.

Statue of Toleration, seen from Forbidden Drive, emphasizes the high rocky promontory on which it is set. Source: GHS

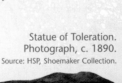

Statue of Toleration.
Photograph, c. 1890.
Source: HSP, Shoemaker Collection.

The statue of the Lenni-Lenape chief Tedyuscung, placed on the top of Indian Rock (also called "Council Rock") in 1902 by the Henry family, was not the only Indian image to stand at this site.[1] Joseph Middleton, a Chestnut Hill resident and president of the Wissahickon Turnpike Company, put the first image here in 1856—a two-dimensional painted wooden cut-out made from an old barn door.[2] By the early 20th century, the wooden Indian had rotted and the Henrys replaced it with a marble statue by J. Massey Rhind, sculptor of the statue of Henry Howard Houston at Harvey Street and Lincoln Drive. Over the years there has been considerable debate about whether the statue was intended to represent the real person of Tedyuscung, or an idealized representation of an American Indian.

Rhind's Tedyuscung was actually a duplicate of four identical Indian figures that he had done for a public fountain in Hartford, Connecticut. But a plaque at the back of the statue clearly identifies it as Tedyuscung, as did the *Annual Report* of the Fairmount Park Commission and the newspaper accounts at the time of the dedication.[3]

Source: Photograph by CLF

Tedyuscung or " he who makes the earth tremble," also called "Honest John," was a Lenni-Lenape of the Munsi band. As pressures mounted on the Delaware following the Walking Purchase, Tedyuscung, who was not a hereditary tribal leader, rose to become a major spokesman for the tribe. Weslager describes him as "an aggressive and eloquent man conversant in the English language."[4]

---

1. *Philadelphia Record*, January 12, 1902.

2. *Germantown Guide*, May 24, 1902; Edwin C. Jellett, Scrapbooks, 7:136.

3. *Independent-Gazette*, June 3, 1902; Edwin C. Jellett, Scrapbooks, 8:137: Edward W. Hocker, "Along the Wissahickon, *Independent-Gazette, 1911*, Council Rock ; " FPC, *Annual Report*, 1912, 14.

4. C.A. Weslager, *The Delaware Indians: A History*, (New Brunswick, NJ, 1996), 210.

Statue of Tedyuscung. Photograph, c. 1902.
Source: GHS

Coming of Age in a New Century

The turn of the century was a time of investment and expansion for the green, open spaces in the city. This era of prosperity and pride provided both the money and the civic will to enlarge and embellish Fairmount park as an essential part of the urban experience. Open spaces were as integral to the planning concepts of the City Beautiful movement as buildings.

The park commission added significant pieces to Wissahickon Park, widening the corridor of the main stem and adding the larger tributary valleys. The original parkland and the additions were acquired as "wilderness park"—and not designed. Under the influence of the City Beautiful movement, both the commission and private individuals added "designed" park elements—everything from a parkway connection from City Hall through the gorge, to new pathways, gateways, pavilions and statues.

At first, the park was shaped by romantic concepts of a scenic wilderness, where the industrial past was seen as intrusive and far too urban. The City Beautiful movement informed the second phase of park development. The third phase would follow quickly on this era of park improvements. Guided by an emerging conservation ethic in the country, public interest would coalesce around protection and restoration of wilderness.

Conservation and Civic Activism

1910-1940

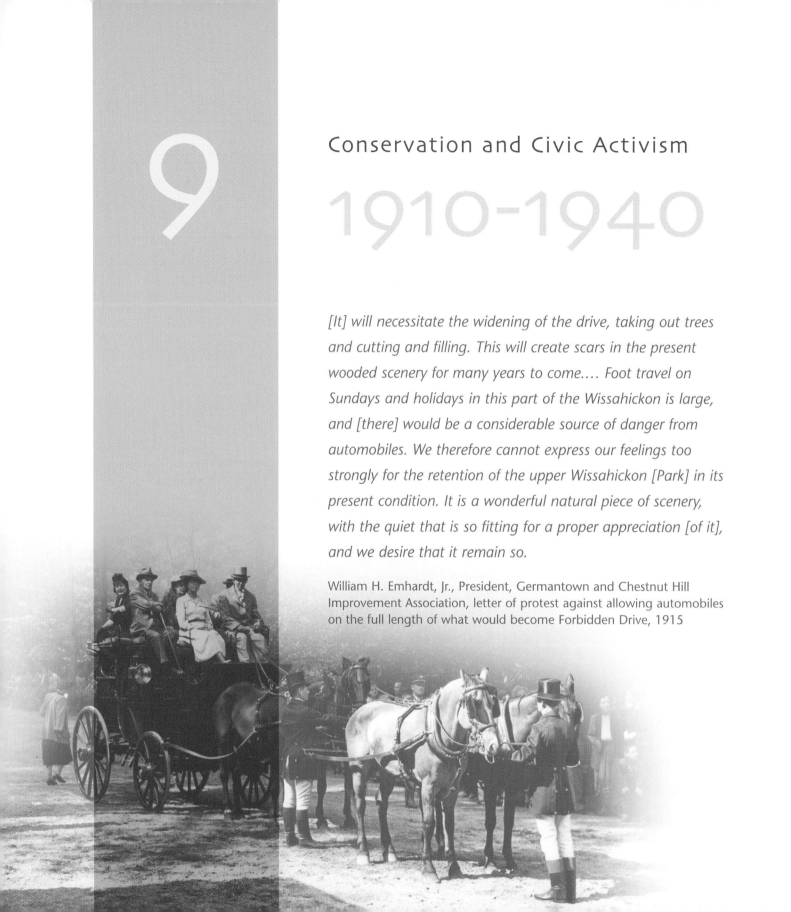

Conservation and Civic Activism
1910-1940

[It] will necessitate the widening of the drive, taking out trees and cutting and filling. This will create scars in the present wooded scenery for many years to come.... Foot travel on Sundays and holidays in this part of the Wissahickon is large, and [there] would be a considerable source of danger from automobiles. We therefore cannot express our feelings too strongly for the retention of the upper Wissahickon [Park] in its present condition. It is a wonderful natural piece of scenery, with the quiet that is so fitting for a proper appreciation [of it], and we desire that it remain so.

William H. Emhardt, Jr., President, Germantown and Chestnut Hill Improvement Association, letter of protest against allowing automobiles on the full length of what would become Forbidden Drive, 1915

P hiladelphia's tradition of civic activism, especially the efforts of powerful and well-connected citizens, was essential to the creation of the Fairmount Park system. Such efforts continued to influence the growth and development of Wissahickon Park and left a legacy of volunteerism and civic activism in defense of park values for future generations.

Since acquiring and protecting the lower Wissahickon Valley, the Fairmount Park Commission had directed much of its energy to erasing the remnants of the industrial era. In doing so, the commissioners hoped to reinforce the park's character as a "scenic wilderness." Paradoxically, and apparently running counter to a desire for wilderness, local residents would organize and run successful campaigns to save two structures—the Valley Green Hotel and Glen Fern (the old Livezey house)—buildings which, for them, evoked the qualities of the colonial era.

At the same time, there were new threats to the park: automobiles, loss of vegetation, the destruction of beloved, historic buildings, new park models of active recreation and a deteriorating or nonexistent infrastructure. These threats found the park commission unprepared and unwilling to act. Spurred by this vacuum, older civic groups in Northwest Philadelphia geared up, and new civic groups were formed to tackle both existing and potential problems.

These organizations were increasingly involved in a series of civic struggles to safeguard the valley. Park improvement and restoration took place within the context of a growing nationwide "conservation" movement.

The Conservation Movement

The Conservation Movement came of age in the decades between 1850 and 1920. "In the United States . . . a heightened conservation consciousness first emerged as a complex, broadly popular political and cultural movement....This movement led to unprecedented public and private initiatives intended to ensure the wise and scientific use of natural resources, and the preservation of wildlife and of landscapes of great natural beauty." Conservation consciousness and actions have continued to expand and evolve in vital ways in the decades ever since.[1]

9:1

The Two Faces of Conservation—Utilitarian and Sacred

People with widely differing interests mounted campaigns to protect and set aside the nation's heritage for the future—for economic, recreational, and aesthetic purposes. Identifying themselves as "conservationists," they tended to divide themselves into two main ideological groups—one led by President Theodore Roosevelt (1858-1919) and his chief forester Gifford Pinchot (1865-1946) and the other by John Muir (1838-1914).

Pinchot, founder of the U.S. Forest Service and later a two-term governor of Pennsylvania, mirrored Roosevelt's belief that the nation's natural resources, particularly its forests, should be used "wisely" so that the country would not only benefit from these economic and recreational resources, but would also conserve them for future use. This attitude was later called "wise use" and has been distorted to justify the private exploitation of public natural resources.

John Muir (1838-1914), a late romantic, prolific writer and founder, in 1892, of the Sierra Club, was horrified at the idea of the natural world as a renewable resource to be exploited for profit and pleasure. "Rocks and sublime canyons, and waters and winds, and all life structures," he wrote, "animals and ouzels, meadows and groves, and all the silver stars ...are works of God, and they flow smooth and ripe from his lips."[1]

Muir and Pinchot became iconic types, whose ideas, exaggerated by others, formed the two poles of the conservation debate—one pole insisting that natural lands be closed off from human presence and preserved as close to its undisturbed state as possible, the other demanding the broadest possible commercial and recreational use.[2]

John Muir and President Theodore Roosevelt at Yosemite National Park. Photograph, c. 1906.
Source: Library of Congress

These contrasting positions were reflected locally in on-going debates, sometimes erupting into acrimonious quarrels over the use and improvement of Wissahickon Park. These differences in attitudes became the foundation of continuing disagreements over whether the Wissahickon should remain a scenic wilderness park or accommodate new and more active recreational facilities. Symbolizing these issues were the "hot-dog wars" of the 1930s. Decades later, this dispute would resurface over the preservation of the WPA shelters, and still later in public debates over mountain bikes and the removal of historic milldams.

The polarization of positions has too often kept these attitudes from fusing together in creative and constructive ways. In the late 20th century, there was a new ecological recognition of human beings as part of the natural world and a realization that there was no "pristine" place on the planet. These attitudes were central to a new paradigm of mutually interdependent and mutually beneficial partnerships with nature.

---

1. John Muir, quoted in, Library of Congress, American Memory: The Evolution of the Conservation Movement, 1850-1920. Website: memory.loc.gov ammem/amrvhtml/conshome.html, 190.

2. Ibid.

President Theodore Roosevelt with Gifford Pinchot on the deck of the steamer "Mississippi." Photograph, c.1907.
Source: Grey Towers National Historic Landmark.
Courtesy Edgar Brannon, Jr., former director

The desire to protect natural and cultural legacies developed, in part, out of a growing recognition and widespread alarm at the increasingly visible losses in a continent that had once been seen as pristine. In his 1913 book, *Our Vanishing Wildlife*, William T. Hornaday, Director of the New York Zoological Society, sounded a battle cry to call citizens to action to save America's natural heritage: "I am appalled by the mass of evidence proving that throughout the entire United States…the existing legal system for the preservation of wild life is fatally defective. There is not a single state in our country from which the killable game is not being rapidly and persistently shot to death, legally or illegally, very much more rapidly than it is breeding, with extermination for the most of it close in sight."[2] Causing this loss on an unprecedented scale were large, formative changes in the western world—widespread industrialization, urbanization, commercial agriculture and extensive natural resource extraction.

Building Social Capital

Private activities to improve Wissahickon Park were part of a long legacy in the communities around the Wissahickon Valley, especially in Germantown / Mt. Airy / Chestnut Hill. For generations, residents had been in the habit of forming small associations to solve problems or meet civic needs that did not fall within the duties of the relatively weak local governments. As immigrants who had come to the American colonies to escape oppressive authorities, and as Protestants who had overthrown traditional religious authorities and believed in a direct relationship between human beings and God, many Americans mistrusted strong governmental authority. Various forms of mutual help were created to fill the gap. This tendency to form small local associations made a strong impression on Alexis de Tocqueville when he visited the United States in the late 1820s. In his classic *Democracy in America*, he wrote, "Americans of all ages, all conditions, and all dispositions, constantly form associations … to give entertainments, to found seminaries, to build inns, to construct churches, to diffuse books, to send missionaries to the antipodes; they found in this manner hospitals, prisons, and schools."[3]

The creation of voluntary organizations and their continued response to crises in the Wissahickon Valley provide examples of "social capital," operating at its best and at its worst. Robert Putnam, in his book *Bowling Alone*, defines "social capital" as "connections among individuals—social networks and the norms of reciprocity and trustworthiness that arise from them." Putnam explains that social capital, while closely related to the concept of "civic virtue," is distinct from it. Social capital "calls attention to the fact that civic virtue is most powerful when embedded in a dense network of reciprocal social relations."[4]

In taking up community causes, some local civic groups would have relatively brief lives, while others would endure and flourish into the next century. They would take advantage of the wealth, leisure, self-confidence and political connections of residents in this relatively prosperous, outlying area of Northwest Philadelphia. At their best, these civic groups would offer bonding opportunities for men and women of similar interests and backgrounds, while building bridges to other civic groups, public and private institutions and various governmental entities, creating reciprocity and trust among those interested in

Nostalgia for ruins led this young woman to have a wedding photograph taken in front of the crumbling walls of the Kitchen's Mill. Photograph, c. 1890.
Source: Courtesy of Richard Wood Snowdon

the park. At their worst, they tended towards social exclusivity and made outsiders, whose support was crucial to their success, feel unwelcome and marginalized.[5] In the Wissahickon Valley, this exclusivity led to a concentration on a narrow spectrum of park uses and interests, and to a lack of imaginative ideas to solve park problems. Despite short-comings, these voluntary organizations would be essential to the vitality of Wissahickon Park.

Nostalgia and Historic Preservation

As new park improvements were going up, many remnants of the past were coming down, causing some local residents to mourn the dissapearance of a familiar fabric. Their reaction was part of a prevailing mood in the older parts of the United States, a mood begun in the early 19th century with writers and artists bemoaning the disappearance of the "wilderness." Heightened by the increasing pace of urban and industrial development, the nostalgia for the past was captured in 1900 by the writer Walter Sargent: "However much one may rejoice in the progress, the development of industries, conveniences and advantages and the whole inspiring energy of the twentieth century, there is still something akin to sadness in the removal of old landmarks which have come to be seen through an atmosphere of fond associations."[6]

The feelings of loss caused a number of prominent individuals to make collections of antiques and handcrafted tools, to revive dying crafts, and/or to preserve historic buildings. In the Philadelphia area this group included Henry Chapman Mercer, collector of 19th

The Colonial Revival

A growing desire to save the past in the park was part of the wider Colonial Revival movement. This movement included restoring buildings, collecting antique furniture and artifacts and designing new structures that imitated the earlier colonial style. Locally, the colonial revival helped to inspire the Germantown Site and Relic Society in 1900, later renamed the Germantown Historical Society.[1] Besides putting plaques on historic houses and sponsoring a series of lectures and publications about "Old Germantown," the society began to gather what would become one of the most extensive and remarkable archival collections of regional culture and society—houses, furniture, clothing, tools, toys, documents, books, articles, photographs and paintings. This collection also includes a large cache of material about the Wissahickon Valley at the center of which are the nine scrapbooks of Edwin Jellett.

The Colonial Revival movement had been building for many years prior to the early 1900s. It had roots in the first important commemorations of the American Revolution in 1825 and 1826, when Americans observed the 50th anniversary of the outbreak of fighting against the British, followed by the Declaration of Independence.[2] Lafayette's visit to the Germantown battlefield in 1825 revived fading memories of old-timers, who remembered the Revolution as children. Philadelphia's 1876 Centennial Exhibition also renewed interest in the colonial period.

By the end of the 19th century, mass immigration from southern and eastern Europe alarmed many Americans descended from northern European settlers (Dutch, Swedes, English and German). They saw the newcomers as inferior beings who would undermine the civilization they and their ancestors had built. Many descendants of old families in the communities bordering the Wissahickon shared this sense of alarm.[2] Determined to maintain their social and cultural dominance, these people founded lineage societies to explore and establish their roots, such as the Daughters of the American Revolution (DAR), Sons of the American Revolution (SAR), and the Society of Colonial Dames.

Board members of the Germantown Historical Society in colonial costume, dressed up for the reenactment of the Battle of Germantown, following a tradition established around the turn of the 20th century. Photograph, 1952.
Source: GHS

Prosperous citizens with colonial ancestry began to erect statues, put plaques on 18th-century buildings, restore colonial-era structures, design new buildings in the colonial style, reenact significant events and put on pageants to commemorate (what they believed to be) a "better and simpler" past. Cornelius Weygandt, Jr. (1872-1957), who lived his entire life in or around Germantown, wrote in his autobiography that the 18th-century furnishings in his house were like sacred relics, providing, "A safe retreat from the ugliness fast pressing in on all sides from a deteriorating world."[3]

Even when genuine colonial era structures were saved in this first great wave of historic preservation, the focus was almost entirely on noteworthy buildings and not on the surrounding landscape or even on related, adjacent structures. Careful research into original styles, materials and craftsmanship (which would later become standard practice) was not yet considered critical.

Valley Green Hotel, renamed (more quaintly) Valley Green Inn, after the 1901 "restoration" by the Valley Green Association. Many members of this group also belonged to the Society of Colonial Dames. Photograph, c. 1901.
Source: GHS

1. On the Colonial Revival in the United States, see Karal Ann Marling, *George Washington Slept Here: Colonial Revivals and American Culture, 1776-1986* (Cambridge, Mass, 1988), 85-114; and William B. Rhoads, "The Colonial Revival and the Americanization of Immigrants," in Alan Axelrod, ed., *The Colonial Revival in America* (New York, 1985), 341-361.

2. See David R. Contosta, "Philadelphia's Miniature Williamsburg," *Pennsylvania Magazine of Hisotry and Biography* (October 1986), 283-320.

3. Cornelius Weygandt, Jr., *On the Edge of Evening: An Autobiography of One Who Holds to the Old Ways* (New York, 1946), 204.

century American tools and artifacts. It also included Samuel Yellin, an enormously talented designer responsible for much of the hand-forged ornamental ironwork in the houses and major buildings of the region. Amateur horticulturalist and historian Edwin Jellet was also a great local collector of the past, devoting much of his life to saving and archiving many documents and illustrations about Germantown and the Wissahickon Valley.

The desire to save the past extended into Wissahickon Park, where some of the mill buildings had survived the initial demolitions. Some mills remained outside park boundaries. Their survival was engineered by owners with political connections to city hall. Among the buildings temporarily saved were the massive Magarge Paper Mills, located on the Chestnut Hill side of the creek near the covered bridge at Thomas Mill and a second complex on the opposite side of the creek, just upstream from Wise's Mill Road.[7] The city had actually purchased these mills in 1871, but allowed them to operate until 1884, when they were finally demolished.[8] A number of residents, now nostalgic about the ruined mills and the passing of an era, mourned the removal of the last of the mills in the local newspapers. According to a 1901 editorial in the *Philadelphia Record*, referring to the recent demolition of the Gorgas Mill, "For a few years past several of the old walls have been standing with a curious old brick oven, overgrown with moss and clinging vines. But these are now being removed, and soon there will not be the slightest trace remaining of these famous old mills."[9]

The Wissahickon inns died a slower death. Although the park commission did not order the inns to close immediately, its decision to ban alcohol sales in the park sealed the fate of nearly all these establishments.[10] The Maple Springs Hotel was torn down around 1900. The Lotus Inn and the Indian Rock Hotel were demolished in 1916.[11]

These two inns survived longer than most because they were located just outside park limits and could continue to serve alcohol. Proprietor Reuben Sands of the Indian Rock Hotel had political connections, as did the owners of the Lotus Inn, which kept the park commission from taking these properties. These privileges did not last forever. In the end only two inn buildings would survive—the Valley Green Hotel/Inn and the old Wissahickon Hall.

Saving Glen Fern and Valley Green

Sentiment for a disappearing era coalesced around campaigns to save two old buildings in Wissahickon gorge—Glen Fern (the old Livezey house at the foot of Allen's Lane), and the Valley Green Hotel, located along the creek below Wise's Mill Road and across from the Springfield Avenue Bridge. Both structures were threatened by continuing efforts to restore the park to a more natural state. Those mobilizing to rescue these buildings saw this undistinguished miller's house and this ramshackle mid-Victorian inn as relics of a "kinder and gentler" past. To justify the expenses of restoration, it was important to find a productive use for the buildings.

Edwin Costley Jellett (1860-1929)

Born in Philadelphia, Jellett spent most of his childhood on a farm in upper Montgomery County, moving to Germantown in the late 1880s. Largely self-educated, working as a gardener as a young man and then as an employee of his brother Stuart's engineering firm, Jellett was a shy bachelor who loved the Wissahickon and walked it as often as he could, camera and notebook in hand. He obsessively collected every scrap of information he could find, interviewing park guards and writing letters to anyone who might give him information about his beloved valley. It could be said that Jellett followed in the footsteps of John Fanning Watson, an early 19th-century amateur historian, both pioneers of what would later be called "oral history." Recording local stories was one of several ways that both men saved information about a place and time that was rapidly disappearing.

The Germantown Historical Society, of which Jellett was a charter member, later organized his mound of material into nine large scrapbooks, essential to anyone researching or writing about the Wissahickon Valley and the communities around it. In the English scientific tradition, Jellett read several papers before the society. One of these, published in 1915 as "Gardens and Gardeners of Germantown," gives some of the only early records of the natural vegetation of the region.[1]

Edwin Jellet in his Germantown home. Photograph, c. 1890s.
Source: GHS

---

1. Lisabeth Holloway, "Germantown Past: Walden in Germantown? Edwin Costley Jellett, 1860-1929," *Germantown Crier*, Spring 1985, 43-44; Lisabeth Holloway," Germantown Historical Society," in Jean Barth Toll and Mildred S. Gillam, *Invisible Philadelphia: Community Through Voluntary Organizations* (Philadelphia, 1995), 884; GHS obituary files, Edwin Costley Jellett, 1860-1929.

Glen Fern before
renovation.
Photograph, c.1890s.
Source: GHS

Renovations and repairs at Glen Fern were prompted by the Fairmount Park Commission's purchase in 1908 of part of the Livezey estate—the mid-18th-century house and the surrounding 75 acres. A year after the purchase, the park commission demolished the Livezey mills and all the surrounding buildings, but saved the house. This separated the house and the property from any association with its former function and meaning, leaving no trace of the indusrial activities that had once animated the area. The house was then rented to the newly formed Valley Green Canoe Club. Members of the club went canoeing in the pond behind the old milldam. They held a variety of social events, including an annual canoe race and a corn roast each fall on the grounds around the house.[12] In adapting the structure for club purposes, they made repairs, exaggerating the colonial character by adding stylized shutters and a curved second-story balcony, additions which had nothing to do with the character of the original miller's house.

In tearing down the old industrial buildings such as the Livezey Mills, the park commission was motivated by a desire to enhance a wilderness park. Nothing that reminded visitors of the dreariness of work would be allowed to remain. All efforts would be made to "restore" the area to its rugged and scenic landscape. Only park improvements, which heightened or dramatized the picturesque features, were considered desirable.

The rescue of the Valley Green Hotel (later known as the Valley Green Inn) was motivated by many of the same considerations as the renovations at Glen Fern. The crusade to preserve the inn began in 1900 following a decision the year before by the Fairmount Park Commission to demolish it. Although tearing down this structure was in line with the commission's goal of maintaining and extending the "wild" landscape of the park, the place had become a familiar and welcome spot for park users.

Built in the early 1850s and operated successfully until the park took it over a decade and a half later, the inn struggled under the alcohol ban. Charles W. Henry, the descendant of a signer of the Declaration of Independence and a member of the Fairmount Park Commission, raised approximately $1,200 from residents of Chestnut Hill, Mt. Airy and Germantown to save the building. In 1901, a group of socially prominent women from the

Glen Fern in 1912, after renovation and "colonialization." Shutters, a balcony and a garden were added, and the last remaining outbuilding was renovated. These changes, although not major, took away the "vernacular integrity" of the old miller's house, making it look like an early suburban house in the colonial style. Vernacular integrity was not a value at the time, and only came to be important in the later half of the 20th century. Photograph, 1912.
Source: GHS

area formed the Valley Green Inn Association. Led by Lydia Morris (whose estate would become the Morris Arboretum), these women directed efforts to renovate the place. Also on the committee were Sallie Henry, the daughter of Henry Howard Houston and wife of Charles W. Henry; Mrs. Samuel Chew who lived at "Cliveden," an authentic 18th-century Colonial house and the epicenter of the Battle of Germantown in 1777; and Mrs. Randall Morgan, whose large estate in Chestnut Hill would later become the Market Square Shopping Center. They and the other women in the group were members of the Society of Colonial Dames, a national lineage society that preserved colonial houses and artifacts, partly as a way of glorifying their own history.[13]

The sources of the ladies' ideas about restoring Valley Green are unknown. Alice Morse Earle, a member of the Society of Colonial Dames in New York, had published a well-illustrated book in 1898 entitled *Home Life in Colonial Days*, and the Valley Green ladies may have been influenced by it, as well as by all the national interest in the colonial period.[14] It is also likely that the women engaged an architect, whose name has not survived, to make suggestions and actually design the renovation.[14]

Although the Valley Green Association used the term "restoration" to describe their efforts, they actually refashioned this unimpressive building into what they imagined a late colonial-era establishment would look like. At the same time they changed its name from the Valley Green Hotel to the quainter sounding Valley Green Inn. Contributing to the faux-colonial flavor was a large open fireplace in the south dining room and reproduction Windsor chairs, along with simple wooden tables and benches on the front porch with scrolled arm rests. A "pretty covered gateway" opening through a new stone wall to the left of the porch replaced one set of stables.

9:4-5

View along Wissahickon Drive looking towards Valley Green Inn. Photograph, c. 1890s.
Source: Free Library of Philadelphia

The Valley Green Inn, after
it had been saved and renovated
by the Valley Green Association.
The new covered gateway can be
seen in the far left corner.
Photograph, c. 1940s.
Source: CHHS

At the time, and even a century later, many people have been fooled by the makeover. In 1901 one newspaper wrote, "[The] Valley Green Inn, a relic of the colonial days, ...has been renovated [by] a committee of society women...along the original lines."[15] As late as the 1960s, a manager of the inn would claim on his menus that Washington and Lafayette had dined there during the American Revolution, a good 75 years before the building was actually constructed.[16] Meticulous research undertaken by Eunice Ullman for the Friends of the Wissahickon in 1970, using early tax lists, historic maps, deeds, and city directories, found no evidence of any structure at the Valley Green Inn site before 1850.[17] The origin of this belief in a colonial date for the inn may have been an early 20th century newspaper article, which alleged that Washington and Lafayette had been invited to dine at the "Valley Green" mansion of a Judge Longstreth, located along the Wissahickon Creek in Whitemarsh Township near the village of Flourtown during the army's encampment in the area in the late autumn of 1777. Later newspaper articles seem to have conflated the two Valley Greens, and had the Revolutionary officers stopping for a meal at a then nonexistent Valley Green Inn.[18] Although not "real colonial" architecture, ironically, the inn has become a fine example of "real Colonial Revival"; and like much of the later colonial face lifting along Germantown Avenue in Chestnut Hill, the makeover has quality and lasting charm.

Valley Green in the Park

Unlike other inns, Valley Green was not torn down when the park was newly established. However, like the other inns within park boundaries, it struggled to survive under the ban on alcohol. Gradually deteriorating, it was saved and refurbished just as it was about to be demolished.

Over time, Valley Green has assumed a greater and greater importance in Wissahickon Park. This destination, halfway along Forbidden Drive—the wide, continuous pathway that follows the creek through the upper gorge— serves many functions. Perhaps, most

critically, Valley Green is the place that brings together a multitude of different experiences—a whiff of history, a setting in the gorge beside the creek and a continuous parade of people.

View of Valley Green Inn, looking south, down the creek along Wissahickon Drive (later Forbidden Drive). The simplicity of the gravel clearing enclosed by a hemlock grove, with the inn seen in the distance—creates a sense of an oasis in the forested valley. These qualities began to erode with the coming of the automobile, although Valley Green is still a special place with extraordinary qualities. Photograph, 1927. Source: CHHS

View of Valley Green from the bridge over Wissahickon Creek, showing the tranquil millpond used for boating.
The banks are now stabilized by a stone wall, but the water's edge is still heavily treed.
The wider floodplain is covered in gravel, making a spacious "plaza" in front of the inn. Photograph, 1938.

Source: FPC

Antiques at Valley Green Inn

A collection of antique furniture, tools and tableware embellished the inn for a number of years. In 1937, the year the inn was again repaired, Samuel S. Fleisher lent some pieces from his antique collection to be displayed there. Fleisher was a member of the Fairmount Park Commission and chairman of its recreation committee. He was also a well-known philanthropist and art collector who would later endow Philadelphia's Fleisher Art Memorial.[1]

A newspaper story about the collection of antiquities at Valley Green Inn gave a lengthy, evocative list of the items: "Entering the hall you find a cupboard with flowered Canton China and a complete Russian samovar. The cream colored walls of the room on the other side are hung with old American implements: Old copper saucepans, fine old brass vessels, horn-handled forks and knives, hay forks, a curiously curved horn, a cradle, the grease bucket from a Conestoga wagon.... In this antique-lover's haven, are found apple butter churns, a sausage grinder, and a foot warmer for ornamental, as well as practical purposes. Here is a flax wheel complete with wooden comb and spindle, a sauerkraut bench... and ox bow, very fine brass candlesticks, much pewter and iron —handwrought—of course. There is a fine collection of glass—most of it of Pennsylvania design. The goblets, some of which date from 1840, bear widely varied patterns. Pennsylvania women designed them and there are over 3000 patterns.... At Valley Green the old world meets the new: Spanish platters, 150 years old; Chinese mirror paintings, hammered copper from India. Long ago a New England sailing captain brought home from China a delicately flowered Canton medallion bowl. Now it stands in the inn, survivor of many voyages."[2]

1. Thora E. Jacobson, "Samuel S. Fleisher Art Memorial," Jean Barth Toll and Mildred S. Gilliam, *Invisible Philadelphia: Community Through Voluntary Organization* (Philadelphia,1995), 975.

2. Unidentified newspaper clipping dated March 31, 1937, Edwin C. Jellet Scrapbooks, 6:72.

Antique "Welsh" dresser in the hallway at the Valley Green Inn.
Source: Photograph by CLF

When the inn first opened after the 1900 renovation, it served only light refreshments—tea, cake, ice cream and lemonade. Not until a decade later did it begin to serve meals. In those days, besides purchasing refreshments, visitors could rent boats and canoes and paddle around on the millpond in front of the inn. This pond, created by the dam downstream at the old Livezey Mill site, gave a "lakeside" setting to the inn.[19] Over time, Valley Green Inn has assumed a greater and greater importance as the anchoring point in the park and as a major gathering place for people from both sides of the creek—Roxborough and Mt. Airy/Chestnut Hill. After walking or riding through the forest, the inn, in its small clearing, once framed by dark hemlocks, appeared as a bright, friendly hamlet at the edge of the woods.

Milldams

Another preservation impulse provoked controversy over the old milldams along the creek. Some individuals and groups at the time, including the Pennsylvania Fish Protective Association, thought the dams were inconsistent with either a wilderness park or with a picturesque, free-flowing stream. They wanted all the dams taken down and the Wissahickon Creek returned to a more "natural" state. They also argued that the cooler, more rapidly moving water would improve conditions for native fish and for fishing. But as the Germantown newspapers pointed out, water levels around 1900 were much lower in the dry months than before European settlement, and without dams, the creek would lose much of its attractiveness.[20] One editorial in 1913 urged the park commission to save the dams and conserve "the stream and keep it in harmony with its picturesque setting."[21] Although the dams and the pools behind them were "man-made" and damaging to certain types of aquatic life, they had established themselves in people's imaginations as an important part of the valley's appeal. The controversy over the dams, with its cultural, scenic, and ecological implications, would not go away and the debate would be repeated in later generations.

Curbing the Automobile

Until the appearance of substantial numbers of automobiles in the park, the area's many civic organizations had not generally included Wissahickon Park in their improvement programs or focused on the park's role in the community. As of 1909, dangerous curves and steep embankments were the main reason given to keep cars off the upper portion of Wissahickon Drive (a stretch of the present Forbidden Drive) that began at the junction with Lincoln Drive and extended to Northwestern Avenue at the city limit. The first reports of significant automobile traffic in the whole of Fairmount Park came in 1899, when park guards counted 696 vehicles in one year. By 1912, the park commission's *Annual Report* put the total number of cars entering the park, including both the Schuylkill and Wissahickon sections, at 900,000. Two years later these figures had risen to 1,333,000 cars.[22]

The Roxborough Board of Trade joined advocates from Mt. Airy and Chestnut Hill to call for improving and opening the upper end of Wissahickon Drive to automobiles as a way of stimulating business and real estate development on the west side of the valley.

9:6

Autos in the Park

As their numbers grew, automobile owners, taking pleasure drives in the park, came in conflict with other park users. Horse riders and carriage drivers would later organize to ban automobiles from the park. This controversy would anticipate the later conflict between horse riders, walkers and mountain bikers. The modern controversy would be resolved in innovative ways with a new coalition of bikers and the FOW working to resolve user conflicts by redesigning the trials.

An early automobile fords a tributary of Wissahickon Creek. Photograph, c. 1905.
Source: David Bowe postcard collection

Making the route along the upper drive safe for automobiles would have required extensive widening and straightening of the road and would have demanded cutting trees and blasting rock from the hillsides.[23]

The first organized protests against this project began in 1910 and were led by the Germantown and Chestnut Hill Improvement Association, founded the year before to lobby the city for a variety of neighborhood enhancements. This group passed a strong resolution against opening the upper drive to automobiles, sent spokesmen to speak against it before the park commission and orchestrated a campaign of editorials and letters in local newspapers. The Pennsylvania Forestry Association and the Automobile Club of Philadelphia joined this coalition. The Fairmount Park Commission gave into the pressure from so many outspoken opponents and decided, for the moment, to ban cars from the drive.

Five years later, in 1915, a new proposal to open this section to automobile traffic came to the park commission again. This time the Germantown and Chestnut Hill Improvement Association collected 2,000 signatures, placing protest petitions in every drugstore in the area. George P. Rich, a Germantown resident, also threatened to sue the park commissioners if they allowed automobiles on the drive. He cited the state legislative act of April 14, 1868, which expressly authorized Wissahickon Park to protect the purity of water in the creek and to preserve the natural beauty of the valley. He added that this act had prohibited riding or driving more than seven miles per hour in the park.[24]

In 1920 these civic groups were horrified to discover that the park commission had agreed to take yet another look at opening the upper park to cars. Members of the Philadelphia Riders and Drivers (founded in 1912 and reorganized in 1952 as the Riders of the Wissahickon) led the fight against this latest threat. Using tactics that had been taken up recently by reformers of all kinds (from labor unions to women's suffrage marchers), the group held an equestrian demonstration around the Valley Green Inn in October 1920, with nearly 200 horseback riders and carriage and coach drivers, to publicize their cause. The demonstration persuaded the commissioners to ban cars from Wissahickon Turnpike and the name of the road was changed to "Forbidden Drive"—open only to carriages, horseback riders, bicyclists and pedestrians.[25]

9:7

Reintroducing Animals and Plants

In the late 19th century, the disappearance of America's wild places and wildlife fueled growing conservation efforts. Wealthy men prided themselves on shooting or catching hundreds of animals a day in contests that often echoed the ruthless attempts of businessmen to monopolize as much of a given market as they could. Between 1850 and 1920 the passenger pigeon (*Ectopistes migratorius*), the Carolina parakeet (*Conuropsis carolinensis*) and woodland bison (*Bison pennsylvanicus*) became extinct, while the wolf (*Canis lupus*), black bear (*Ursus americanus*) and mountain lion (*Puma concolor*), the larger predators, were pushed into remote, isolated areas. As a result of unregulated hunting and trapping, deforestation and pollution, wildlife was dwindling.

In response to this threat, the state legislature established the Pennsylvania Game Commission in 1895 to protect and conserve wildlife. The commission was and is largely supported by hunters and trappers (from the sale of hunting and fur taking licenses on State Game Lands) and not by the Pennsyvania State General Fund appropriations. This dependency has greatly influenced the game commission's agenda and has had important consequences for conservation efforts.[26]

Several decades earlier, in 1866, the founding of the Pennsylvania Fish and Boat Commission was motivated by a similar desire to restore a game fish—the American shad—to the Susquehanna River (by reducing pollution and creating fish ladders). In the late 19th century, this commission was the first state agency in the United States to restock fish, distributing over 90,900 frogs and more than 10.2 million pickerel (*Esox americanus*) to Pennsylvania streams and rivers.[27] The efforts of the Pennsylvania Fish and Boat commission, along with the Pennsylvania Game Commission, were focused entirely on game animals—those "useful" species that could be hunted, trapped or fished.

In the Wissahickon, where hunting was prohibited, park authorities and private individuals nonetheless opted to reintroduce the white tailed deer (*Odocoileus virginianus*)—in this case as a picturesque addition to the forest landscape. Deer had virtually disappeared in Pennsylvania by the end of the 1800s, but were brought back by the game commission, which set aside large areas of Western Pennsylvania as hunting lands, managed for deer. In a parallel gesture, during the mid-1890s, the fish commission restocked Wissahickon Creek with fish raised in state hatcheries. These fish, in contrast to the deer in the park, were primarily released to provide "sport." Many of the species chosen, although native to Pennsylvania—rainbow trout (*Oncorhynchus mykiss*),

9:8

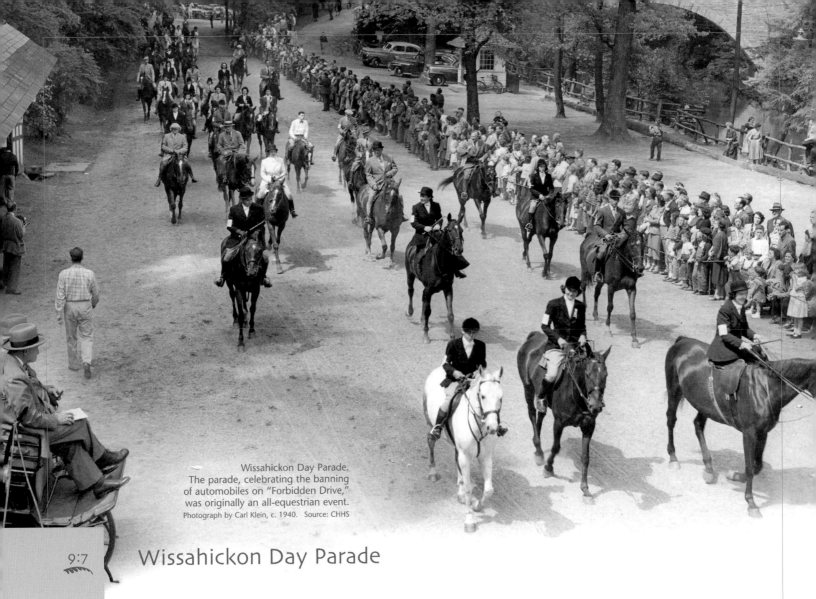

Wissahickon Day Parade.
The parade, celebrating the banning
of automobiles on "Forbidden Drive,"
was originally an all-equestrian event.
Photograph by Carl Klein, c. 1940. Source: CHHS

9:7

Wissahickon Day Parade

To remind people of the importance of keeping the Wissahickon free of automobile traffic, the Philadelphia Riders and Drivers began holding the Wissahickon Day Parade in May 1921, an event that would continue every year except for an interruption during and just after World War II. More than 600 riders and drivers, along with 12,000 spectators, turned out for the first parade.

Over the years a number of celebrities joined the fun and in 1924,

silent screen star Tom Mix and his horse, Tony, appeared in the parade.[1] This event drew wide community participation and included numerous groups and organizations— "mounted Park Guards, mounted police, ... mounted military and fraternal organizations, ... mounted boy scouts, riding academies in units, riding and hunt clubs, polo teams, and various saddle clubs."[2] In later decades, Wissahickon Day became simply a local festival—its initial

purpose as a continuing demonstration of civic activism in the park—largely forgotten.

1. *The Beehive* (monthly periodical published in Germantown), June 1926, 20, 23; *Independent-Gazette*, October 28, 1920, May 19, 1921, May 28, 1925; *Chestnut Hill and Mount Airy Herald*, May 29, 1925; Guide, February 27, 1926; Jane Campbell, Scrapbooks, 41:123, 145; 43:99, 139-142.

2. Francis Burke Brandt, *The Wissahickon Valley Within the City of Philadelphia* (Philadelphia, 1927), 31.

Private Restocking

By 1800, Southeastern Pennsylvania had no deer—hunted out by Indians and early settlers for the commercial trade in hides and for individual food and clothing. The idea of stocking the lower Wissahickon Valley with deer originated with Robert Glendinning, a banker, stockbroker and member of the Fairmount Park Commission, who had a private deer park at his estate on Towanda Street, at the edge of Wissahickon Park in Chestnut Hill. Deeply Anglophile, Glendinning, like a number of other wealthy Philadelphians, saw the English gentry as a model for his own lifestyle. When two of his animals escaped into the Wissahickon and survived, Glendinning offered to purchase 16 deer for the park—13 does and 3 bucks.

Let loose in Wissahickon Park in 1914, with permission from the park commission, these deer roamed into adjoining private properties, munching on shrubbery and young trees. After numerous complaints from residents, the commission agreed, in the spring of 1916, to round up and remove the deer to a preserve in Western Pennsylvania. By 1918, the deer question disappeared from the local press. The remaining animals may have died or been killed, since there was no mention of them in the park between the 1920s and the 1950s. The questions raised by Glendinning's private restocking anticipated the more complex issues and serious philosophical controversies faced when deer later returned to the valley on their own—growing in numbers until they threatened the forest itself.[1]

Knole House

Knole House in Sevenoaks, Kent, England, is an English country house surrounded by 1000 acres of deer park. This Tudor deer park is one of the few to have survived the past 500 years.[2] Deer parks were fenced, wooded pastureland, originally created to raise deer for hunting in the Middle Ages. From the Tudor period to the Restoration, the deer park slowly declined in popularity. However, by the 18th century, they were revived as an important component of the picturesque English "Gentleman's Seat." Economic realities gradually induced large property owners to replace deer with cattle. In a last gasp in the 19th century, new deer parks were created on the smaller properties of the newly wealthy, upper middle class.[3]

---

1. FPC, *Annual Report*, 1914, 10; *Germantown Telegraph*, November 12, 1913; *Independent-Gazette*, April 18, 1918; Campbell, Scrapbooks, 25:68; 28:27-28,120,136; 29:173; 30:155, 181; 31:37; 34:166; Edwin C. Jellett, Scrapbooks, 1:142.

2. Website: www.gardens-too.org.uk/Knole.htm

3. Tom Williamson, *Polite Landscapes: Gardens & Society in Eighteenth-Century England* (Gloucestershire, U.K., 1995), 22-24, 93-94.

Tudor Deer Park with red deer (*Cervus elaphus*) at Knole House.
Source: Courtesy of Knole House

black bass (*Micropterus salmoides*) and rock bass (*Ambloplites rupestris*)—were unsuited to the Wissahickon's increasingly warm and muddy waters. They remained alive for only for a few weeks or months, but did not reproduce. [28]

As a result of the desire to fish in the creek, local fishermen became conservation advocates. As early as 1911, the Germantown chapter of the United Sportsmen of Pennsylvania protested to local newspapers about pollution in Monoshone Creek, alleging that it was killing fish in the Wissahickon, and demanding that the dumping of raw sewage be stopped immediately.[29]

The ecological thinking of the later 20th century did not inform the early conservation movement. Scientific ideas about ecosystem function and organization had not yet been developed. For example, the concept of "habitat,"(the unique conditions required for species to live) and "keystone species" (species critical to the survival of other plants and animals) were not yet understood. Instead, efforts to protect and preserve singled out "appealing" individual animals and "horticulturally desirable" plants. These efforts paralleled the approach to the protection and preservation of historic buildings. In both cases, the focus was on individual elements. The complexity of the systems in which these elements were embedded was neither recognized nor integrated into conservation plans.

A Very Different Forest

The American chestnut (*Castenea dentata*) and the Canadian hemlock (*Tsuga canadensis*) were major forest canopy trees in the valley when Europeans first arrived in the area. By the early 20th century, several forces—both natural and human—gradually eliminated the chestnut and greatly reduced the hemlock.

The ridges of the Wissahickon Valley had once been covered almost entirely with chestnut trees. In late June, the hilltops were white with chestnut blossoms and in the fall, when the leaves changed color, these hilltops turned a deep yellow-orange. The prolific nut production of the chestnut tree was one reason for its great success as a species. Other reasons for its success were late flowering, which kept the blossoms from being killed by spring frosts, and an early maturation, which allowed this tree to produce nuts when only four years old. The chestnut was also one of a number of native trees called "sprout hardwoods." This adaptation allowed these trees to persist by growing new stems from the stump even if blown over in a storm—or cut down for timber. The unmistakable predominance of chestnut trees on the highest areas led early colonists to name a number of their new communities "Chestnut Hill."[30]

The chestnut blight was the first in a series of devastating exotic pests and diseases that decimated native forest trees throughout the 20th century. The fungus was discovered in 1904 on American chestnut trees at the New York Zoological Gardens. The disease was brought into the country as the result of efforts to increase the commercial value of chestnuts by crossing the American tree, known for its great size, with the Asian species, known for its larger nuts.

Imported with the Asian species was a deadly fungus called *Cryphonectria parasitica*. This fungus destroyed chestnut trees by clogging their circulatory systems so that they were unable to move water and nutrients from their roots to their branches and back again—a kind of hardening of the arteries. The American chestnut, unlike its Asian counterpart, had

9:9

Facing Page
Late in the month of October or early in November, Fairmount Park held a "Nutting Day" when children and adults filled baskets and bags with shiny brown chestnuts as well as beech and hickory nuts that covered the ground in great numbers. Engraving by J.W. Laudebach, first published in *The Art Journal*, 1878.
Source: Chris Bolgiano ed., *Mighty Giants: An American Chestnut Anthology* (Bennington, Vt., 2007)

no immunity to this fungus and it spread swiftly from tree to tree, radically changing the character of the Northeastern Deciduous Forest and the entire Wissahickon Valley. This blight arrived in Wissahickon Park around 1914, and moved with terrifying rapidity. By the early 1920s most chestnuts in the valley were infected.[31]

Fungicides were tried unsuccessfully. Chemical treatment proved ineffective. Wide "firebreak" barriers were cut to prevent the advance of the disease, but the blight jumped past it, spreading as much as 50 miles a year. Plant quarantine legislation was passed in 1912; and in hopes of preventing the blight from spreading throughout the country, the U.S. Forest Service directed that all diseased trees be cut down. This policy had the unintended consequence of eliminating the possibility that a few immune trees would survive and become the basis for "recolonization." All the chestnuts in the Wissahickon Valley were cut, and by the late 1930s a park visitor would have found only spindly stems sprouting from stumps. Well into the 1950s these sprouts struggled to become new trees, but succumbed to the disease when they were five to six years old, doomed since the fungus remained in the bark of any surviving chestnut trees and from there spread to any nearby sprouts.[32]

At the same time that the chestnut was disappearing from the Wissahickon Valley, many of the great, old groves of hemlock that lined the slopes of the gorge, and that had been such a signature, were also being lost. Cornelius Weygandt wrote in 1929 that "many of these ancient trees were blown down by heavy storms, cut for new projects or succumbed to old age .... Time was when I should have said that the hemlock was the dominant tree of the Wissahickon Valley. Now, however, a walk from the mouth of the creek to its gorge's end at the Reading Pike [Germantown Pike] will tell you that the tulip poplar [*Liriodendron tulipifera*]

The American Chestnut Blight

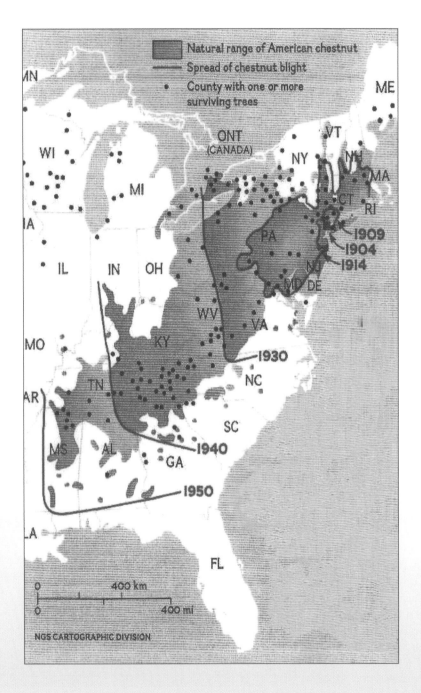

The American chestnut tree (*Castenea dentata*) was the single most important and most abundant tree in the Wissahickon valley. This tree was almost wiped out by an orange fungal pathogen (*Cryphonectria parasitica*) from China (apparently introduced on nursery stock, possibly as early as 1893). In Asia, this fungus is only a weak parasite. On the trees it infests small cankers occur but they do not kill Asian chestnuts.

Chestnut blight is a canker disease. The cankers are diffuse and grow rapidly. They infect stems and branches of any size. A canker forms on the chestnut stem when the fungus enters through an open wound. The fungus grows in and under the bark, eventually killing the cambium— the layer of living tree tissue responsible for growth and the transport of nutrients. The spores are carried from tree to tree by wind or by animals and insects that have touched the cankers. They are also disseminated by water after rainstorms.[1]

The map shows the spread of the chestnut blight, from its first recorded appearance at the New York Zoological Gardens in 1904. The blight spread up to 50 miles a year and appeared in the Wissahickon by 1914.

Source: *National Geographic Magazine*, "Back from the Brink," February, 1990, 133.

After the tree dies, sprouts will develop from a burl-like tissue at the base of the tree called the "root collar," which contains dormant embryos. These sprouts grow from the old root systems into small multi-stemmed shrubs. Reinfected and killed back to the ground, these stems resprout until the root system is exhausted.[2] For many years after the blight had toppled the mature chestnut trees in the Wissahickon Valley, such sprouts could still be seen on the ridges and upper slopes.

1. Sandra L. Anagnostakis, Connecticut Agricultural Experiment, New Haven, Conn., "Revitalization of the Majestic Chestnut: Chestnut Blight Disease." Website: apsnet.org/online/feature/chestnut/

2. The American Chestnut Society, also Website: forestpathology.org/dis_chestnut.html, article by James Worall, May, 2007.

Right
Stems of American chestnuts infected by the fungal parasite (*Cryphonectria parasitica*). The orange cankers shown here have destroyed the bark of the tree.
Source: The American Chestnut Society

Below
The flowers of the American Chestnut.
Source: Chris Bolgiano, ed., *Mighty Giants: An American Chestnut Anthology* (Bennington, Vt., 2008)

outnumbers all other trees for these miles…. There was once a noble wood of [hemlocks] from the site of "The Woman in the Wilderness" above Hermit's Lane. Today that wood … is sadly decimated…. The forest of old hemlocks that used to be a feature of the east slope of the valley just above the Monastery is nearly all gone…." [33]

Construction projects within the park took a severe toll on the hemlocks. In 1900, in an effort to address the problem of sewage flowing into Wissahickon Creek, the Fairmount Park Commission agreed to allow the construction of the first of several intercepting sewers that would run parallel to the creek. These sewers were generally considered to be a public good, since they would take raw sewage from trunk sewers in the community and separate it from stormwater. With separate sewers, only rainwater flowing off the land and into the storm sewers would be carried into the creek. Raw sewage would be taken to treatment plants. Building these interceptor sewers was a conservation action, as well as a health measure, since it would mean cleaner water in the creek. However, to build this sewer, large stands of very old trees were cut and the ground disturbed along a corridor over 50-feet wide.

A stone aqueduct was built across Cresheim Creek, just above Devil's Pool to carry the sewer pipe. In a letter to the editor of a Germantown newspaper, a resident bitterly criticized the damage: "Thirty years ago [c. 1870] this was the fairest spot on the Wissahickon. . . . Then came employees of the Park Commission. The fantastic tangle of laurel and vines was ruthlessly destroyed. . . .Next the Commission threw a bridge across the Devil's Pool and in doing this work cut down some of the fine hemlock trees which shaded the pool."[34]

Just six years later, a second major construction project—the building of the Walnut Lane Bridge across Wissahickon Creek—decimated another major hemlock grove. Part of the much-loved "Hemlock Glen," this stand had some of the largest and oldest hemlocks in the lower valley.

Natural forces also contributed to the decline of the hemlock in Wissahickon Valley. A devastating sleet and ice storm during the winter of 1923-24 toppled hundreds of trees in the gorge, some estimated to be "200 years old [and] the glory of the Wissahickon."[35] Vandalism of young trees—for Christmas trees as well as transplanted to private gardens—also reduced the numbers of hemlock. The worst threat to the remaining hemlocks and to hemlock reproduction would come after World War II, with the arrival and spread of new pests—the wooly adegid (*Adelges tsugae*) and hemlock scale (*Fiorinia externa Ferris*).

Friends of the Wissahickon (FOW)

The Fairmount Park Commission did little or nothing to restore the forest, citing a shortage of funds to undertake the work of clearing and replanting.[36] This failure to take the initiative galvanized local civic leaders to form a new group in October 1924. Called the Friends of the Wissahickon (FOW), its mission was, "To preserve the natural beauty and wildness of the Valley and to stimulate public interest therein."[37] The FOW became the largest, most important and longest surviving civic organization directly concerned with safeguarding and restoring the Wissahickon. The social capital that this group would garner has been unmatched by any other organization in the valley, in any of the other of the Fairmount Park system's stream corridor parks and perhaps in the country at large.

"Heavy Hitters"

Druim Moir, a large house on the edge of the Wissahickon valley, was the site of the first Friends of the Wissahickon (FOW) meeting. This house belonged to Samuel F. Houston, one of three heirs to the immense fortune left by his railroad magnate father, Henry Howard Houston. Fifty or so other men and women attended this first meeting, Including Henry Howard's daughter, Gertrude, and her husband, Dr. George Woodward. Woodward was by then a well-known Pennsylvania State Senator and outspoken progressive reformer. These men and women, self-confident and with the money and leisure to spend in volunteer civic activities, were not easily intimidated by government officials or by the Fairmount Park Commission.

Charles F. Jenkins, a Germantown resident, publisher of the *Farm Journal* and president of the Germantown Site and Relic Society. He was elected as the first president of the Friends of the Wissahickon in 1924. Photograph, c. 1920s.
Source: CHHS

In 1926, in a letter to the membership, the FOW summed up the most pressing threats to the Wissahickon: "The erection of many buildings adjacent to the Valley is bringing about conditions which are not conducive to the growth of certain forest trees; there ha[s] been little or no planting to take the place of the trees that [have] died, notably the chestnut trees, which were annihilated by the terrible blight of twelve years ago; a third cause is the most deplorable of all, and the one that should be most easily rectified, the wanton destruction of plants, flowers and small trees by the very persons who should be most eager to protect the property of the citizens of Philadelphia."[38] These threats—the impact of construction along park boundaries, the loss of important stands of trees and vandalism—would continue to be major concerns for this organization and for the park as a whole.

To publicize their plans and to attract additional members and support, the FOW brought their work to the attention of both community and Philadelphia metropolitan newspapers, and even gave a series of radio talks during the mid-1920s. By 1930, FOW membership increased tenfold—from 50 to 500 people. With this publicity, they raised approximately $58,000 during their first decade (equivalent to about $1 million in early 21st-century values). This money was given to Fairmount Park to buy nearly 14,000 trees.[39] Park staff planted the trees (mainly from Andorra Nurseries), and this extensive replanting project began a long, fruitful private-public partnership between Fairmount Park and the FOW.[40]

As part of this partnership, the FOW formed a tree committee to establish guidelines for replanting. The members of this committee were George Woodward, Samuel Newman Baker, chief landscape gardener for the Fairmount Park Commission, and W. Warner Harper, head of the Andorra Nurseries. The Committee used aerial photographs of the valley to identify "bare places" and urged that trees be placed "on the borders of Wissahickon Park to cut off undesirable views of building operations...."[41] They also recommended that only native species be planted in the park. The Fairmount Park Commission did not always honor this goal. Some of what they planted were non-native exotics that ultimately became invasive. Although board minutes and newsletters of the FOW carried partial accounts of the numbers and types of trees planted—and sometimes even the locations of these plantings—the picture of what was actually accomplished is not clear. Nor is there any record of the percentage of plantings that survived.[42]

Perhaps the FOW's most significant work at this time was securing additional property to enlarge park boundaries in places vunerable to development. New construction adjacent to the narrower parts of the park would have compromised the feeling of being "removed" from the city. In the early 1920s, the FOW board resolved to make "a systematic effort ... to increase the area of the Wissahickon Park by gifts of adjacent land, or by legacies, or gifts of money, which could be used to purchase such land."[43]

When a developer planned to build several dozen small houses on a large property at the corner of Germantown and Northwestern Avenues, adjacent to the creek, the FOW took action. Learning that the park commission, citing lack of funds, had declined to purchase the property, members of the FOW contributed $19,000 to buy the site and hold it until the commission could pay. In 1937, under a grant from the Depression-era Works Progress Administration (WPA), the FOW donated this property as memorial to William Warner Harper, a founder and long-time board member of the FOW. Landscape architect, Arthur Paul, Harper's successor at Andorra Nurseries, designed the new parkland, now called Harper's Meadow.[44]

The Depression and Private Work Projects

In its *Annual Report* for 1933, the Fairmount Park Commission lamented that "forced economies" over the past several years had "made it impossible to adequately maintain and improve the park system and [have] resulted in a decided lowering of our standards."[45] That year the appropriation for wages had been slashed more than 25 percent, from $421,200 to $315,000. For the years 1936, 1937 and 1938 the commission had been prohibited by city council from filling park guard vacancies, reducing the force by 21 officers.[52] With the park commission unable to act for lack of funds, the FOW stepped up its work in Wissahickon Park. During the worst years of the Great Depression, between 1930 and 1934, the organization raised nearly $50,000, beginning with a donation of $5,000 from George and Gertrude Woodward, for work projects in the valley to assist unemployed men in the local communities. Approximately 180 men worked for $3.50 per day under the supervision of Fairmount Park staff. By May 1931, the FOW had spent over $22,000 on relief projects, with the men taking on a wide variety of jobs.[46]

Relief workers cleared dead chestnut trees, sawed them into logs and sold them for firewood at special yards set up at the edges of the park at Allen's Lane in Mt. Airy and at Rex Avenue in Chestnut Hill. They improved older trails, especially on the west side of the valley, covering them with cinders, building new foot bridges, and putting drainage pipes under trails where necessary. They also began work on a road-building project that extended Cresheim Valley Drive from Germantown Avenue to Stenton Avenue. Land for this road beside Cresheim Creek was donated to the park by Randall Morgan and by the Woodward family. [47]

The FOW was justly proud of its relief work, since it helped the unemployed as well as providing labor for worthwhile projects in the Wissahickon. Beyond these benefits, the FOW board recognized that the work in the valley—and the fund drives to sustain it—had produced a new enthusiasm for the park. According to the FOW secretary's report for May 2, 1931, "One great good that has resulted from [this relief work] is the added interest and sense of ownership in the Wissahickon Valley, that has come to the ever increasing number of those who live near it and enjoy its beauties…. In the past year alone, membership has increased by 124, for a total of 604."[48]

The Depression and Public Work Projects

As the Depression deepened and showed no signs of ending, the majority of Americans began to look to the federal government for help. Franklin D. Roosevelt was elected president in 1932 and launched his "New Deal" the following year. A distant cousin of earlier conservation crusader Theodore Roosevelt, Franklin Roosevelt also considered himself a conservationist and believed that giving jobs to the unemployed would provide both the labor and the funds for conservation projects.[49]

By 1934, the Fairmount Park Commission was using workers from two public relief programs—the Civil Works Administration (CWA) and the Local Works Division (LWD)— to carry out a variety of projects in the Wissahickon Valley. The CWA was an early New Deal agency, while the LWD was funded by the City of Philadelphia. Enlargement of the public golf course along Walnut Lane was one of their first, joint projects.[50]

A New Park Model

Many of these Depression-era projects reflected a new park model. By the late 1920s and early 1930s, the more genteel uses of the park—boating, fishing, walking, hiking, horseback riding, ice skating, painting, sketching, and photography—appeared to be on a collision course with new concerns, both national and local. There was now a desire to provide more "active" recreation facilities for the public. In 1924, the National Conference on Outdoor Recreation, convened by President Calvin Coolidge, had brought these new concerns to wide public attention. The conference report suggested that the older parks, as designed by Olmsted and others for "peaceful enjoyment amid beautiful surroundings of a naturalistic type," were no longer adequate to accommodate an expanded idea of recreation. "Play for the child, sport for youth and recreation for adults" had become a national battle cry.[51]

The national conference report recommended that parks should now provide a number of active recreational facilities: "playgrounds, playfields, athletic fields, stadiums, neighborhood recreation parks, swimming and boating centers, [and] golf courses...."[52] To the FOW and many area residents, park proposals based on these ideas threatened the wilderness character of the Wissahickon Valley. Opponents of expanded recreation reacted angrily and with fierce determination, waging campaigns in the press and using their influence with the Fairmount Park Commission to preserve the park as a natural haven in the city.

In 1934, The Fairmount Park Commission hired L.H. Weir to make a report on Philadelphia's parks. Weir had been the director and editor of the 1928 study, *Parks: A Manual of Municipal and County Parks*, commissioned six years earlier by the National Conference on Outdoor Recreation. His report for Philadelphia recommended an array of new recreational amenities—picnic shelters, tennis courts, and baseball diamonds in Fairmount Park.[53] Fortunately for Wissahickon Park, the commission rejected Weir's recommendations and suppressed the report. However, interest in active recreation was so great that the following year a committee of the Pennsylvania House of Representatives harshly criticized The Fairmount Park commission for not acting on the Weir report and its "expanded recreational" model.[54] Philadelphia newspapers sided with the park commission and one editorial suggested that if the new model were adopted, "There would be precious little room left for a Park.... There is no need to turn the Park into a gigantic recreation center, supervised by an army of teachers. The people of Philadelphia enjoy this great Park as it is today."[55]

The federal relief system built suppport for state and local Democrats. In 1936 a Democrat, S. Davis Wilson was elected mayor and opened the city to New Deal funding rejected by his predecessor, the Republican mayor, J.Hampton Moore.[56] Wilson, disagreed with the local press, and charged that the park commission was "undemocratic" and "not responsible to anyone." Foreshadowing the attitudes that later spurred the city takeover of Fairmount Park, Wilson believed that the park's problems stemmed from the method of choosing the commissioners—appointment by judges. He strongly urged that the selection method should be changed to popular election, or that the commission should be abolished and its functions absorbed by the appropriate city departments.[57] Like so many other early park controversies, these arguments over democracy, appropriate use of the park, and the structure of park administration would be repeated in subsequent generations and with new casts of characters.

Different types of recreational facilities needed in a modern park, as recommended by L.H. Weir in *Parks: A Manual of Municipal and County Parks*.

Source: L.H. Weir, ed., *Parks: A Manual of Municipal and County Parks* (New York., 1928), Plate 14, 62

The WPA in the Wissahickon

When Congress enacted the Works Progress Administration (WPA) in 1935, it had become clear that the Depression would not end any time soon and that a more massive government jobs program would have to be instituted. Headed by Harry Hopkins, one of Roosevelt's closest confidants, the WPA provided jobs for workers with all sorts of abilities and experiences, from unskilled laborers to artists and musicians. It was a program of impressive scope and budget.[58] A large grant from the WPA to the Fairmount Park Commission resulted in plans for wide-ranging improvements to Wissahickon Park that would employ some 1,000 men at a cost of over $800,000.[59]

White City | 1898-1912

The official name of this private park was the Chestnut Hill Amusement Park, although it was located just outside Chestnut Hill and the city boundaries. The park was popularly known as "White City" possibly because of the limewashed buildings or possibly after "White City," a part of the 1893 Columbian Exposition in Chicago.

This amusement park was constructed on the site of old Yeakle farm (owned by Daniel Yeakle) that included a mill and millpond in the floodplain of Paper Mill Run, a tributary of Wissahickon Creek. A comparison of the two historical maps shows that the old millpond was reconfigured and a canal loop added to the southeastern end when White City was built.

Popular in the last decades of the 1800s, amusement parks often began as picnic groves on the outskirts of cities, offering "swings and merry-go rounds, target shootings, footraces, donkey rides, music and dancing, and bowling matches."[1] By the 1890s, with the development of the electric streetcar, "trolley-car" amusement parks were built at the end of these lines, to bring new riders to outlying areas on summer evenings and weekends.

With the creation of Fairmount Park, the inns and beer gardens within its boundaries were forbidden to serve alcohol, foreshadowing their end as viable commercial establishments.

White City was built in 1897 and open for the 1898-1911 seasons. During the dozen years of its existence, White City offered many of the activities and amusements not allowed in the public park system. It attracted a wide group of people, mainly from Northwest Philadelphia.

View of the boating pond at White City, framed by the carousel pavilion and encircled by a broad promenade.
Source: Springfield Township Historical Society

The amusement park included a toboggan (roller coaster), other rides, a dance hall, a music pavilion, long promenades, flowerbeds and a small lake for boating. Couples could come here without chaperones and families were attracted to the rides, the picnic areas and the musical performances. It provided safe, "wholesome" entertainment outdoors at an affordable price. However, well-to-do residents of Chestnut Hill wanted no part of this "low-brow" recreational facility, and for years, many claimed that this establishment attracted a rowdy crowd and "lowered the tone of the entire suburb... depreciat[ing] the value of the land and... [keeping] desirable persons away from Chestnut Hill."[2]

In February 1912, George C. Thomas, Jr. (former owner of Bloomfield Farm and the designer of the Whitemarsh Valley Country Club's golf course), Charles N. Welsh, Wilson Potter, and Jay Cook III bought the property for approximately $500,000 and tore down the park. The site was then subdivided into two portions

Trolley terminus at White City. Photograph, c. early 1900s.
Source: Free Library of Philadelphia

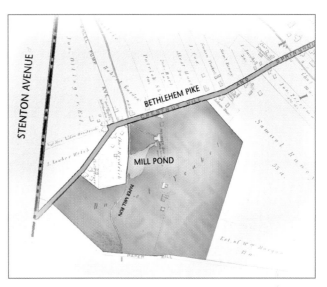

Detail of the 1885 map of Springfield Township, showing an industrial property and farm (with the Reliance Saw Mill and Machine Works and a mill pond in Yeakel's meadow) that later became the site of White City.
Source: Hopkins, Atlas of Chestnut Hill/Springfield Township, Montgomery County, Pa., 1885

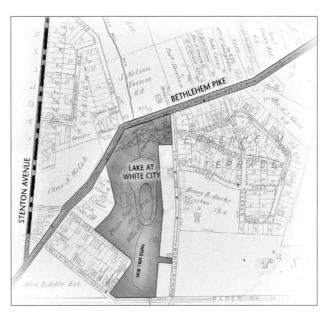

Detail of the 1916 map of Springfield Township, showing the site of White City after the park had been closed. The Union Traction Company ran trolleys from Philadelphia through Chestnut Hill to White City and the Lehigh Valley Transit Company operated trolleys from White City along Bethlehem Pike. The map shows the trolley lines and terminus.
Source: A.H. Mueller, Atlas of the North Penn Section of Montgomery County, Pa., 1916

White City | 1898-1912 *(Continued)*

and reused. In 1923 one portion was sold to Springfield Township for $1 for the former Springfield Township High School; and the other portion for a township park (including the pond). While these elitist attitudes helped preserve the Wissahickon Valley, they have also deprived the larger community of some of the richness of recreational opportunities. Once White City was torn down, only the more "genteel" pastimes of Wissahickon Park were available.[3]

1. Galen Cranz, *The Politics of Park Design: A History of Urban Parks in America* (Cambridge, Mass., 1982), 3-59.

2. *Germantown Telegraph*, February 28, 1912. See also Contosta, *Suburb in the City*, 157-58.

3. The authors are indebted to Edward Zwicker for his lecture on White City, July 2009, and for his review of these pages.

Boat Basin, looking towards the rear of the Casino, designed by Horace Trumbauer, a well-known Philadelphia architect. The Casino was the most impressive building on the site. Photograph, c. early 1900s.
Source: GHS

View of Palace the Theatre and bridge over the dam at White City. Photograph, c. early 1900s.
Source: unknown

Unlike the earlier public works programs in the Wissahickon, which were smaller and could function side by side with private programs, these new massive proposals—and their embrace of the fashionable recreational model—led to considerable friction between the FOW and the WPA.

The park commission, stung by criticism heaped on it by the state investigative committee and by Mayor Wilson, agreed to go along with the WPA. This led to a head-on collision between the FOW and the WPA that erupted in 1937 over plans to add tennis courts, baseball diamonds, picnic shelters, and refreshment stands to the lower valley.[67] In December 1937, the FOW came out against several WPA projects proposed for the park—especially the refreshment stands, which they believed would commercialize the park and lead to serious litter problems. Philadelphia newspapers played up this dispute, writing a series of articles on the "the hot dog stand menace." *The Philadelphia Inquirer*, reflecting the FOW position, predicted that, "Ere next summer arrives, the blossoming trees may vie for honors with Coney Island stands and the scent of new-born violets and arbutus may be lost in the blanketing odor of fresh hot dogs."[60]

The FOW also opposed the construction of picnic shelters and other structures along the Wissahickon, charging that they would mar the wilderness appearance of the park. According to George Woodward, "Such structures would make the valley lose its naturalist[ic] appearance and give [it] a semblance of an amusement park."[61] This viewpoint, although characterized by some as elitist, ultimately helped to preserve the valley and its wilderness ambience for future generations of all classes and backgrounds to enjoy.

Despite the "hot dog war," the FOW, the Fairmount Park Commission, and the WPA arranged a meeting on November 13, 1937 at Valley Green Inn, where the warring parties agreed to a compromise. There would be no refreshment stands, and all shelters, some for park guards and some for picnickers, would be constructed only of indigenous materials—Wissahickon schist and lumber from trees native to the region. They also agreed to place the structures at "well established gathering areas so that the valley would be disrupted as little as possible."[62]

New Structures

Altogether, the WPA designed and built 13 new structures in the Wissahickon—guard-houses, picnic shelters, and restrooms. They took their design guidelines from the book *Park Structures and Facilities*, by Albert Good and published by the National Park Service in 1935. Good summarized his guidelines for park structures as "the use of native materials at the proper scale, through the avoidance of rigid, straight lines, and over simplification, [which] gives the feeling of having been executed by a pioneer craftsman with limited hand tools."[63] This approach would achieve "sympathy with natural surroundings and with the past."[64]

For many, the rustic but sturdy structures built along the creek, like the statues and even the large, protruding sewers, have added a friendly, humanizing touch. In time they would become so familiar and blend so well into the scenery that park users would take them for granted. Ironically, a later generation of the FOW would raise money to repair and restore these structures as a treasured layer in the park palimpsest.

View of Wissahickon Hall, one of the old inns along the creek, reused as the headquarters
for the Fairmount Park Guard. Photograph, 1938.
Source: Philadelphia City Archives

Built on the site of the first Wissahickon Turnpike toll booth, "Ten Box," so called because it housed the tenth park guard call box, had multiple functions: trailhead with park information, guardhouse, shelter, restrooms, refreshment stand and bicycle rental. Photograph, c.1950.
Source: Free Library of Philadelphia

9:12

The WPA in the Park

Between 1938 and 1943, Fairmount Park, under a grant from the Depression-era Works Progress Administration (WPA), carried out numerous projects in the Wissahickon. Crews repaired dams, repaired and built trails and retaining walls and put up 13 structures in the park, including picnic shelters, guardhouses and combination guardhouses/ shelters and restrooms. In accordance with an agreement worked out with the Friends of the Wissahickon (FOW), the structures were placed in areas that had already been disturbed—on the sites of earlier guardhouses, mill buildings or tollbooths.

The lower half of these WPA structures (and the chimneys for small stoves or fireplaces) were generally made of Wissahickon schist, laid in random courses—with large stones taking up several courses, mixed with smaller stones to create a rustic effect. The upper half of these little buildings were constructed like a Southeastern Pennsylvania log cabin of an earlier era, using oak and ash native to the valley. All the joints were mortise and tenon, held together with wooden pegs. The roofs were moderately pitched and covered in cedar shakes.

Like the National Park structures of the time, built with fine traditional craftsmanship and local materials, these buildings had a simplicity and character that grew out of the place. Later (post-World War II) park struc-

tures would lose this integrity. They were frequently uniform, sterile, poorly constructed, made of cheap materials and painted a dismal brown.

Despite the fact that many members of the community during the Depression era did not want any man-made structures in this wilderness park, two generations later, a growing constituency would increasingly value this cultural layer and work to repair and restore the best of these WPA structures. Along with the Valley Green Inn, the steps, leaps, lookouts, statues and the variety of path journeys, these friendly little huts have made the park experience so much richer than a simple trail through urban woodlands.

WPA Guardhouses & Shelters

A WPA picnic shelter seen from Harper's Meadow. Located several hundred feet from the actual entance to Wissahickon Park at Northwestern Aveune, it is a self-contained pavilion recessed below the Forbidden Drive. This structure was envisioned as a "trailhead" or gateway into the park from Montgomery County. However, unlike the other park gateways, this shelter only works as a picnic facility and does not signal the beginning or ending of this major trail.
Source: CHHS

Left
Guardhouse at Bell's Mill Road.
Photograph, c. late 1930s.
Source: CHHS

Facing Page:
Park guard with his horse at the guardhouse at Rex Avenue. This building was a shelter with a small attached porch.
Photograph, c. late 1930s.
Source: CHHS

Depression-Era Trails

New Deal projects included an extensive network of new trails, as well as the improvement of older trails. In the photograph on the right, relief workers are constructing a new trail on the east side of Wissahickon Creek, opposite Forbidden Drive, between Bell's Mill Road and Germantown Avenue. This new pathway was extended as far south as Hartwell Lane and later called the "Orange Trail." The route followed the one proposed four decades earlier as the first section of a parkway extension that was to have traveled from the upper end of the gorge to Fort Washington.

Steps to the Tedyuscung statue. These steps and trail were constructed at the turn of the century, before the New Deal improvements of the 1930s. Photograph, c. 1910. Source: GHS

Trail constructed by the WPA, north
of Bell's Mill Road, on the east side
of Wissahickon Creek.
Photograph, c. late 1930s.
Source: CHHS

Repairing Valley Green

By 1937, the Valley Green Inn was deteriorating and the Park Commission once again threatened to close it. The Valley Green Association had saved the inn a generation before. Members of the association suggested that the FOW take charge of the inn. The organization raised $30,000 to repair the inn and save it from being demolished. The growing FOW needed a place to hold meetings and social events. Preservation of this increasingly important landmark seemed consistent with its overall conservation goals. The Fairmount Park Commission handed over responsibility for the Inn to the FOW and gave the organization a sublease for $1 a year. They then had the right to collect rent and share in any profits made by the restaurant—provided this revenue was used to maintain the inn and its surroundings. The FOW has continued to manage the Valley Green Inn, leasing the operation to professional restaurateurs. Assuming stewardship of the inn in the 1930s may have generated a tenacious but false oral tradition that the organization was founded expressly to save this legacy.[65]

Valley Green after repairs.
Photograph, 1938.
Source: FPC

Park Trails

During the Depression, the FOW and New Deal agencies cooperated on park trail projects. Although paths of varying lengths had been built in the Wissahickon before the 1930s, New Deal agencies, in cooperation with the Fairmount Park Commission and the FOW, created the first trail system within the park, incorporating older trails and establishing new ones. The largest and most widely used trail in this more comprehensive network remained Forbidden Drive—the old Wissahickon Turnpike that followed Wissahickon Creek. Higher up on each side of the valley, and roughly parallel to Forbidden Drive, two new trails were constructed. When completed, each trail ran from the entrance to Wissahickon Park at Ridge Avenue to the other end of the park at Northwestern Avenue. Connector trails were built to knit together a number of older pathways and remnant mill roads that descended into the park from the surrounding communities. New loop trails were built in several places where the park widened out, and special "destination" trails were constructed (or improved) to sites like Indian Rock and the Toleration statue.[66]

Altogether, there would now be a total of about 65 miles of trails, old and new, in Wissahickon Park. These trails were in line with FOW conservation goals—encouraging the traditional park uses of walking, hiking, and horseback riding. In 1940, to promote these trails, the organization published the first comprehensive map of Wissahickon Park.[67] This map has become a very important contributor to park identity and visitor orientation. The FOW continues to issue updated versions.

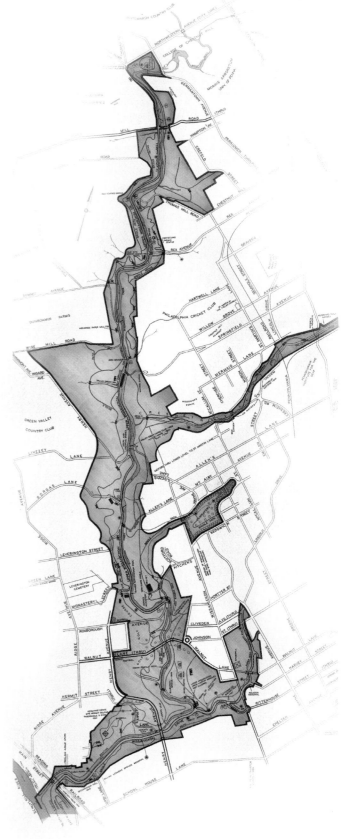

The first trail map of Wissahickon Park published by the Friends of the Wissahickon, in 1940.
Source: CHHS

Conservation and Civic Activism

During the first four decades of the 20th century, attitudes to the natural world changed throughout the country. Like the larger Conservation Movement, with all its complexities, contradictions and compromises, early conservation efforts in the lower Wissahickon Valley left a formidable legacy: "Conservationists reasserted the moral obligation human beings have to one another in their use of the natural world, and established that obligation as a primary principle of the nation's public life. At a time when fewer and fewer [citizens] found their identity in the soil, conservationists reconfigured the character of Americans' moral relationship with nature. Most fundamentally, perhaps, those who shaped the early American conservation movement recovered for their nation the abiding truth that what is human and what is natural are parts of a single whole, and devised a repertoire of formal structures and cultural strategies for giving that insight creative and enduring form."[68]

In the lower Wissahickon Valley, serious losses and threats created a desire to "conserve" what had been initially "protected" as a park. By the late 1930s, the FOW and other civic organizations in Northwest Philadelphia could look back with pride on the fact that they had established an effective framework for action and had successfully tackled a number of projects. This legacy of civic activism built a strong base of social capital, which would resurface after World War II and lead to a renewal of community involvement in the park.

Five Wissahickon Communities

1900-1920

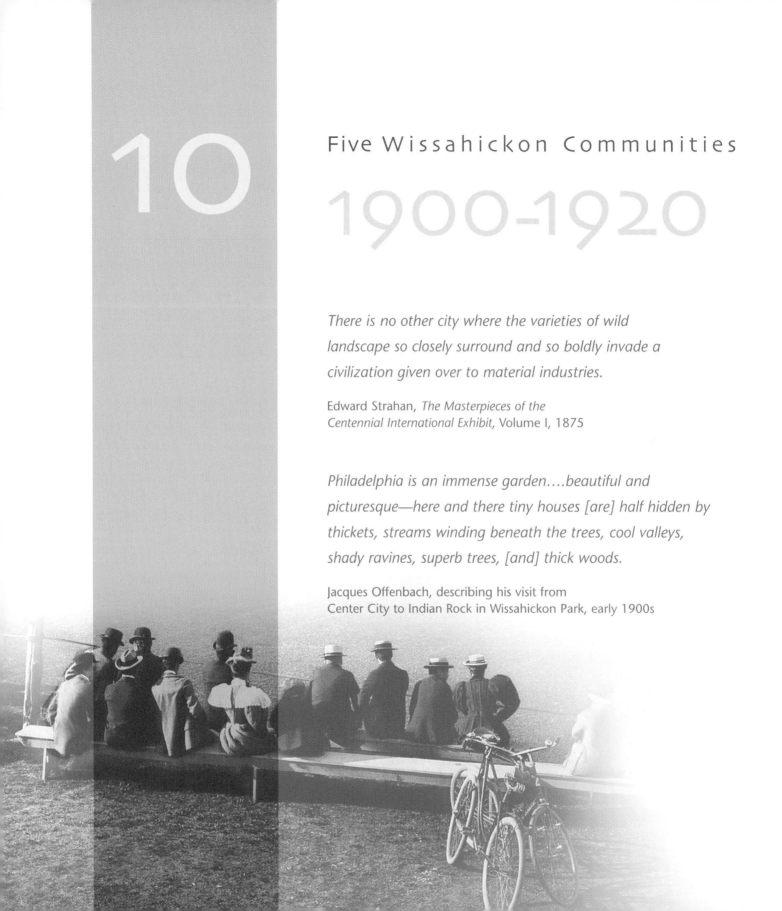

10

Five Wissahickon Communities
1900-1920

There is no other city where the varieties of wild landscape so closely surround and so boldly invade a civilization given over to material industries.

Edward Strahan, *The Masterpieces of the Centennial International Exhibit,* Volume I, 1875

Philadelphia is an immense garden....beautiful and picturesque—here and there tiny houses [are] half hidden by thickets, streams winding beneath the trees, cool valleys, shady ravines, superb trees, [and] thick woods.

Jacques Offenbach, describing his visit from Center City to Indian Rock in Wissahickon Park, early 1900s

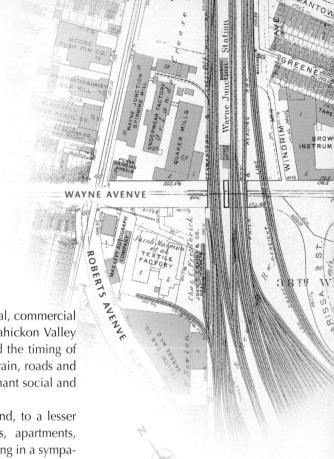

By the early 20th century, five distinct communities—with residential, commercial and industrial neighborhoods—had grown up on both sides of the Wissahickon Valley within the city. A complex mix of topography, economics, technology and the timing of development gave shape to community patterns. These factors included terrain, roads and other transportation systems, the decisions of key individuals and the dominant social and economic currents at the time of the most intense development.

In three of these communities—West Chestnut Hill, West Mt. Airy and, to a lesser extent, East Falls—developers and architects wove residential enclaves, apartments, individual houses and institutions into the fabric of Wissahickon Park, resulting in a sympathetic bond between the natural and built environments. The other two communities—Germantown and Roxborough—developed in more conventional ways, and did not forge strong connections to the park.

Germantown: Close to the City and Densely Developed

Of these five communities, Germantown was the earliest to be developed. Closest to the center of Philadelphia, none of the town fabric borders directly on the main stem of Wissahickon Creek, although several small tributaries drain through it.

Situated on a plateau between two stream valleys—the Wissahickon and the Wingohocking—Germantown was relatively flat, making dense development easier here than in other parts of Northwest Philadelphia. The wide, flat plateau encouraged the extension of Philadelphia's street grid into the community and, later, promoted the growth of extensive rail connections. Developers quickly filled these blocks with factories and houses, effectively blocking the intermingling of park and community. As Germantown became more urban and industrial, East Falls, Mt. Airy and Chestnut Hill evolved partially as suburbs of this community.

Since locomotives could not climb more than a five-percent grade, Germantown's relatively level land provided convenient locations for railyards, sidings and factory buildings. The first of these rail lines (the Philadelphia, Germantown & Norristown Railroad) reached Germantown in 1832. Closely paralleling Germantown Avenue—the main

At Wayne Junction, in southeastern Germantown, an intense industrial development grew up around the junction of several Reading Railroad lines. The map shows a number of the smaller industries as well as the long monotonous lines of workers row houses, Wayne Junction station and the many converging rail lines.
Source: G.W. Bromley and Company, *Atlas of the City of Philadelphia, 22d Ward*, 1923

commercial street—this railroad entered from the southeast at Wayne Junction. The rail connection to downtown Philadelphia opened the east side to intense industrial development. By the end of the 19th century, large industrial complexes—Midvale Steel, the Kendrick Knitting Mill and Glen Echo Mills—were located here. In the early 20th century, smaller, specialized industries also grew up around this transportation hub, such as the Max Levy Autograph Company, which made special cameras and ground glass screens to create and print half-tone images.[1]

With the coming of the railroad and the resultant spurt in population, developers bought the long properties extending back from Germantown Avenue and ran streets down the middle of each, making building lots on either side. West Tulpehocken Street, one of these new developments, was part of the old Haines farm, and included the house and property known locally as Wyck. This country house, a portion of which may date from the late 17th century, claims to be the last, remaining colonial farmhouse in Philadelphia.[2]

By the 1860s mid-Victorian houses appeared on both sides of Tulpehocken and nearby streets, in wonderfully ornate Gothic Revival and stately Italianate styles. One of these, the Ebenezer Maxwell Mansion, has been purchased by a non-profit group, and has been partially restored as the only Victorian house and garden museum in Philadelphia. Meanwhile, industrialization had led to an explosive demand for workers' housing, with developers putting up block after block of small row houses around the factories of East Germantown.

This community pattern of a working-class east side, with small row houses along stark streets with little tree planting and very small gardens, contrasted with the more well-to-do west side, with free-standing houses on extensively planted lots bordering tree-lined streets.[3] This east-west dichotomy would be repeated, if less relentlessly, in both Chestnut Hill and Mt. Airy.

10:1

Typical row houses on the east side of Germantown. Note that the street has no trees or plantings of any sort. Photograph, c.1900.
Source: GHS

Victorian Germantown Side Streets

Plan and sketch of Maxwell Mansion, a house for a well-to-do Germantown family, in the Victorian Gothic style. Note that the house is placed in the center of a lot that is almost square. Source: Drawings by Rolf Sauer

Henry Howard Houston's house in Germantown, at the corner of Wayne and Tulpehocken Streets. Houses such as this one in the Victorian Italianate style co-existed with Gothic styles in the post-Civil War period. Photograph, c. 1875. Source: GHS

View of tree-lined West Tulpehocken Street, showing large, freestanding Victorian houses on well-planted lots. Photograph, c. late 1800s.
Source: GHS

Looking across the
Schuylkill River at the mills
in East Falls. The scenic
drive along the east side of
the river has not yet been
built and factories come
directly down to
the water. The covered
wooden bridge was later
replaced by the 1895
decorative iron bridge.
Engraving, c. 1860s.
Source: GHS, Jellett Scrapbooks

10:2

By the early 1900s many of the old farms and country estates in and around Germantown had been sold to developers. Boosters saw these new houses and the burgeoning population as signs of progress, declaring that Germantown, with over 70,000 people, was actually "a city within a city."[4] Some Germantowners were uncomfortable with these changes and local newspapers were flooded with letters decrying the loss of open space and the cutting down of huge, old trees for new factories and houses.[5] Many who objected to this destructive development went on to found Germantown's Site and Relic Society, later the Germantown Historical Society.

East Falls: Suburb of Germantown

South and west of Germantown, East Falls parallels Wissahickon Creek, extending along the plateau, and then down to its confluence with the Schuylkill River. Many of the storied Wissahickon inns were located beside the creek in this community. A portion of East Falls, largely in the Schuylkill River floodplain, was once heavily industrialized.

East Falls developed originally along the Schuylkill floodplain. Schoolhouse Lane ran along the plateau above the valley, and, with Germantown and Ridge Avenues, made a third ridge road.[6] By the late-19th century, looking to escape increasing urbanization and industrialization, Germantowners built country houses on large properties that extended down to the park on Schoolhouse Lane. Later, many of these estates became institutions or the sites of large apartment complexes, while others were redeveloped into smaller houses.

"Raven Hill" was one of the large estates along Schoolhouse Lane. The property later became Raven Hill Academy, a Catholic girls school and still later a part of the Philadelphia University campus. Photograph, c.1890s.
Source: GHS

Map showing East Falls and the large properties along Schoolhouse Lane.
Source: Hopkins, *Philadelphia Atlas, 21st Ward*, 1885

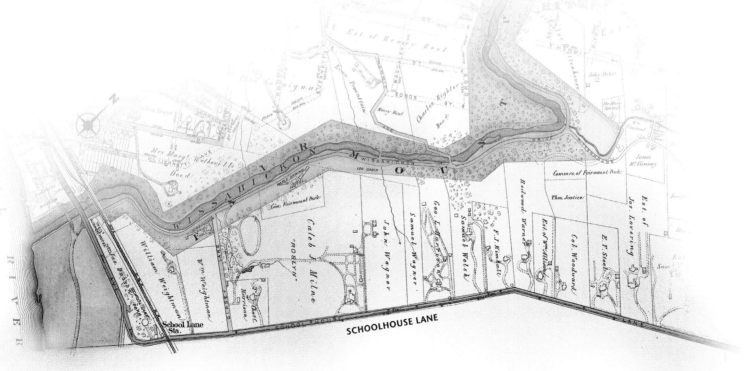

Alden Park

The Alden Park apartment complex opened in 1925. Seven buildings, clustered in three groups, were called the Manor, the Kennilworth and the Cambridge. Set in 38 acres, on the old estate of Frederick H. Strawbridge and bordering Wissahickon Park, these apartments had underground garages, formal gardens, an indoor/outdoor swimming pool, a nine-hole golf course, tennis courts, sweeping lawns and huge specimen trees. The old Strawbridge Mansion was saved and readapted as a restaurant open to the public.

Each individual apartment looked out onto the estate landscape or into Wissahickon Park. With huge elegant lobbies, large rooms, wood-burning fireplaces and open balconies, these units had the grandeur and amenities of a spacious English country house. The winding roads that led through the estate landscape to the rose-colored towers reinforced this perception. Unfortunately, as the estates in East Falls continued to be broken up in the post-World War II period and as the neighborhood deteriorated, this model would be abandoned. Denser and far less sensitive low-rise apartment blocks, surrounded by parking lots, would fill in the remaining open spaces on the slopes facing the Wissahickon Park.

While it has no direct connection to the Wissahickon, the pool at Alden Park is a magical evocation of a Roman bath and part of the unexpected richness of this apartment complex.
Source: Alden Park Apartments

Veiw of one of the towers (Kennilworth) of the Alden Park Apartments. Source: Photograph by CLF

Aerial photograph of Alden Park Apartments, c.1928. Wissahickon Park
is clearly visible as the context for the grounds. The Walnut Lane Bridge
can be seen in the background.
Source: Richard H. MacNeal, *Growing up in Alden Park* (Burbank, Ca.,1998)

Path into Wissahickon Park beyond the
Kenilworth Towers. The Walnut Lane Bridge is barely visible
in the background, middle left. Photograph, c.1931.
Source: Richard H. MacNeal, Growing up in *Alden Park* (Burbank, Ca.,1998)

Roxborough: Between the River and the Creek

Across the Wissahickon Valley from Germantown and East Falls, Roxborough was sandwiched between the Schuylkill River and Wissahickon Creek. Most of this community is in the Schuylkill watershed, but the western side of the Wissahickon gorge is in Roxborough.

First settled about 1690, much of Roxborough was isolated on a steep hillside that made access difficult until better roads were built after World War II. Ridge Avenue, the only route into Roxborough from center city Philadelphia, climbed a steep valley wall as it left the flat floodplain of the Schuylkill River at a grade approaching 8 percent. Wagon drivers dreaded this ascent, even after its improvement by a private turnpike company in 1811. The alternatives were even worse. Shurs Lane or Green Lane ran directly uphill from the Schuylkill at Manayunk's Main Street, with grades as high as 12 percent. Residents unsuccessfully tried to overcome their isolation with a horse car line in 1874, and with an electrified trolley line in 1894, both of which ran up the steep hill of Ridge Avenue. Until 1924 this road remained unpaved, rough and frequently muddy, contributing to the difficulty of getting in and out of the community.[7]

Before the city/county consolidation of 1854, Roxborough was an entire township. It later evolved into four districts—Manayunk (briefly established as a separate borough shortly before consolidation), Lower Roxborough, Upper Roxborough and Andorra.[7] The development of the township paralleled the development of Germantown, with most of the initial growth occurring closest to center city, and with the upper portions of both townships remaining largely undeveloped until railroads came into the area. Much of Upper Roxborough, which belonged primarily to the Houston Estate, remained in farms until after World War II and the widespread use of the automobile. The northwestern corner of Roxborough was called Andorra, after the mid-19th-century estate of Richard Wistar.

With the building of the Schuylkill Canal in 1825 and the completion of the Philadelphia, Germantown and Norristown Railroad in the 1830s, steam-powered industry came to lower Roxborough. Digging the canal and building the railroad erased the old village, known as "Flat Rock," at the confluence of Wissahickon Creek

Map of Lower Roxborough and Manyunk showing small working-class houses down by the river and the larger mill-owners' properties on the east side of Ridge Avenue.
Source: Hopkins, *Philadelphia Atlas*, 21st Ward, 1885

Aerial view of Manayunk, showing the mills along the Schuylkill River, the dense hillside and the larger houses further up the hill. Photograph, c. late 1920s.
Source: Roxborough Historical Society

with the Schuylkill River. As in other mill towns along the Schuylkill River, early mill owners and wealthy residents settled on the heights where they built large, freestanding Victorian houses along tree-lined streets.[8] On the plateau and the upper slopes, they escaped the noise and fumes of the industry below, avoided the "vapors" and "miasmas" of the wetlands and commanded a view of their possessions and the surrounding countryside. On or near

the floodplain of the Schuylkill River, and along the lower portions of the steep streets that ran up to "the Ridge," row houses and semi-detached houses for the workers were pressed up against the sidewalk, their lots devoid of trees or other vegetation. Roxborough came to take its reputation from this working-class character, not unlike the gritty, industrial quality of south-eastern Germantown.

1924 sketch of workers housing on the hillside is in Manayunk/Roxborough. Dense, interconnected buildings piled into the steep hillside, high stone retaining walls, flying foot bridges, the intrusion of bedrock through the built fabric, all give this community a romantic likeness to an Italian hill town. Sketch by Joseph H. Miles in the *Roxborough Review*.
Source: "Roxborough-Manayunk-Wissahickon,"Special Supplement to *The Review*, June 1965, Roxborough Historical Society

Large houses near the top of the hill in Roxborough.
Source: Roxborough Historical Society

Mt. Airy: A Parkway Community

Located in the upper reaches of the old Germantown Township, Mt. Airy and Chestnut Hill became "suburbs" of Germantown, even though, after 1854, these communities were, in fact, part of the consolidated City of Philadelphia. Many of the residents were prosperous former Germantowners fleeing the increasingly dense and industrialized surroundings. Although both Mt. Airy and Chestnut Hill supported small, craft industries at various times, both became largely residential with a considerable commercial spine along Germantown Avenue.

A more rugged terrain and greater proximity to the park in West Mt. Airy and West Chestnut Hill offered varied sites for development and greater opportunities for these communities to be woven into the fabric of the park. Over time, boundaries between park and community were blurred and the larger natural systems of the place—bedrock, water, and native vegetation—found rich and multiple expressions in the community.

Lincoln Drive, conceived as the completion of the "northwestern parkway," was one of the four boulevards envisioned by the City Beautiful Movement around 1900. This scenic carriage drive, built just before the advent of extensive automobile traffic, shaped the dominant patterns of West Mt. Airy.[9] Lincoln Drive followed the meandering corridor of Monoshone Creek. Frequent intersections gave access to leafy and often sloping side streets. Direct access to the neighborhood street grid and the winding configuration of the road slowed the traffic and kept Lincoln Drive from becoming a high-speed arterial.

Lincoln Drive at McCallum Street. Seen here is Lincoln Drive, the parkway that bisects the community with its winding alignment, maturing trees and large, heavily planted front yards. Photograph, 1916.
Source: Philadelphia City Archives

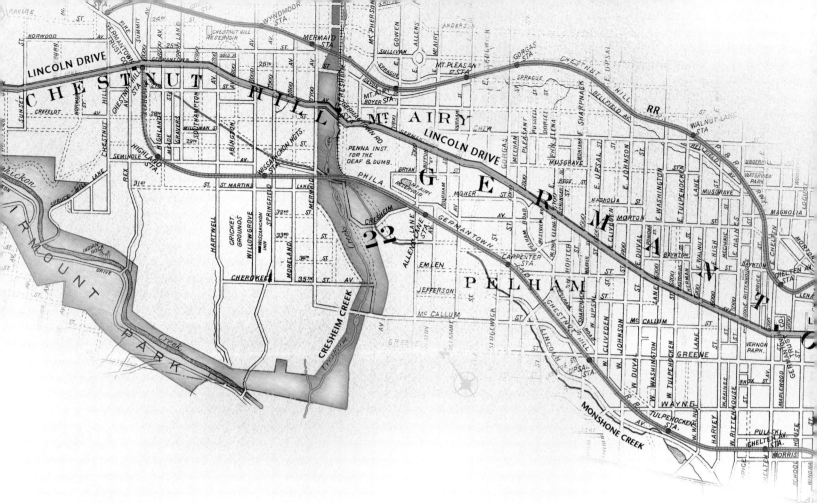

Much of the forested character of West Mt. Airy came from preserving the larger tributaries—Monoshone Creek, the Carpenter Woods stream and Cresheim Creek—allowing them to penetrate the built fabric. The institutional grounds and open spaces around the railroad stations and railroad rights-of-way allowed fragments of the Wissahickon forest, or pieces of open land, to "finger" into the community. Often, as with the small woods on the grounds of the Unitarian Church, these remnant forest pieces remained or grew up around small tributaries and drainage swales. Along with these forest fragments, the large canopy trees planted along the streets and in the front yards extended the perceived boundaries of parkland.

While Lincoln Drive enhanced the scenic character of West Mt. Airy, the alignment badly damaged the integrity of historic Rittenhouse Town—lopping off and obliterating its southeastern portion. The park commission had already demolished most of the Rittenhouse mills, leaving only a few of the houses. The drive also took out a portion of old Rittenhouse Street, required the demolition of an abandoned blanket mill that had been part of the complex, encroached on the millrace of the second paper mill and erased its millpond, further compromising the site. This fragmentation would make it nearly impossible to restore and coherently present one of the earliest industrial villages in colonial America.

Map showing Lincoln Drive. Coming out of Wissahickon Park at Johnson Street, this parkway follows the stream valley of the Monoshone Creek and cuts across the grid. Originally planned to cross the park at Cresheim Creek and continue through Chestnut Hill as it runs through Mt. Airy, the drive was, mercifully, cut off.

Source: G.W. Bromley and Company, *Atlas of the City of Philadelphia, 22nd Ward*, 1923

10:3

Tributary Fingers | Carpenter's Meadow

Following its purchase in 1916 by Fairmount Park, Carpenter's Meadow (later Carpenter's Woods) became a bird sanctuary. The scanctuary was organized in 1923 by the Fairmount Park Bird Club, under the presidency of Dr. Whitmer Stone, head of the ornithology department at the Philadelphia Academy of Natural Sciences. In the late 1920s, with approximately 700 members, this bird club claimed to be the largest organization of its kind in the United States. The club renovated two old houses in the woods (both later demolished by Fairmount Park). One of these houses was originally used as a headquarters and bird museum, with a library and exhibits of stuffed birds. The second house became a residence for Caroline Moffett, the principal of the nearby Charles Wolcott Henry Elementary School.

Each May, Miss Moffett and her students put on a "Bird Masque" in the clearing in the central bowl. According to a 1924 newspaper account, "More than 250 children staged a production which charmed. It was a colorful combination of pantomime, music and dancing, which appealed to grown-ups as well as children, to cherish and protect the small wild, living creatures which inhabit the woods."[1]

This performance, and frequent visits to the bird sanctuary by Henry School students, made this extension of Wissahickon Park into an intimate part of both the physical design and the social structure of the community.

1. *Philadelphia Evening Bulletin*, May 16, 1923; *Beehive*, April 1923; GHS, Jane Campbell, Scrapbooks, 31:49, 50:61, 48:138.

Above
Children taking their bows at the end of the Bird Masque. This play was staged in the central meadow. Photograph, 1924.
Source: GHS

Left
An earlier photograph showing children playing around Carpenter's Run, the tiny stream that flowed through the open meadow. Photograph, c. 1910.
Source: GHS

Chestnut Hill: On the Heights

Adjacent Chestnut Hill shared a number of key community shaping elements with West Mt. Airy—a commuter railroad, the largely residential neighborhoods with a creative mix of housing types, a commercial spine, a parkway following a major tributary of Wissahickon Creek and an extensive border along the park. Whereas West Mt. Airy had a number of developers, much of Chestnut Hill was shaped by several generations of a single family. This unique circumstance gave Chestnut Hill a wider range of innovative housing types and a greater integration of park and institutions into the residential fabric.

Although Chestnut Hill has two parkways—Cresheim Valley Drive and the upper portion of Lincoln Drive—they never influenced the patterns of development in Chestnut Hill in the way that Lincoln Drive shaped Mt. Airy. Although Cresheim Valley Drive is the more extensive of the two, it runs through parkland and is not primarily part of a residential neighborhood. Lincoln Drive was originally proposed to run through both communities and join Bethlehem Pike. This plan was never realized. The upper portion of Lincoln Drive is cut off from its lower portion in Mt. Airy and remains a relatively short stretch of road in Chestnut Hill. Instead it ends at the edge of Pastorius Park—a small public green space that was the source of a tributary to Cresheim Creek.

Entrance to Cresheim Valley Drive in Mt. Airy. Two gates signal the beginning of this road as it dips into the valley to follow Cresheim Creek. Source: *The Architectural Record*, July 1929, CHHS

A view to the northeast, at the beginning of Cresheim Valley Drive looking towards Cresheim Creek.
Source: Photograph by CLF

10:4

10:5-6

Like Mt. Airy, Chestnut Hill originated as a farm and mill community, but after the Civil War it developed into a summer retreat from the dirty, crowded and unsanitary city. At several hundred feet above sea level, Chestnut Hill offered a retreat from muggy Philadelphia summers, when cholera and yellow fever were rampant in the lower parts of a city located between two rivers. At a time before it was easy for wealthy Philadelphians to pack up and "summer" in Maine, Chestnut Hill, with its trees, breezy heights, and close proximity to the Wissahickon Valley, was an appealing site for a summer retreat. Year-round living "on the heights" became more feasible once railroad connections to downtown Philadelphia allowed the family breadwinner to commute daily to a job in the city.[10]

Two commuter railroads connected Chestnut Hill to downtown Philadelphia. The first of these lines was the Chestnut Hill Railroad, completed in 1854 and later acquired by the Reading Company. The second was a spur of the Pennsylvania Railroad, completed through the west side of Chestnut Hill in 1884. Along this second route, from the 1880s to the 1920s, several remarkable planned neighborhoods were built, where the natural systems of the valley were allowed to penetrate and to become an integral part of the community.[11] A number of factors fostered this remarkable fusion—protected stream corridors, community institutions with large open grounds abutting the park and a wide variety of housing types set in a gradient of density.

Wissahickon Heights, a name that celebrated a high knoll above the gorge, was the first planned neighborhood on the west side of Chestnut Hill. This neighborhood was built over a ten-year period beginning in the 1880s. It extended east from the edge of Wissahickon Park to approximately the railroad station on the Pennsylvania line (the Wissahickon Heights station, later called St. Martin's). Its developer, Henry Howard Houston, was an executive with the Pennsylvania Railroad and a many-faceted entrepreneur and multi-millionaire.[12] The sources of Houston's planning ideas are unknown, and if other planned communities in the United States inspired him, no record has survived.

The housing designs of Houston's architects (the brothers William D. and George W. Hewitt) were relatively undistinguished, but a number of the elements that went into creating Wissahickon Heights set the stage for the more imaginative housing and community designs undertaken a generation later by other members of the family.

In this pre-automobile age, railroad transportation was central to Houston's plans. Houston himself persuaded the Pennsylvania Railroad to construct a commuter line into the west side of Chestnut Hill, donating much of the right-of-way from his huge land holdings. This railroad corridor was particularly well-sited along the first shallow break in the plateau, placing the tracks either in cuts below the houses, or on trestle bridges above them. Consequently, the railroad did not divide a neighborhood or interrupt the flow of the landscape through the community. In Chestnut Hill, there was no "wrong side of the tracks."

The railroad stations were designed by talented architects. Many of the stations had apartments on the second floor where the stationmaster and his family lived. Commuters knew the stationmaster by name, and he and his family were part of the neighborhood. In time, forest vegetation from the nearby valley filled the large open spaces around the stations. At several of them, this vegetation eventually spread around the adjacent houses and the railroad parking lots. Instead of being eyesores or disreputable places, as in many other communities in the United States, these railroad stations became focal points of neighborhood pride. Later, local preservation groups would adopt these stations and repair them, when the local transit authority, the Southeastern Pennsylvania Transportation Authority (SEPTA), inheritor of the earlier railroad lines, could no longer afford to keep them up.

Just beyond the Wissahickon Heights station, Houston built about 80 houses and several important community institutions on the relatively flat plateau—the easiest land to develop. All these houses were built of Wissahickon schist. Houston rented most of the houses instead of selling them. His rationale was to control the type of resident (favoring white Anglo-Saxon Protestants) and to make sure that the properties were well-maintained. Nearer Germantown Avenue, Houston built spacious twins set close to the streets with relatively generous back yards. The density of housing in this area allowed him to set aside land closer to the park for a summer hotel, a church, a cricket club and horseshow grounds. Ample open space surrounded them and these properties were resources for neighborhood residents.

Chestnut Hill has two parkways; Cresheim Valley Drive and the Upper portion of Lincoln Drive. Cresheim Valley Drive runs mainly through parkland. Tradition holds that the Woodward Family kept Lincoln Drive from running through both Cresheim Valley and Pastorius Park.
Source: Hopkins, *Philadelphia Atlas, 22nd Ward*, 1911

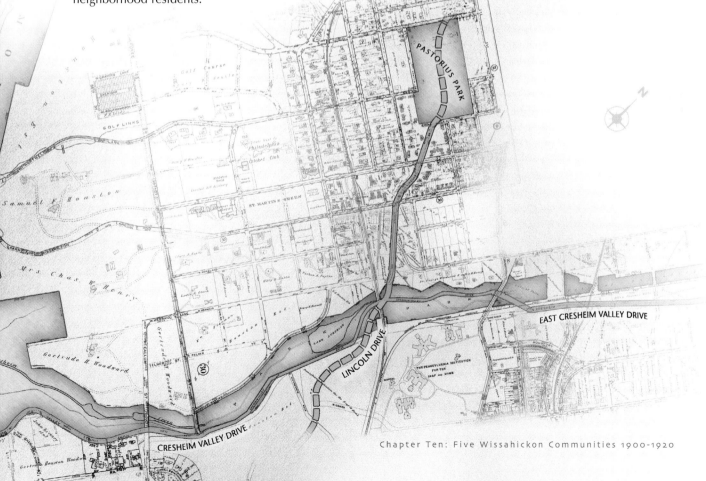

Wissahickon Heights and the Development of West Chestnut Hill

This map of Chestnut Hill in 1911 shows the Houston Estate properties. The yellow square marks Wissahickon Heights, including the Philadelphia Cricket Club and its golf course, the Philadelphia Horse Show grounds, St. Martin's Church, the Wissahickon Inn (later Chestnut Hill Academy), St. Martin's Green, Wissahickon Heights station (later St Martin's station) and the Houston rental houses.

From the park to the ridge road (Germantown Avenue), a gradient of density of development is visible. Wissahickon Park merges into the large properties of the three Houston estates, which in turn merge into the shared landscape of the community institutions. This landscape then grades into a denser development, closer to the ridge—the Houston houses built around Wissahickon Heights railroad station.

Source: Hopkins, *Philadelphia Atlas, 22 Ward*, 1911.

The Wissahickon Inn, acquired in 1900 by Chestnut Hill Academy as a private boys' school, looking up from Springfield Avenue. The inn was built in 1884 by Henry Howard Houston as a summer resort and part of his Wissahickon Heights development. Photograph, c. 1905.
Source: David Bower postcard collection

A match at the Philadelphia Cricket Club. The club was across the street from the Wissahickon Inn and St. Martin's Green. This green was a large, rectangular strolling garden that belonged to the inn. It was later used as the football field and track for Chestnut Hill Academy. Photograph, 1895.
Source: CHHS

Aerial view of the Philadelphia Cricket Club, looking southeast from Hartwell Lane towards St. Martin's Church. These semi–public community facilities were the heart of the Wissahickon Heights neighborhood (later renamed St. Martin's). The residential development can be seen in the upper left, the Cricket Club in the center and the former horse show grounds in the lower right. Photograph, 1925.
Source: LCP

Henry Howard Houston (1820–1895)

Henry Howard Houston's contributions to the development of Chestnut Hill were many and his influence on the shape of the community was profound. His plan for Wissahickon Heights included large open spaces and a series of institutions that continue to enhance the social and civic life of the neighborhood more than a century later. He established the Andorra Nurseries on terrain that was difficult to develop, providing a source of a wide variety of plants—both native and exotic—that would become an essential element of the later Wissahickon style.

Photographic portrait of Henry Howard Houston. Photograph, c. 1880s.
Source: GHS

Houston came to Philadelphia in 1847 from his native Wrightsville in York County, Pennsylvania. In 1851, he became the general freight agent for the Pennsylvania Railroad and after his retirement became a member of the railroad's board of directors. He used his influence to establish a fast freight line during the Civil War and made a great deal of money on this investment. By the time of his death in 1895, he left an estate worth over $14 million.

During the 1860s, Houston became interested in developing housing, after moving with his family to Tulpehocken Street, then one of the fashionable addresses in Germantown. He bought land in Germantown and built a number of large houses along Wayne Avenue.

Houston then looked to the west side of Chestnut Hill—still made up of small farms and a few country estates—and in the 1880s, he amassed a huge swath of almost contiguous property.

This property started at the corner of Allens Lane and Cresheim Valley Drive in West Mt. Airy and extended all the way into Montgomery County, some six miles away. His holdings ultimately included nearly the entire west side of Chestnut Hill and most of Upper Roxborough, totaling almost 3,000 acres, making him both the largest landowner and the largest taxpayer in the City of Philadelphia.[1]

1. David R. Contosta, *A Philadelphia Family: The Houston and Woodwards of Chestnut Hill* (*Philadelphia, 1988*), 3-35.

No "Wrong Side of the Tracks"

In Chestnut Hill and Mt Airy, where the topography is steeper, the railroads take advantage of the terrain to unify rather than separate the community. The railroad corridor goes either below or above the street grid, allowing the landscape of the neighborhoods to be uninterrupted by the tracks. This unimpeded flow is even more apparent a century later, when the forest has reclaimed parts of the right-of-way and the surrounding neighborhoods.

The stations contributed to this unity of fabric. They were designed to have a residential scale and character and blended into the community.

Like the later, high bridges over Wissahickon Creek, a trestle over the Cresheim Valley, built in the early 1880s, allowed the landscape to flow under it. The bridge carried trains of the Pennsylvania Railroad commuter line (now Chestnut Hill-West) from plateau to plateau on a level crossing. After the land was acquired by Fairmount Park, (between 1909 and 1914), the surrounding valley walls returned to forest, and Cresheim Valley Drive was built as a parkway that followed the creek through the valley to the edge of the city at Stenton Avenue.

Trestle railroad bridge across Cresheim Creek. The Cresheim Valley is the unofficial boundary between Mt. Airy and Chestnut Hill. The photograph is taken from the Mt. Airy side. Photograph, c. early 1900s. Source: GHS

Wissahickon Heights Station (later St. Martin's), designed by W. Bleddyn Powell, 1884.
Source: CHHS

Context of the Three Houston Estates

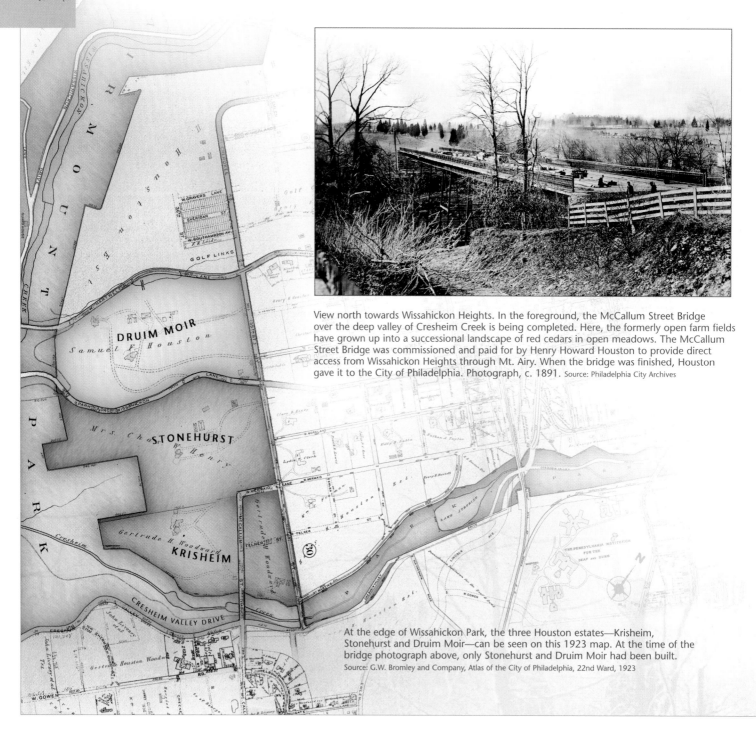

View north towards Wissahickon Heights. In the foreground, the McCallum Street Bridge over the deep valley of Cresheim Creek is being completed. Here, the formerly open farm fields have grown up into a successional landscape of red cedars in open meadows. The McCallum Street Bridge was commissioned and paid for by Henry Howard Houston to provide direct access from Wissahickon Heights through Mt. Airy. When the bridge was finished, Houston gave it to the City of Philadelphia. Photograph, c. 1891. Source: Philadelphia City Archives

At the edge of Wissahickon Park, the three Houston estates—Krisheim, Stonehurst and Druim Moir—can be seen on this 1923 map. At the time of the bridge photograph above, only Stonehurst and Druim Moir had been built. Source: G.W. Bromley and Company, Atlas of the City of Philadelphia, 22nd Ward, 1923

The open fields below Gertrude Woodward's property at Krisheim blended gradually into the forest of the lower Cresheim Valley. Black and white photograph (colorized for this volume), c. 1910. Source: LCP

Three Houston Estates | Druim Moir *(Continued)*

In the early 1920s, Samuel F. Houston commissioned Robert Rodes McGoodwin to design the Druim Moir gardens. These gardens, inspired by Italian Renaissance models, step down in a series of terraces to the Wissahickon Valley, ending visually in the park.

Source: CHHS

A great, crenellated Victorian mansion, designed by George W. and William D. Hewitt, and completed in 1886, Druim Moir was the home of Henry Howard Houston until his death in 1895. His son Sam inherited the estate and lived there until his death in 1952.

Source: Moses King, *Philadelphia and Notable Philadelphians* (New York, 1901)

Three Houston Estates | StoneHurst *(Continued)*

The Stonehurst house and property, immediately south of Druim Moir, was a wedding gift from Henry Howard Houston to his daughter Sallie, who married Charles Wolcott Henry. Designed by the famous beaux-arts firm of McKim, Mead and White, it was completed in 1887. This house was demolished in 1940. The grounds were later developed by the Henry heirs as the Cherokee Apartments.
Source: CHHS

The Stonehurst Estate was probably photographed from the tower of Druim Moir looking southeast. The lower part of West Chestnut Hill can be seen in the background. A returning forest is visible on the steep slopes of the Cresheim Valley. The plateau is largely open, fringed in an "old field" with red cedars and meadow at the edge of the forest.
Photograph, c. late 1880s.
Source: CHHS

Three Houston Estates | Krisheim (Continued)

Shortly after acquiring Krisheim,
the Woodwards hired the Olmsted Brothers
(the landscape architecture firm that suceeded
Frederick Law Olmsted) to design both the formal
gardens, seen here, and the larger grounds.
Photograph, c. 1912. Source: CHHS

Krisheim, seen from the back of the house.
Built on a large property given by Houston to his
second daughter, Gertrude Woodward, the house
was designed by Peabody and Sterns of Boston,
Massachusetts and completed in 1911.
The slopes were originally meadow, but over time
the forest returned and was allowed to encircle the
house, dissolving into a large shadow lawn
at the front of the property.
Photograph, c. 1912. Source: CHHS

Although separate entities, these institutions shared their landscapes. St. Martin-in-the-Fields Episcopal Church sat at the edge of the Philadelphia Cricket Club playing fields. Next to this club, the Philadelphia Horse Show grounds remained active until this facility left the area in 1908. The horse show grounds later became the athletic fields of Chestnut Hill Academy, a private school that took over the Wissahickon Inn after it closed in 1900. The cricket club added a golf course in 1895, located just north of the horse show grounds, which extended the shared open space up to the edge of the park. Forest vegetation from the park flowed into and around the edges of these community open spaces and extended a sense of the "park."[13]

Three large Houston family country houses at the edge of Wissahickon Park also allowed forest vegetation to filter up into the community through private land and blur park boundaries. These country houses were Druim Moir, which Houston built for himself; Stonehurst, which he built for his daughter Sallie and her husband, Charles Wolcott Henry; and Krisheim, built for Houston's other daughter, Gertrude and her husband George Woodward.

The forested matrix in which these large houses and the rest of the community sat, would become one of the hallmarks of the west side of Chestnut Hill. Misunderstandings of this idea have led new residents to cut down the forest remnants and open up the landscape with big sunny lawns, undermining the character of the area.

10:7

The Philadelphia Cricket Club laid out a small nine hole golf course in 1895. Located north of St Martin's Church, the Wissahickon Inn and the cricket fields and clubhouse, this course abutted Wissahickon Park. Black and white photograph, c. 1900 (colorized for book).
Source: CHHS

Five Wissahickon Communities

West Chestnut Hill, West Mt. Airy, and to a lesser extent East Falls, were characterized by connected open spaces that filtered through the park and into the community. This connecting tissue would be a central characteristic of a unique "Wissahickon style" of architecture and landscape design during the first three decades of the 20th century. In contrast, Roxborough and Germantown (although with many charming houses and streets) would continue to develop in a more conventional way. Upper Roxborough, still farmland when Mt. Airy and Chestnut Hill were reaching their peak, would become prey to the pressures ofpost-World War II development and the ascent of the automobile.

The Wissahickon Style

1920-1935

11

11

The Wissahickon Style

1920-1935

With a property of modest size, within the city limits, the boundaries of a public park have been used to such advantage as to incorporate the park woods in the composition.

Paul P. Cret, "High Hollow, The Property of George Howe Esq., Chestnut Hill Philadelphia," *The Architectural Record*, August, 1920

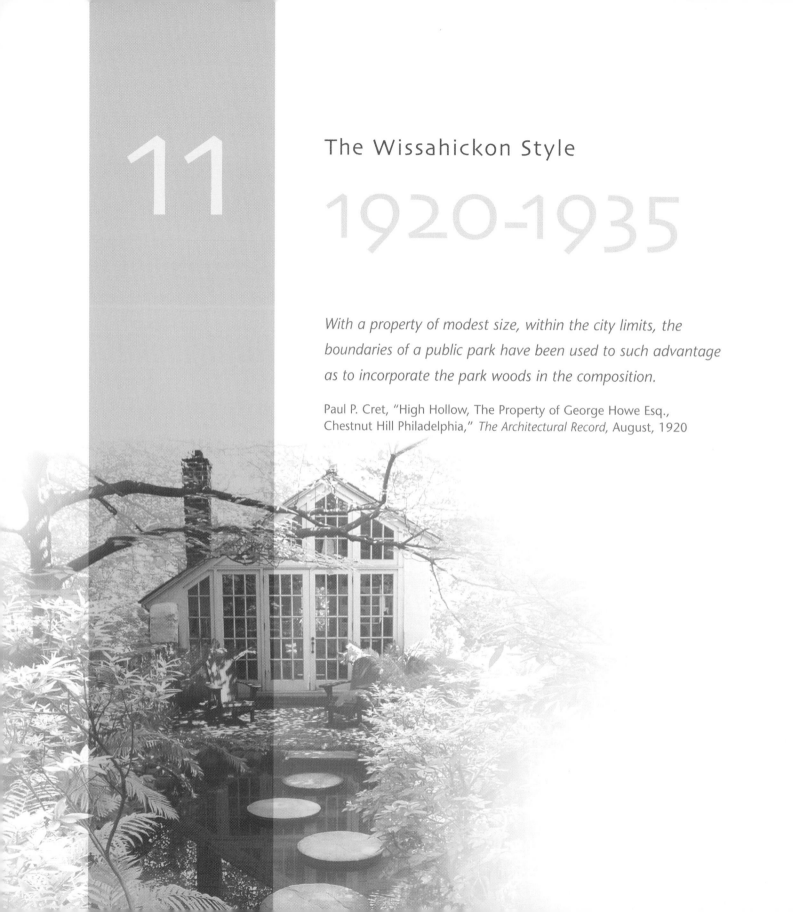

Residents of the five communities surrounding Wissahickon Park had built a strong tradition of civic activism, accumulating social capital and preserving natural capital. In two of these communities—West Mt. Airy and West Chestnut Hill—there is a track record of park stewardship and a history of physical development that responded in sympathetic ways to their proximity to Wissahickon Park.

In these communities farthest from the city center, the pattern of density, the street layout, the preservation of the natural drainage system, the lot configurations, the design of the buildings and gardens themselves and even their "delectable" details—either purposefully crafted or serendipitous—evolved into a "Wissahickon style." In the face of the later destructive forces of suburban sprawl and the sometimes even more destructive forces of dense infill, these two Philadelphia communities provide a new and better community model. This model offers all the liveability and pedestrian scale of a small town or European village and gives an astonishing variety of housing choices fused with community institutions and a commercial spine. Most importantly, it blurs the boundaries between nature and the built environment, and allows the larger natural systems of the place to find rich expression.

Although the Wissahickon Style developed in an affluent area of Philadelphia, the variety of lot sizes and housing types—from individual mansions on 50-acre estates to humble quaduplexes on one-eighth acre lots—allowed people of different backgrounds and incomes to live together. The difference, ultimately, was not in resources, but in attitude and vision.

The contribution of these communities to planning and design has grown out of an unarticulated but powerful commitment to the importance of the natural world and its integration into the built world. It has also grown out of a social ideal that stressed the importance of multiple choices in housing to allow a multi-faceted, multi-aged community to flourish. Lastly, these communities built on a heritage of mixed use, where housing was never far away from recreation in the park and shopping along the commercial strip. Between the end of World War I in 1918 and the full onset of the Great Depression in the early 1930s, developers and architects, working in a freer vernacular style, capitalized in remarkably imaginative ways on these opportunities.

Beyond Victorian Styles

A multitude of forces came together to produce the Wissahickon Style. Beginning in the late 19th century, and intensifying after World War I, there was a general revolt against the rigidity and heaviness of the Victorian lifestyle. In domestic architecture, the rigid divisions of internal spaces and activities were abandoned in favor of a more open and informal floor plan, where rooms and functions flowed into one another, and where interior and exterior spaces echoed and complimented each other. In some cases, this sensibility extended to an interest in organic forms. In Pennsylvania, architects began to explore rambling old farmhouses, where the buildings grew incrementally out into the landscape to meet the needs of successive generations. In these farm complexes, a variety of positive spaces were defined by extensions and outbuildings.

The military service of many American architects in England and France during World War I reinforced an interest in vernacular forms. These architects discovered Cotswold villages as well as Norman farms and "châteaux." Such building traditions responded to the climate, materials and landforms of temperate Northwestern Europe—similar in many ways to Southeastern Pennsylvania.

In the postwar building boom of the 1920s, fed by spreading affluence, American architects evolved a "country house style." These architects were inspired by late 19th century English architects—H. Ballie Scott, C.F.A. Voysey and Edwin Lutyens—who had pioneered new "suburban house" styles. As public parks were one expression of American democracy, the individual house and garden for the middle classes became another.[1]

Unlike the oversized and hard-to-maintain Victorian residences, the new American country houses were more modest. A burgeoning middle class and innovations in technology led to changes in lifestyle that came together to encourage economies in house design. Modern amenities—indoor plumbing, electrical wiring, and central heating—now amounted to as much as 25 percent of the total cost of a house. Servants became expensive and scarce, their numbers diminished by restrictive immigration laws or by better paying factory jobs. With fewer servants in the home, architects and builders could eliminate the servants' quarters (typical of the earlier Victorian house) and give the homeowner rooms that were easier to maintain.[2] New "life style" magazines—*House and Garden* and *The Ladies Home Journal*—promoted "easier living" with smaller, simpler and less compartmentalized households. As the architectural critic Matlack Price wrote in 1921, "There are a great many new valuations in effect since the war. A great many people are wanting simple, straight-forward things, free from much of the unusable excess which was once indulged in for show."[3]

As industrialization took over in Northern Europe and North America, a countervailing Arts and Crafts Movement flourished on both sides of the Atlantic. Supporters of this movement mourned the loss of hand craftsmanship and the growing emphasis on standardization, uniformity and machine production. In the late 19th and early 20th centuries, well-known figures such as the Englishman William Morris and the American Henry Chapman Mercer devoted their lives to reviving and reinterpreting handcrafts. They looked for ways to adapt pre-industrial traditions by making handmade wallpaper, textiles, furniture, ironwork and ceramic tiles.[4] Others emphasized local building materials, extensive hand-carved decoration and a return to the older building techniques of tile setting and masonry.

A Flowering of Local Architects

Philadelphia in the 1920s and early 1930s was home to a number of remarkably talented architects interested in vernacular styles, the use of local materials and the ornamentation of their buildings with revived local crafts. This architectural renaissance in Philadelphia included the firms of Mellor, Meigs, & Howe, Duhring, Okie & Ziegler, Willing, Sims & Talbutt and individual practitioners such as H. Lewis Duhring, Robert Rodes McGoodwin and Edmund Gilchrist. Development opportunities in Mt. Airy and Chestnut Hill brought them together to explore a wide variety of residential designs—from large houses on individual lots to "quads" and courts.

11:1

Mellor, Meigs, & Howe (1916 to 1928) was perhaps the best known of Philadelphia's architectural firms to work in the country house style. In his book, Daniel Wilson Randle describes the firm's design philosophy and practice: "While there was a clear aesthetic in the firm's picturesque compositions, the relaxed approach to planning also had the enormous benefit of allowing for complex arrangements of highly varied spaces which could deal with the demanding topography surrounding Philadelphia....The volumes of the structures could be freely expressed on the exterior, and with a freedom of fenestration, the interior rooms could be sensitively aligned with light, principle views and the exterior spaces into which they were often visually extended."[5] As the firm matured, it adapted vernacular styles more freely, creating buildings that responded inventively to the materials and landforms of Northwest Philadelphia.

Craftsmen

From the beginning of a project, Philadelphia architects often collaborated with nationally known arts and crafts firms. Their imaginative designs and high quality workmanship gave Philadelphia a lasting reputation as a center of artisanship. Metalworker, Samuel Yellin, and artist, William Willet, who founded the Willet Stained Glass Studios, were among those who revived pre-industrial craft traditions. Equally important were the firms that designed and crafted art tiles and ceramics. The now defunct Enfield Pottery and Tile Works was located just outside Philadelphia in Springfield Township. The Moravian Pottery and Tile Works, popularly known as Mercer Tiles, in Doylestown, survives to this day. One hallmark of the Wissahickon Style was the seamless integration of tile, ironwork and stained glass into building designs.

11:2-3

Mellor, Meigs & Howe

In 1906, Walter Mellor (1880-1949) joined with Arthur Ingersoll Meigs (1882-1956) to form the firm of Mellor and Meigs. Mellor studied architecture at the University of Pennsylvania and then worked in the office of Theophilus Chandler where he met Arthur Meigs, a graduate of Princeton University. In 1916 George Howe (1886-1955), who had studied architecture at Harvard as well as at the Ecole des Beaux Arts in Paris, joined the firm after a brief stint with Furness, Evans and Company, the office of Philadelphia's great 19th-century architect, Frank Furness. With Howe on board, the office became the highly successful firm of Mellor, Meigs, & Howe, designing some of the most creative and comfortable houses built in and around Philadelphia. The office lasted from 1916 to 1928.

Like a number of other architects serving in Northern France during World War I, both Meigs and Howe, "Came to the conclusion that the region's unaffected rural architecture provided the basis for a new type of American vernacular architecture."[1] For this generation, a style that emerged from their experiences was a fortuitous fusion of vernacular traditions—"unconscious architecture" —that included Pennsylvania farmhouses, large Norman country houses, Italian courtyards and terraced gardens and Cotswold villages. While the new building designs borrowed many elements from these architectural traditions (sometimes wholesale), architects were also developing a uniquely American synthesis. In Mt. Airy, Chestnut Hill and the Philadelphia Mainline, they pioneered a style that was a "creative partnership" with the local landscape.

High Hollow, the large country house George Howe designed for himself in Chestnut Hill at the edge of Wissahickon Park. This 1914 house, one of the earliest examples of a country house in the Wissahickon Style, is still heavily based on European models. However, it is built partly of local materials. It stepped down into the valley, and the walls of the house embraced positive space, reaching out into the forested landscape to create garden rooms.   Source: Photograph by CLF

Looking very much like a large house in the Cotwolds, this 1928 house in Mt. Airy was designed by Walter Mellor for A.T. Malmed, after the departure of George Howe from the firm. Built into the side of the hill and stepping down into the valley, the large entry court is framed by the L-shaped house on two sides, and on the third by the hill and by the retaining wall of the neighboring property.
Source: Photograph by CLF

Three photographs of Square Shadows, Whitemarsh Township, Pa., designed by George Howe for William Wasserman and built in 1932, after Howe left the firm. Although a "modern" building, this house is another demonstration that the Wissahickon Style can be realized in many different architectural vocabularies.
Source: University of Pennsylvania, Architectural Archives

High Hollow (1914), the house Howe designed for himself in Chestnut Hill two years before joining the firm, shows the vitality and originality that he brought to the office. By the late 1920s, Howe—a restless, creative spirit—was dissatisfied with what he viewed as the romantic nostalgia of the office, and he began to experiment with "the clearer, more austere" forms of modern architecture, moving away from the design of houses for the wealthy to large-scale commercial and institutional buildings. Quitting the firm in 1928, to become, as he put it, "a priest of the modern faith," he went into partnership with William Lescaze, a young Swiss architect, who had studied with Karl Moser in

Switzerland and was an eclectic modernist.[1] Together these men designed an elegant, tall building with curtain walls of glass and stainless steel—Philadelphia's first modern skyscraper—for the Philadelphia Savings Fund Society (PSFS) at 12th and Market Streets. In 1940, Howe took on a new partner, the then unknown Louis I. Kahn, who would go on to become Philadelphia's greatest architect.[2]

---

1. Daniel Wilson Randle, new edition, *A Monograph of the Works of Mellor*, Meigs and Howe (Boulder, Colorado, 1991), introduction.

2. Robert A. M. Stern, *George Howe: Towards A Modern American Architecture* (New Haven, 1975), 54-65.

Samuel Yellin, Metalworker (1885–1940)

Source: Courtesy of Samuel Yellin Metalworkers Co.

Samuel Yellin was one of the most talented and successful individuals in the American arts and crafts movement. He was born in Mogilera in the province of Galicia, a small village in present-day Poland, near the Austrian border. His father died when he was twelve years old, and he was apprenticed to a local Russian black-smith. He then traveled widely in Europe where he admired and copied the designs of medieval and renais-sance artists and craftsmen.[1]

Immigrating to Philadelphia in 1906 when he was only 21, he enrolled in evening classes at the Pennsylvania Museum School of Industrial Arts (later renamed the Philadelphia College of Art and, still later, the University of the Arts), where he developed a new class teaching wrought iron.

With increasing success and 29 employees calling him "maestro," Yellin engaged Mellor, Meigs, & Howe to design new quarters for his operation at 5520 Arch Street. When this new office was completed in 1915 he rechristened his firm "Samuel Yellin, Metalworker."

Like Henry Mercer and the best country house architects of the 1920s, Yellin was a talented and original artist who adapted earlier architec-tural styles. For Yellin these works were never simply copies of old masters or of anonymous historical craftsmen. In a speech given to the Architectural Club of Chicago in 1926, Yellin said," I do not mean that we should copy from books or examples just what they did, but it is advisable to always have their examples before us and to work upon the suggestions made by the best of them."[2]

Source: Courtesy of Samuel Yellin Metalworkers Co.

He insisted on close collaborations with architects and believed that the ironwork was an organic part of the whole building, not incidental ornamentation. Architects were delighted to work with a craftsman like Yellin, whose knowledge, skills, and business acumen were exceptional. As a result, he collaborated with some of the best architects of the day, on some of the most important buildings in Eastern United States. According to Yellin himself, "It is this spirit of camaraderie between the architect and craftsman that develops a true conception of organic architecture and makes possible its final accomplishment." [3]

1. Jack Andrews, *Samuel Yellin, Metalworker* (Ocean Pines Md, 2000), 1.

2. Quoted in Ibid., 3.

3. Quoted in Ibid., 73.

Wrought iron lantern, originally with sheets of mica as the glazing (now plastic), and wrought iron window grill by Samuel Yellin. This lamp hangs over the front door at the house that Arthur Mellor (of Mellor, Meigs & Howe) designed for himself in Mt. Airy, Philadelphia, Pa., c. 1934.
Source: Photographs of details by CLF

Henry Chapman Mercer (1856–1930)

Independently wealthy and a brilliant, renaissance man, Henry Mercer established the first arts and crafts tile works in the United States on land belonging to his family in Doylestown, about 30 miles northeast of downtown Philadelphia. His interest in crafts of all sorts began while he was a student of Harvard professor Charles Eliot Norton. Norton believed that art reflected the "volksgeist"—the spirit of the people and the era that produced them. Later, bored by his study of law at the University of Pennsylvania, Mercer became a gentleman archaeologist and worldwide traveler.

In 1897, while browsing through a junkyard in Bucks County, Mercer had the very modern revelation that one could read the whole history of Pennsylvania in discarded objects. He began a life-long mission to preserve the remains of America's handcraft traditions before they disappeared. According to historian Cleota Reed, Mercer "assembled relics of every trade, craft, and calling: implements for making barrels, wallpaper, cheese, tinware, sausages, shoes, pottery, hats, books, baskets, shingles; tools of the gunsmith, weaver, fisher, housewife, miner, sign painter, barber, blacksmith, teacher, doctor, musician, farmer."[1]

To house this eclectic collection, Mercer built a faux French château to be used as a museum, and opened it to the public in 1916. The museum's interior layout was as imaginative as the structure itself. Anticipating Frank Lloyd Wright's Guggenheim Museum by eighty years, it was designed as a spiral. Unlike the Guggenheim, Mercer's result was astoundingly complex with dozens of ante-chambers off the central core. It was also slightly forbidding and somewhat resembled a Piranasi drawing of a prison.

For many craftsmen in this era, Gothic architecture came to mean a visible—and therefore honest—building style, both in the construction techniques and in the organically integrated decoration. Mercer, however, was not simply a "revivalist." A complex and brillant man, he looked both backwards and forwards,

"Spring," a Mercer tile, Special Edition, 2007.
Source: Website: buckscounty.org/government/departments/Tileworks/misc_tile/07_tile.aspx

constructing his Gothic museum of state-of-the-art and highly experimental reinforced concrete.

Besides collecting craft tools and artifacts, Mercer was determined to revive local handcrafts and settled on ceramics because of the tradition of Pennsylvania German potters in and around Bucks County. Apprenticing himself to one of the last of these potters (although never actually mastering the art), he combined

Henry Mercer, working on archeological artifacts in the archeological workshop and studio he constructed at his family home, "Aldie." Photograph, 1895.
Source: Mercer Museum, Bucks County Historical Society, "Mercer Mosaic," Spring/Summer 1989

potter's techniques with his archaeological knowledge to establish the Moravian Pottery and Tile Works in Doylestown in 1912. For inspiration, Mercer drew on medieval European tiles, on stove plates by Bucks County ironworkers and on objects in his own museum. The tiles themselves grew from Mercer's own art and imagination and had the quality of folk art.[2]

Mercer offered over 500 designs in his catalogs. Architects throughout the Northeast used these tiles in major public buildings such as the Pennsylvania State Capitol at Harrisburg, as well as in private homes such as the Morris Estate and the Woodward mansion in Chestnut Hill. Nearly a century after its founding, Mercer tiles are still produced and were used recently at the Widener Education Building at the Morris Arboretum. Mercer's house and tile factory are now also museums open to the public.

---

1. Cleota Reed, "Henry Chapman Mercer and the Crafts Tradition," in *The Genius Belt: The Story of the Arts in Bucks County, Pennsylvania* (Doylestown, Pa., 1996), 89.

2. Ibid., 89-96.

View of the wonderfully cluttered interior of the Mercer Museum, Doylestown, Pa. Mercer had these artifacts hung so that the visitor could see the bottoms as well as the sides and tops. The square spiral staircase was another device to view these objects from every possible angle. Photograph, c. 1988.

Source: Mercer Museum, Bucks County Historical Society

Quarries, Quarrymen and Stone Masons

Since the earliest European settlement, Wissahickon schist had been used for construction in Northwest Philadelphia, giving it a unique texture and color that blended the buildings into the surrounding bedrock. In the 1890s, a wave of highly skilled stonemasons, many from the northern Italian province of Friuli, settled in the five communities adjacent to Wissahickon Valley. Among these masons and quarry operators were members of the Caruso, DiLauro, Galanti, Lorenzon, Marcolina, Morasco, Sabia, Vecchione and Yanni families, whose descendents still live and work in the vicinity.[6] The fortuitous combination of available local stone and skilled craftmen flourished until the height of the Great Depression and contributed to the flowering of the Wissahickon Style.

At one point, more than a half dozen quarries in the area supplied Wissahickon schist for all types of construction.[7] Some of these quarries have been completely filled in. The exposed bedrock of others, only partially filled, have become part of the community landscape and help to tie the community to its geology.

A Nursery Tradition

11:4–5

Two nurserymen, Thomas Meehan of the Germantown and Wissahickon Nurseries, and William Warner Harper of the Andorra Nurseries, also made important contributions to the Wissahickon Style. Meehan was a strong advocate for the use of native plants, while Harper, rooted in a late Victorian frame of mind, prized the exotic and the eclectic, and advocated a mixed palette of oriental and native species.

At its best, the use of exotic plants collected from Northeast Asia enriched the palette of the gardens of Chestnut Hill and Mt. Airy, while blending with the character of the Wissahickon forest. At its worst, this love affair with ornamentals allowed many pernicious and aggressive plants to escape into the adjoining natural areas, later causing major environmental problems.

Components of the Wissahickon Style:
A "Gradient of Wildness"

Decades before the concepts of "smart growth" and the development of a "Smart Growth Code," the Wissahickon Style was characterized by an unlegislated "gradient of density" that was used to organize the community. This gradient of density was also a "gradient of wildness" and is directly equivalent to the "transect" described in the Smart Growth Code as, "a geographical cross-section of a region used to reveal a sequence of environments. For human environments, this cross-section can be used to identify a set of habitats that vary by their level and intensity of urban character, a continuum that ranges from rural to urban."[8]

In the communities of West Mt. Airy and West Chestnut Hill, this transect runs from the commercial spine along the ridgeline to the natural area preserved in the valley. Four broad zones can be identified. In the first zone, small, deep lots and tightly packed two-and three-story buildings characterize the commercial street. Moving away from the ridge onto the plateau, housing in the second zone is mainly small individual houses or

Thomas Meehan (1826–1901)

Thomas Meehan. Photograph, 1901.
Source: GHS

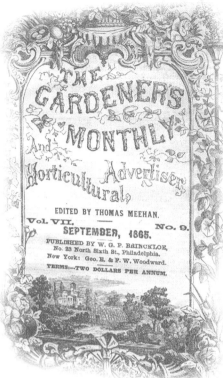

An issue of Meehan's
Gardener's Monthly.
Source: GHS

Meehan was a widely respected, internationally known botanist and nurseryman. A member of Philadelphia's Academy of Natural Sciences, he traveled extensively in the Western United States, bringing back plant specimens. When alerted by Harvard's Charles Sprague Sargent that specimens from the Lewis and Clark Expedition were stored (but uncatalogued) at the American Philosophical Society in Philadelphia, Meehan took on the job of documenting and identifying the collection.[1] He even corresponded with Charles Darwin and sent him North American plant specimens.

Meehan's childhood was spent on the Isle of Wight where his father was the head gardener for Colonel Francis Vernon Harcurt. A precocious child, he wrote a horticultural paper when he was only 12, and at age 15, he propagated the first hybrid fushia.[2] Trained at London's Kew Garden, he came to Philadelphia in 1848. Among other jobs, he worked as a botanist and landscape gardener at Bartram's Garden and later became an advocate for the preservation of this important Philadelphia botanical site.[3]

Meehan owned and operated extensive nurseries in Germantown, located between Germantown Avenue and Chew Streets, where he concentrated on American species. He believed that these native plants were best suited to thrive locally. According to a September, 1893 article in the magazine *Garden and Forest*, "In no other establishment are American trees and shrubs raised in such numbers. Long ago Mr. Meehan recognized two facts—that the climate of eastern America is particularly suited to deciduous-leafed plants, which grow more satisfactorily here than any other country of the world, and that American plants are best for America."[4]

From 1859 to 1888, Meehan explained his ideas on garden design as editor of the national magazine, *The Gardener's Monthly*—the premier horticultural publication of its time. His magazine was influential in establishing an informal landscape style in the Northeastern United States that emphasized the broad use of native plants.

1. Website: panteek.com/Meehan/pages/ meh41a.htm2.

2. Thomas Meehan, American Botanist Wikipedia website: en.wikipedia.org/wiki/Thomas Meehan.

3. Stephanie Ginsberg Oberle, "The Influence of Thomas Meehan on Horticulture in the United States," *Germantown Crier* (Spring, 1999), 4-25.

4. Quoted in Ibid., 7.

William Warner Harper (1867–1934)

Born and raised in the Germantown section of Philadelphia, William Warner Harper learned the nursery trade working for the Yates and Miller Nursery in Mt. Airy. Charles Miller, one of the owners, was the chief horticulturalist for Fairmount Park and in charge of the design of the landscape of Horticultural Hall at the 1876 Centennial Exhibition.

In 1891, when Harper was just 24, Henry Howard Houston hired him as the business manager of the Andorra Nursery. When Houston died in 1895, Harper took a 99-year lease from the Houston Estate on the original nursery site. An expert horti-culturalist, with a genius for merchandizing, Harper offered his customers landscape design services along with his large and varied nursery stock—all keys to the phenomenal success of the Andorra Nursery. Over the years, he provided plants and created garden designs for numerous properties in the region, including the Houston and Woodward estates (Druim Moir and Krisheim) and the many Houston and Woodward develop-ments in Mt. Airy and Chestnut Hill.

By the early 1920s, Harper had expanded his business, buying farms in Springfield and Whitemarsh Townships and eventually bringing together over 1,400 acres. The nurseries ultimately extended as far as Ridge and Butler Pikes—largely around the old village of Spring Mill.

Harper highlighted many of his landscape ideas in the introduction to his nursery catalogs, calling for a treatment that blended the regional landscape with a "freedom of choice of the best that the world has to offer."[1] He also promoted a close connection between the house and a series of carefully defined garden rooms.

Harper shared John and Lydia Morrises' fascination with plants from Northeastern Asia and acquired considerable seed stock from E. H. "Chinese" Wilson. Harper introduced temple cedars, Hinoki cypress, Japanese pagoda trees, a variety of Japanese maples and the Chinese toon tree. Harper's influence led to the characteristic mixture of plants from the Northeastern Deciduous Forests of Asia and North America.

Surprisingly, several of Harper's many enterprises still survive (in scaled-down versions), including the Andorra Spring Water Company. Adjacent to the nursery at Spring Mill Road and Ridge Pike, in Whitemarsh Township, Harper laid out the Marble Hall Golf Course in the mid-1920s, now the Green Valley Country Club.[2]

An early member of the Friends of the Wissahickon, Harper served for many years on its planting committee. To honor this service, the Friends donated what came to be known as "Harper's Meadow" at the intersection of Northwestern and Germantown Avenues. This property was a large wet meadow in the crook of the sharp bend in Wissahickon Creek just below the city–county boundary. The Friends of the Wissahickon bought this property from the Houston Estate for $30,000 and presented it to Fairmount Park in 1937.[3]

1. Andorra Nurseries brochure, Autumn 1919, 4, GHS.

2. Thomas Keels,"Andorra: From Private Estate to Public Preserve," unpublished typescript, GHS; Thomas Keels, interview by authors, December 11, 2002.

3. Thomas Keels, "Andorra"; Campbell, Scrapbooks, 48:38, 491. An extensive obituary of Harper appeared in the *Philadelphia Public Ledger*, December 27, 1934. The authors are grateful to Keels for sharing this obituary with them.

Harper's office at the Andorra Nursery. This building is located on Wissahickon Drive (later Forbidden Drive) where the road ended, just south of the edge of the city. Photograph, c. 1910. Source: CHHS

twins on modest lots. Further west, where the plateau begins to dip into the valley, the third zone is made up of boxy, Victorian houses, in the center of bigger lots. As the slope becomes steeper, there is a fourth zone of large, rambling country houses that abut Wissahickon Park. This gradient of wildness is repeated, at a smaller scale, within individual lots. It is particularly well expressed within the more generous properties of the country houses, where there is a gradual transition from house to managed landscape of garden rooms and shadow lawns that, in turn, blends into the forest adjoining the park.

The natural vegetation encircling these country houses brought the forest up into the community. From there, streets, drainage channels and planting on the smaller properties continued to draw the natural systems through the neighborhoods. Unlike the post-World War II suburbs, West Mt. Airy and West Chestnut Hill were "forested communities," and much of their quality and character stemmed from the celebration of the Wissahickon forest within the built fabric.

Source: *CHCA Land Use Guildlines*, revised 1982. from original drawing by Baldev Lambda

 Public   Private   Institutional

Wissahickon Park and the adjacent large private, semi-public and public properties within the community of Chestnut Hill. These properties, with extensive forested open space, extend the perceived boundaries of the park.

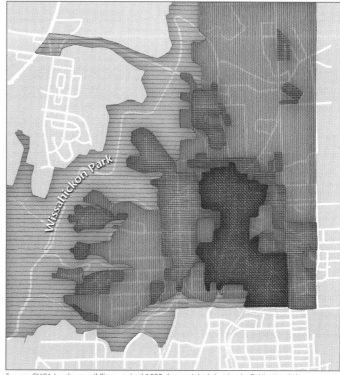

Source: CHCA Land use guildlines, revised 1982. from original drawing by Baldev Lambda

 Park Land   Low Density   Medium Density High Density

The "gradient of wildness" in the community of Chestnut Hill. The map shows a gradient from the most dense development along the ridge to the least dense development next to Wissahichon Park.

Water

The natural drainage system is visible throughout the community—expressed both formally and informally across the gradient of wildness. In the most urban parts (the first zone), water is seen and articulated where tributary streams cross the main commercial spine and where water seeps out of old quarry walls. In the second and third zones, surface water flows are formalized in gutters, stone channels, pools and spillways. In the fourth and outermost zone (where the properties are largest), seeps and swales have been preserved in a nearly natural state. Intermittent streams meander through the private lots of whole mini-neighborhoods, and drainage channels have been kept open as public rights-of-way between private properties. By keeping the natural drainage system relatively intact, these neighborhoods have preserved a "distributed" water system. Water is slowed and allowed to seep into the soil, minimizing flooding and recharging groundwater.

11:6–8

Water | Garden along Upper Lincoln Drive

11:6

A small tributary originated in a spring in Pastorius Park that once fed an ice pond. The icehouse itself was down the road on what would later become the corner of Lincoln Drive and Springfield Avenue. The Woodwards converted the icehouse into the Willet Stained Glass Studio.

The map shows Lincoln Drive running through the middle of Pastorious Park, but this section was never completed and was, after pressure from the Woodward family, finally taken off the city maps in the early 1960s.

South of Pastorius Park the small tributary was elaborated into a series of water features and gardens. Over time, these springs have run dry, the result of development around the park. The water features have been filled in or abandoned.

Remains of the Lincoln Drive water garden. In the early 20th century, the Woodwards developed a long, linear water garden that was an articulated channel with a series of pools, fountains and small waterfalls. This stepped water garden formalized a small tributary that flowed down beside Lincoln Drive to join Cresheim Creek.
Source: Photograph by CLF

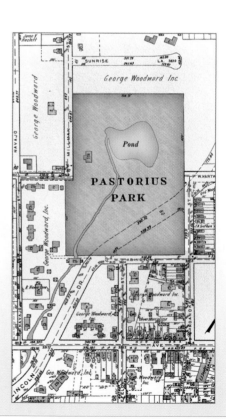

Map showing route of streamlet that fed the water gardens along Lincoln Drive in Chestnut Hill.
Source: Franklin Survey Company, Atlas of Philadelphia, 1954

Water | Gutters

Many of the streets on the west sides of Chestnut Hill and Mt. Airy carried stormwater in gutters. These gutters were made of rough materials—small modular units (of Wissahickon schist, Belgian blocks, or the brownish-yellow bricks once used to pave the streets of downtown Philadelphia). These rough modular pieces slowed the journey of water downhill, and the spaces between each piece allowed water to seep into the ground.

The open channels exposed the flowing water to air and sunlight, permitting a variety of plants and micro-organisms to flourish. These plants as well as the insects and microbes that lived on them, all worked to improve the quality of water carried into Wissahickon Creek.

Later engineering practices and building codes mandated curbs that channeled stormwater into inlets and from there into underground pipes. Unlike the older gutters, these pipes were smooth, largely impervious conduits that concentrated the flow and increased the speed and amount of water arriving at an already swollen creek.

Cobble gutter along Kitchen's Lane in Mt. Airy. Photograph, c. 1968.
Source: Photograph by CLF

Stone gutter made of Wissahickon schist along Scotforth Road, Mt. Airy. The City of Philadelphia's Streets Department has routinely extended the road paving over most of the gutters in Northwest Philadelphia and only a few remain.
Source: Photograph by CLF

This photograph shows one of the last remaining brick gutters in Mt. Airy/Chestnut Hill. It was covered over in the late 1990s when the Philadelphia Streets Department widened West Mermaid Lane.

Here, the bluestone sidewalk, a strip of grass with marching columns of canopy trees and, finally, the yellow brick gutter create a series of bands paralleling the roadway. This series of bands edging the road has added great richness to the community fabric.
Source: Photograph by CLF

Water | Preserved Tributaries

Throughout the community of Chestnut Hill, "headwater" streams (the finest capillaries of the drainage network) have often been preserved. Some of these rivulets were allowed to flow freely through lots of relatively modest size. Others were left open at the bottom of small valleys where they formed the boundary between private properties on opposite sides.

Source: Photograph by CLF

Wissahickon Park often intersects the streets that follow the contours of the shallow slopes at the edge of the plateau, allowing the forest to finger into the community and giving access to the park at many points.
Source: Photograph by CLF

Streets, Alleys and Sidewalks

Local roads also form a distributed system. Instead of concentrating traffic on a single major artery, there are no central collector roads. In Mt. Airy and Chestnut Hill, the streets are a grid system punctuated by parkways and roads that curve along the edges of the park. This loose grid offers many choices for traffic. Cars and trucks percolate through the neighborhoods on many different streets, and no single street takes the lion's share of the vehicles. Each street is human in scale. The traffic is generally moderate and, as a result, there are no undesirable streets where houses and buildings have decayed because of the blighting influence of a busy thoroughfare.

Other factors blunt and divert the flow of traffic. The parkways that cut across the grid follow the contours of the tributary valleys and do not encourage fast moving cars and trucks. Roads closest to the park edges follow the winding contours of the valley. The railroad tracks cut off many streets and force roads to "weasel" around the neighborhoods. Vehicular movement across the valley is limited, and only a few bridges cross the gorge. However, there are multiple points of access into the park for pedestrians and bikers, where the grid stops and people can continue along former wagon roads that lead down to the creek.

Streets and sidewalks on the west side of Chestnut Hill and in West Mt. Airy are forested corridors, extending the sense of the park into the public right of way. Streets are treated as linear gardens with elegant, clearly defined edges. Sidewalk, grass strip, gutter and cartway create a series of parallel bands. This basic pattern of streets and sidewalks resembles a living cathedral, with the street itself as the nave, the sidewalks as the side aisles, the overarching trees as columns and their canopies as Gothic vaults.

11:9-11

Streets

At the edge of the upper slopes, streets follow the curving contours to provide access to houses abutting the park. These streets make occasional sharp turns that help to slow traffic through the community and discourage their use as arterials. From the park, the forest breaks through to frame one side of the street. Small pull-offs along these streets allow people to drive to trailheads and enter the park on foot.

Most of the streets in Mt. Airy and Chestnut Hill are tree-lined, reminiscent of an American small town. The overarching canopy trees planted along the sidewalk combine with the trees in the yards above, to reinforce the sense of a village in the forest. Streets are often more expressive when the trees are planted in a more imaginative pattern—not simply in a single row, 30-foot-on-center. After World War II, when municipalities enacted strict codes mandating uniform road widths and building setbacks, the street tree planting shown below would not have been allowed.

A hedgerow, a remnant from the agricultural past, has been left to line a new street in a very conventional 1980s residential development at the northern end of Chestnut Hill. This dancing line of locusts (*Robinia pseudoacacia*) makes an unusual, but very lively and attractive street tree planting.
Source: Photograph by CLF

At the entrance to the French Village at Elbow Lane, two double rows of lindens (*Tilia europaea*) on either side of the street form an arcade of trees. This arcade reaches only a short distance and makes an elegant, rather formal gateway to the main body of the street which becomes more rural as it curves around to form the "elbow." Source: Photograph by CLF

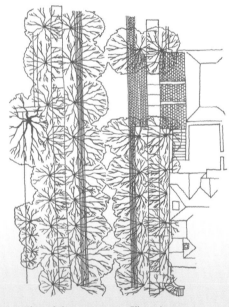

Plan of the entrance to Elbow Lane.
Source: Andropogon, drawing by Rolf Sauer

Facing page
Most of the streets in Mt. Airy and Chestnut Hill are tree-lined, reminiscent of an American small town. The overarching canopy trees planted along the sidewalk in the 200 block of West Springfield Avenue combine with the trees in the yards above, to reinforce the sense of a village in the forest.
Source: Photograph by CLF

Alleys

Behind the backyards, alleys gave access to stables and later to early automobile garages. In many other communities, the alley was poorly tended and often unplanted—the disreputable backend of the property. In the post-World War II suburban developments, alleys disappeared. A half-century later, alleys are reappearing in New Urbanist designs.

In the Wissahickon style, alleys were treated as country lanes and were magical places where forest fragments made intimate, leafy corridors. Part of their charm came from the close relationship between the back of the house and the alley itself.

In the many parts of Chestnut Hill and Mt. Airy, parking in alleys was accommodated either by informal or formal communal parking courts and/or by a series of grouped garages that formed part of the spatial enclosure of the site.

Source: Photographs by CLF

Sidewalks

A "cathedral-like" space is created by the sidewalks and the large canopy trees overarching the street. The street is the "nave" and the sidewalks are the "side aisles." Reinforcing this effect, the trees are often planted on both sides of the path. Photographs by CLF

Walls extend from the "gatehouses" (one either side of the entrance to Cresheim Valley Drive) to create a "gateway" into the park. Source: Andropogon, drawing by Rolf Sauer

A Remarkable Variety

11:12-17

The key elements of the Wissahickon Style were expressed throughout the community fabric in a wide variety of housing types, lot sizes and architectural styles from different eras. Housing types include single-family homes (from huge to modest), an unusual range of twins (some larger than the typical individual house) and innovative high-density units—triplets, quads and courts. Lot sizes reflected these housing types and ranged in size from 50-acre estates to one-eighth acre properties. Part of the success of the denser housing types was that they were not seen as multiple units, but appeared to be one large, rambling village or a manor house.

The same long history that has given Wissahickon Park a rich heritage has also given all the communities surrounding the park a remarkable range of architectural expression: Colonial "town houses" and farm buildings, a plethora of Victorian houses and commercial buildings, early 20th-century Colonial Revival and vernacular and country houses. Later, "modern" architectural designs would also become an important part of the fabric—with houses by Louis I. Kahn, Robert Venturi and apartments by Oscar Stonorov. By the late 20th century, the adaptive re-use of the large estates added to the richness of these offerings.

11:12

Housing Types

In this three block area of Chestnut Hill, there are an astonishing variety of high density housing types. These types include row houses, twins of all sizes, triplets, quads and courts. This area has an urban grid, but the grid is distorted in a number of places by diagonal roads running across it— in this case by Germantown Avenue (the commercial spine) and by Winston Road. Within the strict rationale of the grid there are quirky bends and curved streets that alter the vistas to show the different faces and angles of the buildings and give deep views through and into the gardens, reinforcing the sense of a borrowed landscape.

Map showing an area of east Chestnut Hill around Germantown Avenue and Winston Road.
Source: G.W. Bromley and Company, Atlas of the City of Philadelphia, 22d Ward, 1923

A narrow path, a sitting area in a grove of white pines and a rhododendron hedge to screen the neighbors, are all that is needed to create a forested garden in this tiny space. Source: Photograph by CLF

Housing Types | Architectural Style and Lot Sizes

The Wissahickon Style does not depend on any particular architectural expression, house type or lot size. A Colonial Revival duplex, on a one-eighth-acre lot and a country estate on several acres, both incorporate the local forest into the landscape matrix of the property.

View of the Arthur Mellor house and garden on Scotforth Road, showing the forested landscape caught between the house and the bellevedere. Source: Photograph by Peter Benton

Housing Types | Twins

The Woodwards' Benezet Street "twins" were part of a larger, planned residential enclave. Directly across the street from the twins, there were two sets of "quads." The Woodwards rented to many income levels and all age groups to establish a complete community. The Benezet Street houses were generally assigned to young couples. The many babies born on this street gave it the nickname "Basinette Street."

The sidewalk space between the street trees and the open porches forms a green and porous corridor that makes a friendly, shared, public place. The porch is another kind of "half-room"—half building and half outdoor space—a transition from the public to the private domain.

The sets of twins are separated by heavily planted pathways, which lead to back gardens that surround the little houses in tall canopy trees. Despite the density of this housing, walking along the sidewalk, or driving along the street, is an experience of houses peeping out of a shared, forested landscape.

Twins on Benezet Street, a small residential street, directly perpendicular to the main commercial strip in Chestnut Hill.
Source: Photographs by CLF

Housing Types | Triplets

These three adjoining houses belong to a larger Woodward residential development just east of Germantown Avenue. This triplet, like other multiple housing units in the neighborhood, actually appears to be one large house with a single front yard. Pinkish tan and pale yellow stucco has been used since the colonial era in Northwest Philadelphia. Slate roofs and bluestone paving are also a familiar part of the local vocabulary.

A triplet on Winston Road in Chestnut Hill.
Source: Photograph by CLF

Housing Types | Quadruple Houses

The quadruple houses that the Woodwards built in both Chestnut Hill and Mt. Airy were constructed about 1912 and designed by architect H. Louis Durhing. These "quads" were made of Wissahickon schist and had four housing units under one roof. They resembled two sets of twin houses back to back, each fronting on parallel residential streets. Along with the economies realized from eliminating the additional exterior walls, the quads did away with unsightly back alleys and back yards. Instead, these houses were surrounded on all four sides by gardens and trees.

Porches were placed at the corners of each quad unit to avoid blocking light into the living and dining rooms, and a skylight on the third floor illuminated the stair hall. On the second floor, screened-in sleeping porches opened out from the master bedroom, adaptations to the hot Philadelphia summers in an era without air conditioning and in line with then current ideas about the healthfulness of sleeping in the fresh air. Years later, after the trees along the streets and in the yards had grown above the housetops, the sleeping porches came to resemble

tree houses, perched high up in the tree canopy.[1]

---

1. See David R. Contosta, *A Philadelphia Family: The Houstons and Woodwards of Chestnut Hill* (Philadelphia, 1988), 66-67. See also George Woodward, "Another Aspect of the Quadruple House," *Architectural Record* (July 1913), 51-55, and Matlack Price, "Architecture and the Housing Problem: Recent Work of Durhing, Oakie, and Ziegler," *Architectural Record* (September 1913), 240-247.

Two views of the quadruple houses in West Mt. Airy between Nippon Street and Mt. Airy Avenue. The photograph on the left is looking from the street, between two quads, along their side gardens. The photograph on the right shows the front of one of the four units from the street, with the screened sleeping porch above the lower porch. A little journey through a front gate takes the resident and visitors along the length of the front yard before climbing the porch steps to the front door.

Source: Photographs by CLF

Housing Types | Courts

A court is an adaptation to density, with houses grouped around a shared, central open space. These houses can be large or small, attached or free-standing. Without fences or walls between the houses, the common landscape gives each resident a sense of living in a spacious green setting instead of being hemmed in on a tiny lot.

Roanoake Court is another compact Woodward development. In this multi-leveled enclave, eight houses frame a landscaped central space. The court was designed by H. Louis Duhring in 1931-1933. The central, shared space flows into the private side and back yards. A change of elevation, where the upper green steps down to a lower green at the back of the property gives an added spatial richness.

Winston Court, designed by H. Louis Durhing in 1923, is one of several Woodward courts. Here, the road separates the house from the commons. Parking is along the driveway, which ends in a turn-around at the back.
Source: Photographs by CLF

The "Borrowed Landscape"

With the larger properties and particularly the country houses of the 1920s and 1930s, the organization of the lot was critical to the seamless flow of vegetation between street, lot and forested valley. In the best of the Wissahickon Style, the individual houses did not face the street but were internally organized around the views and the character of the site. Barely visible from the street, these houses were seen through a curtain of forest, and once entry was gained, the street beyond was nearly invisible. Where the house was closer to the street, it was screened by walls, fences and thick forest. The functional elements of the lot—driveway, forecourt, house footprint, garden rooms and the "delectable details" that embellished the design—were transformed into gardens and became part of the community landscape. Shared building materials allowed the individual elements to contribute to and to "borrow"[9] the communal fabric. In Chestnut Hill and Mt. Airy, the wall of one large house often defined the courtyard of a neighbor's property. A single belvedere, built of the same materials, could be seen from several gardens. These materials reflected the local geology and Philadelphia building traditions—Wissahickon schist, bluestone from the quarries of Northwest Pennsylvania, granite cobbles, once ballast for the colonial ships and the wrought iron (later steel) shipped up from New Orleans.

Like the streets, the driveways were treated as a long linear gap in an implied, continuous forest. The conventional driveway and parking areas were replaced by a forested tunnel, ending in a garden court. These components formed a "vestibule" between the house and street. Where the house was close to the street, the forested front was little more than symbolic, with an abbreviated entry through a thick hedge or an arched opening in a wall. In the largest properties, the journey through the forest was indirect and drawn out, heightening the drama of arrival into a large, open courtyard. These entry courtyards were gracious garden spaces, created by the embrace of the wings of the house and high garden walls. Whatever the size of the lot, all the elements were there, and the functions of access and parking were an integral part of the experience of house and garden and pleasant places in themselves.

Properties appear to flow together and are perceived as one large landscape because all the houses and garden walls are built of the same local stone, and the lot edges are heavily planted with native forest trees.

Source: Andropogon, drawing by Rolf Sauer

11:18-23

Two properties, seen from a third, all blend together in one common landscape.   Source: Photograph by CLF

Driveways

Although driveways are a practical necessity, in the Wissahickon Style they become part of the charm of the property. Whether just a short access to a garage or a long, winding entry road, these driveways are part of the forested fabric.

Source: Photographs by CLF

Longer driveways, found on properties closest to the park, are drawn out journeys, often ending in a forecourt, which is the "outdoor foyer" to the house.

On a large estate at the edge of the park, a long formal driveway travels through the different landscapes of the property before arriving at the house. The house, stepping down the hill, Is glimpsed below the shadow lawn.

Source: Photographs by CLF

In yet another example, driveways run parallel to each other, separated by a forested median.

Parking | Courts

Right
A communal parking court, defined by two sets of four adjoining garages with extending walls, creates an anti-chamber to the main residential court. Source: Photographs by CLF

Below
At Sulgrave Manor (a supposed replica of George Washington's family's ancestral home in Surrey, England, brought to Chestnut Hill from the Sesqui-Centennial Exhibition of 1926), the house and extending walls frame the driveway and parking court and enfold the garage into an organic whole.

Parking | Informal Communal Areas

11:20

In contrast to the more formal parking courts shown on the opposite page, there are also informal, shared parking places—for example, pull-offs along an alley defined by forest vegetation. These more casual parking places allow numerous adjacent houses to use the same space for parking, eliminating the need for individual driveways.
Source: Photographs by CLF

Fronts and Forecourts

In the Wissahickon Style, the front of the house is not only a presentation, but also a journey. This journey is often indirect, and contributes to a sense of mystery and of anticipation. These qualities are enhanced because the house is generally screened by vegetation and/or by walls.

A forecourt provides a transition from the street to the house. This transition can be small and compressed or large and elongated. In the old Willet Stained Glass Studio, the arch, the wall and the wrought iron gate both frame and hide the front of the building.
Source: Photographs by CLF

The driveway is separated from the front and entrance, and a small path steps down to give a sense of invitation to a house nestled in the woods.

The "front" of the Willing House, showing the Wissahickon woods coming up into the community through an adjacent right of way. The forest of Wissackickon Park wraps around the house to become the front garden.

Completely engulfed in the landscape of adjoining Wissahickon Park, this house and the front countyard are a mysterious destination, bathed in a pool of light. Source: Photographs by CLF

Creating Positive Outdoor Space | Courts and Half-Rooms

Perhaps the most spectacular half-room in Chestnut Hill is at the Willing House. Here, a pierced wall extends from the house to create "windows" into the forested, public landscape (Wissahickon Park), which is borrowed as the frame for the garden. A multi-stemmed oak has hopped the wall and brings the forest into the garden.

Source: Photograph by CLF

Typically, the individual Wissahickon Style house was one room deep, with an L-shaped, T-shaped or attenuated I-shaped floor plan. From the outside, there was always a view through the house into the garden. From the inside, all the rooms looked out into the landscape. Entryway and ground floor corridors were often treated as garden rooms, reinforcing this inside/outside connection. French doors opened onto terraces from many first floor rooms, and balconies peered over the gardens and into the forested valley

The wings of the house and the walls extended out into the garden and pulled the house outward so that it dissolved into the landscape. These extensions formed a series of complex and multileveled "half-rooms" or small, protected garden spaces and service courts—half architecture and half vegetation. They created a sense of being partly inside and partly outside, with the walls of the house sheltering these positive outdoor spaces. These half-rooms came in different sizes and shapes and accommodated a multitude of outdoor uses, from swimming pools to eating areas. These rooms could be paved with many types of "floors," from grass to bluestone. The "walls" could be entirely green—made of hedges or shrub masses or, alternatively, they could be an architectural garden feature such as a trellis or belvedere. Walls could be solid—house walls, free-standing garden walls and retaining walls—or they could be perforated, screens of stone, wood, brick or wrought iron. In some cases, these walls incorporated the bedrock, making it difficult to know where the rocky ground ended and the house began.

Source: Andropogon, drawing by Rolf Sauer

Half-Rooms

Half rooms are open-air architecture. This little garden pavilion, at the Woodwards' Krisheim estate, is perched at the edge of the garden and anchors the outer boundary of the property. It is surrounded by the formal garden on one side and by a grove of tall white pines on the other. From everywhere in the house and garden, there is a view down into the Wissahickon Valley.

A large medallion by the Mercer Tile Works marks the threshold into the room. Houston and Woodward had earlier bought up and demolished the remaining mills along adjacent Cresheim Creek. This tile, showing an old mill, was perhaps Woodward's nod to the valley's history.
Source: Photographs by CLF

The McCracken House "Garth"

Designed by Arthur Meigs of Mellor, Meigs & Howe, for attorney Robert McCracken, this house on Westview Street, in West Mt. Airy was built in two stages. The first stage was finished in 1919 while McCracken was still a bachelor. The second stage was constructed seven years later, after he had married and the couple wanted more space. The McCracken house was called "Garth." Arthur Meigs wrote, "Garth means a piece of ground, usually small, set aside or enclosed by a wall or other barrier. It is a modest name for a modest place."[1]

The completed house is L-shaped, with both wings just one room deep, so that the garden could be seen from all parts of the house. This footprint allowed the house to form two walls of the garden. The house, pushed to the front and to one side of the property, gave the garden the maximum amount of space. The garden itself began in a paved area covered by a "sheltering vine." It stepped down into a series of terraces surrounded by plantings. Stonewalls enclosed the lot, defining and protecting the outdoor spaces. At the opposite corner from the house entrance at the angle of the "L," a conical-roofed belvedere sat on a small paved terrace and anchored the garden.

An indoor "garden room" connected the 1919 and 1927 wings. The outdoor character of this garden room was typical of entrances and hallways in the Wissahickon style. These rooms functioned as a gentle transition from outdoors to indoors, or vice versa. The side of the house facing the garden was all glass. The floor was bluestone—the same material as the paved terraces and paths in the garden. This gem of a house demonstrated, through many design devices, the possibility of making the most of a half-acre lot.

1. Arthur I. Meigs "Garth: House of Robert T. McCracken, Esq./ Germantown, Philadelphia," *The Architectural Record*, November 1928, 356.

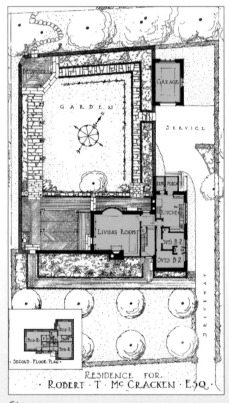

Stage 1

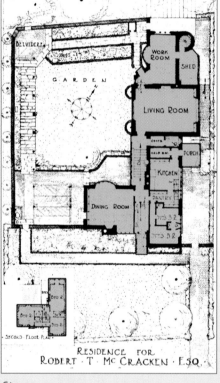

Stage 2

Plans of the McCracken House, before the old garage and service court became a new wing of the house and after the new addition. In this later plan, the hallway is extended and becomes a "garden room" and the house becomes L-shaped, wrapping around the garden on two sides and giving the new living room a direct opening onto the garden. Source: *The Architectural Record*, November, 1928

Formed by the living room wall and two garden walls, this half room was the first of a series of terraces that stepped down towards a small tributary valley in Wissahickon Park.

On the lower terrace, a belvedere sat diagonally across from the house. A path from this little half room led down into the park.

Looking down the stone hallway from the entrance foyer through the house, this room—the connecting corridor between the house and its new addition—was once a piece of the original garden. The new addition incorporated the former garden wall with its small fountain.

Source: *Architectural Record,* November, 1928

Lawns

Minimal Lawns

A minimal lawn is the floor of a small gap in the forest—a little, sunny glade, surrounded by tall trees and lush understory. In climatic regions that would normally support forests, small, grassy openings reduce the environmental problems created by large areas of turf. These minimal lawns, combined with paved terraces, still provide enough flat, walkable area for entertainment and recreation.

A small, grassy opening in a private garden in Chestnut Hill.

View of the shadow lawn at Pastorius Park in Chestnut Hill. Source: Photographs by CLF

Shadow Lawns

In the Eastern United States, campuses and large private properties typically have shadow lawns as a major organizing element. Cool and sheltering, they often function as large outdoor gathering places. Modeled on the English estate "park," they have a gracious quality that invites leisurely activities.

Essentially a forest with the understory and shrub layer cleared out, the shadow lawn is a large grassy area, shaded by scattered canopy trees. Tree trunks cast long, columnar shadows across the ground. In the Wissahickon Style these lawns often grade into the forest beyond. In contrast, the baked, open lawns of post-World War II suburbia, bereft of trees, require copious watering to keep them green, are visually uninteresting and are uncomfortable in hot weather.

Alternatives to Grass

Lawn grass in the middle Atlantic region is generally a European turf plant, which grows by "running" roots, to form a smooth carpet.

Moss, on the other hand, is found throughout the forested areas of the Wissahickon Valley and will establish itself in shady, open places, gradually taking over an untended lawn. The Japanese have traditionally cultivated moss in their forest gardens and this plant can be an alternative to grass in parks and private gardens.

Different mosses have different requirements. The acid-loving mosses of the Wissahickon Valley will flourish and create a remarkably sturdy ground layer that can be walked, sat and played on. Moss does not require mowing or liming, but must be raked of leaves to prevent rotting, and weeded to keep the forest from growing back.

11:25

Source: Photograph by CLF

A Forested Community

In a forested community most of the houses are set into a matrix of layered vegetation—tall trees, understory shrub and a rich herbaceous ground. The plants of the Wissahickon Valley and the multi-tiered structure of the forest was preserved in the gardens, fronts, alleys, streets, driveways and left over spaces.

11:24-28

Canopy trees came out of the forest and encircled the house, defining the outer edge of the garden rooms and forming small glades. Open, sunny places without trees were small, even when the property was enormous, and they were treated like the gaps that occurred naturally in woodlands—kept to a minimum and defined by garden spaces, walls and forest edges. As in the forest beyond, flowering understory trees—dogwoods (*Cornus officinalis*), redbuds (*Cercis canadensis ssp.*), sassafras (*Sassafras albidum*) and shadbush (*Amelanchier canadensis*)—ringed these glades. There was no foundation planting, only masses of understory trees, shrubs, ferns, woody ground covers and wildflowers. The forest that surrounded the largest houses at the edge of the park crept into the community, even into the densest parts.

Much of the land that would ordinarily be lawn in a typical American community— the soft, open, walkable surface—was instead treated as a forest ground layer. The house at Crefeld Street and Hampton Road, by architect Charles Willing, (of Willing, Sims & Talbot), had a ground layer in the front of carefully tended moss, bordered by ferns and woodland wildflowers. On other properties lawns were kept to a minimum—and were used as a softer alternate to paving. On the largest properties, a "shadow lawn," a stretch of mown grass, was shaded by large canopy trees. Often this shadow lawn was carpeted with tiny, native wild flowers like bluets or dogtoothed violets. These shadow lawns, with their native trees and occasional flowering understory, graded gently into the forest with all its natural layers.

Delectible Details

The many delectible details that exist throughout Chestnut Hill and Mt. Airy, illustrate an attitude where even the smallest piece of the built fabric intermingles with the natural world.

Where there were existing large trees, the builders curved the wall to save and showcase the trunks in their own "balcony."

The roots of a beech tree grow down through the spaces left between the cobbles of the gutter.

Ferns grow out of a stone wall of Wissahickon schist, mimicking the ferns in the park that grow out of tiny pockets in the rock outcrops.

Source: Photographs by CLF

Delectible Details | Paths

Mt. Airy and Chestnut Hill are rich in communal footpaths that run between private properties and are accessible from alleys and streets. A number of these paths lead from residential areas into the park. The walls and forest vegetation define a mysterious and shady passage, another level of the conecting fabric, and perfect for children's play.

A formal bluestone path is the entrance to both house and garden.

The Wissahickon garden is a forest garden—a series of small openings or "glades" of varying formality. These openings are connected by paths whose character matches the openings.

An informal bluestone path, almost Japanese in its indirection and its blend of pavers, cut stone and intertwined ferns.

Source: Photographs by CLF

Delectible Details | Steps

Informal steps made of gravel are held in place by bluestone risers. The steps create a transition between a small formal garden bordered by a wall on the left and the Wissahickon forest on the right. Moss has grown at the sides of the steps where foot traffic is light. Source: Photograph by CLF

Steps from a terrace at the back of the house descend into the public landscape of the Wissahickon Valley.
Source: Andropogon, drawing by Rolf Sauer

The Woodwards and the Wissahickon Style

Some of the variety and success of the two communities of Chestnut Hill and Mt. Airy resulted from the involvement of an extraordinary family. This involvement began in the late 19th century with Henry Howard Houston (1820-1895), a railroad magnate and multifaceted entrepreneur, who built Wissahickon Heights. This complete neighborhood on the west side of Chestnut Hill had a church, a cricket club, a summer hotel and approximately 80 houses. Houston's daughter, Gertrude, and son-in-law George Woodward, continued this tradition of community development, making major contributions to the Wissahickon Style.

Although Wissahickon Heights had respected the landscape, the layout of streets and the design of houses were relatively conventional—big boxy houses set back on their lots and evenly lined up along the street grid. The Woodwards, working with three young, imaginative and sensitive architects, broke away to create remarkably innovative and responsive house types and lot configurations.

11:29-30

George (1863–1952) and Gertrude (1868–1961) Woodward

George Woodward grew up in Wilkes Barre, Pennsylvania. Trained as a medical doctor, he worked as an elected official, and led important social and political reforms in the city, especially creating in housing for the working poor. From 1919 to 1947, he served as a progressive Republican state senator. For several decades, Woodward was a central figure in the Friends of the Wissahickon, a member of its board and the head of its tree planting committee.

Gertrude Houston Woodward, George Woodward's wife, was also deeply involved in progressive causes. She was an important supporter of Wissahickon Park as well as a patron of women artists, including her neighbor Violet Oakley, a major figure of the Brandywine School. Gertrude's inheritance from her father, Henry Howard Houston, funded the Woodward development projects.

Like many Victorian women, Gertrude let her husband take the credit, but she shared her husband's interest in architecture and was deeply involved in the decision-making for their innovative housing projects. Their son Stanley remembers both his parents pouring over blueprints spread out over the floor at home. It was George who negotiated with the architects, handled all the business details, and appeared in the public eye as the developer.[1]

---

1. Stanley Woodward, Sr., interview by David Contosta, June 21, 1985.

George and Gertrude Woodward, in the center, photographed on their 50th wedding anniversary, in 1944.
Source: Courtesy Stanley Woodward, Sr.

The Woodward Developments in Chestnut Hill and Mt. Airy

1. Winston Court

2. Benezet Street

3. Pastorius Park

4. Cotswold Village

5. St. Martin's Church

6. Philadelphia Cricket Club

7. Chestnut Hill Academy
   (Wissahickon Inn)

8. Druim Moir

9. French Village

Source: Woodward House Corporation

The Woodward Three

H. Louis Duhring
(1874-1953)

H. Louis Duhring was the oldest of the Woodwards' three architects and the one responsible for the designs of many of the "cluster" houses, which included quads, courts, crescents and other groupings of attached houses. These extraordinary complexes seemed to be an architectural parallel to the "borrowed" landscape, an organic composition where the buildings are knit together with the richness of forms and spaces found in a small, rambling European village.

Duhring studied architecture at University of Pennsylvania and was the first recipient of the prestigious Stewardson Traveling Prize that enabled him to study and sketch in Italy. In 1899, he formed the architectural firm of Duhring, Okie, and Ziegler with Brognard Okie (1875-1945) and Carl A. Ziegler (1878-1953). In 1918, Okie withdrew and the firm continued as Duhring and Ziegler until 1924, when Duhring went out on his own.[1]

Edmund B. Gilchrist
(1885-1953)

Born in Germantown, Edmund B. Gilchrist, like Duhring, was a Philadelphian. He went to Germantown Friends School, Dexel Institute of Technology (now Drexel University) and to the University of Pennsylvania as an undergraduate. Unlike the other two Woodward architects, he did not earn a degree in architecture, instead apprenticing briefly with Horace Trumbauer and then for five years with Wilson Eyre, both important Philadelphia architects. Gilchrist opened his own firm in 1911, and went to work for the Woodwards in the 1920s. His best-known commissions for them was Linden Court on Willow Grove Avenue and Lincoln Drive and a few single-family houses in the area.[2]

Robert Rodes McGoodwin
(1886-1967)

Of the three Woodward architects, Robert Rodes McGoodwin was George Woodward's favorite. He received the greatest number of commissions from him. McGoodwin studied architecture at the University of Pennsylvania and the Pennsylvania Academy of Fine Arts. He won the university's Arthur Spayd Brooke Medal for Design (1907) and the academy's Cresson Traveling Scholarship (1908) for study in Europe. Before leaving, he worked briefly for Trumbauer. Returning to the United States, he teamed up with fellow University of Pennsylvania student, Samuel D. Hawley, and it was from this office that he first began to work for George Woodward.[3]

In 1912 the McGoodwin & Hawley partnership dissolved, but McGoodwin retained his ties to Woodward and developed a flourishing office on his own, designing the master plans and a number of the houses for both the "French" and "English" Villages. In 1942 he wrote a monograph, arranged by themes, which included chapters on the "Influence of Colonial America," the "Influence of England," the "Influence of France," and the "Influence of Italy." These chapters give a good deal of insight into the design inspiration of the Woodward architects.

---

1. Tatman and Moss, *Biographical Dictionary of Philadelphia Architects*, 221, 514-15, 304-5.

2. Ibid.

3. Ibid.

George Woodward, in his *Memoirs*, complained that the land adjacent to Wissahickon Heights "was not so attractive nor so easy to develop as the Houston properties. Some of it was lower and had ponds on it."[10] The more irregular nature of this land pushed the Woodwards and their architects to create an inspired integration of houses and landscape terraced into the gently sloping hillside.

The Woodwards commissioned approximately 180 houses in West Chestnut Hill and West Mt. Airy, generally building out from the edges of Wissahickon Heights. They disliked the name "Wissahickon Heights" and had it changed to St. Martin's, after the local church that Houston had built. Over a 30-year period, beginning in 1904, the Woodwards built a variety of housing types, along with an English and a French "Village" in Mt. Airy and Chestnut Hill.[11] These village developments gave the feeling of a neighborhood within a neighborhood and greatly enriched the community experience.

Almost everything the Woodwards commissioned in Chestnut Hill and Mt. Airy was designed by three Philadelphia architects—H. Louis Duhring, Robert Rodes McGoodwin, and Edmund B. Gilchrist. Not as well known as Mellor, Meigs & Howe, their work for the Woodwards made their reputations. For a number of years George Woodward gathered in his office once a week with these men to go over plans and ideas. He wrote, "Each architect had to submit his designs to the other two and myself for criticism. [It was] a happy, harmonious group working for the common good."[12]

Woodward realized that, with the high cost of property in cities, it was important to make the most efficient use of the land. For two decades, he commissioned his architects to design a remarkable diversity of housing types—single houses, twins and triplets of varying sizes, quads (essentially two twins back to back), larger clusters of six to eight attached houses (which often looked like one enormous, rambling manor house), courts of different configurations, crescents and "villages." The density of these housing types reflect the different zones of density structuring West Chestnut Hill and West Mt. Airy, with the smaller, tighter house types and lots located closer to the ridge road (Germantown Avenue) and the larger ones bordering Wissahickon Park.

Following the precedent of Henry Howard Houston, the Woodwards rented their houses, lived in the neighborhood themselves, and took a personal interest in maintaining the houses and streetscapes. Tenants were responsible for keeping up the interiors, and the Woodwards assumed responsibility for the exteriors, as well as for the landscape. This policy gave them continuing control over the design.

The Woodwards maintained rents below market value, expecting only a six-percent return on investment to keep tenants for long periods and to compensate them for the equity they would have gained through home ownership.[13] The Woodwards also feared that high rents and house prices would exclude young couples. They wanted Chestnut Hill and Mt. Airy to have a variety of age groups and created a system that accommodated changes in family size. Young tenants could start out in one of the smaller rentals and "graduate" to a larger house after they had children. Once the children were grown and had left home, the parents could move into a court, where the units were smaller, more compact and often joined together.

The French Village

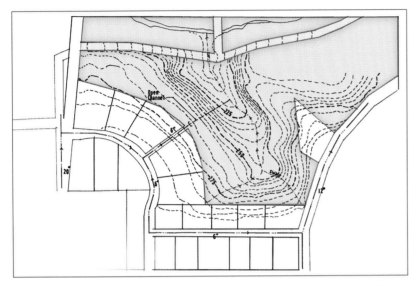

The French Village is the most varied and interesting of all the Woodward developments. It created a special enclave without gates or barriers to the rest of the community. The development provided an unusual mix of different house sizes and types, all built of local materials. Using the plants found in Wissahickon Park, the back gardens, streets and fronts of the properties appeared to be extensions of the forest in the valley.

Topographic map of the French Village, showing the individual properties wrapped around a tributary finger of the Cresheim Creek. This finger reaches deep into the built fabric. The meadows and woodlands of the park come directly up to the backs of the private lots and merge into the gardens. Source: Drawing by Neil Kirkwood for an "Independent Study" with Leslie Sauer and Carol Franklin at the Department of Landscape Architecture, University of Pennsylvania, 1983. Kirkland is now chairman of the Department of Landscape Architecture at Harvard University

At Elbow Lane in the French Village, the houses on the park side are below the street and step down into Cresheim Valley. The houses on the opposite side are above the street. In this way, the entire development responds to the original landforms. Gutters made of Wissahickon schist border the streets. Where the house lots are bigger, a thick band of forest on the property edge reinforces the feeling of a country lane. Source: Photograph by CLF

The French Village
Designed by Robert Rodes McGoodwin
Developer George and Gertrude Woodward 1920–1930

Located just below Chestnut Hill in West Mt. Airy, the French Village sits on a wooded site along the upper slopes of the Cresheim Valley, the largest of the tributary extensions within Wissahickon Park. The development has two quite separate pieces. Gate Lane was designed around a small, straight road, lined on one side with modest houses on half-acre lots, each for rental only. Elbow Lane was designed as a long, curving road, with a variety of lot sizes on both sides of the street for families of different requirements and incomes. These lots were sold to private owners who commissioned the Woodward architects to build their houses. McGoodwin designed the roads, lot layouts, gardens, most of the houses on Elbow Lane and all the houses on Gate Lane, assuring high quality design and craftsmanship.[1]

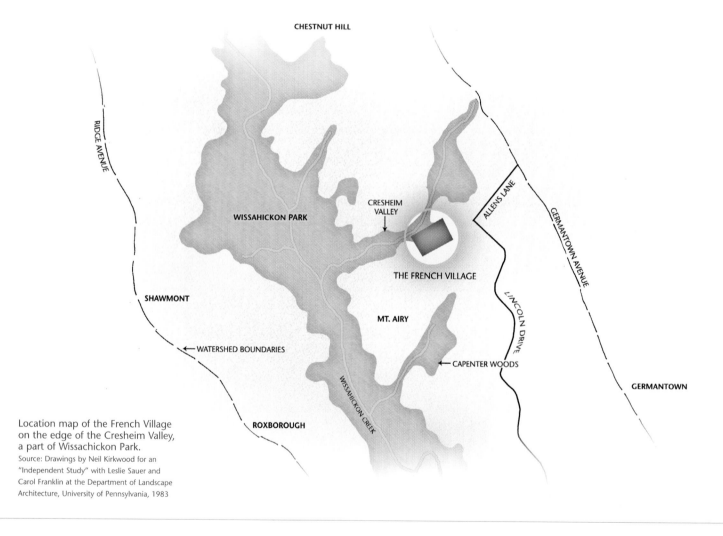

Location map of the French Village on the edge of the Cresheim Valley, a part of Wissachickon Park.
Source: Drawings by Neil Kirkwood for an "Independent Study" with Leslie Sauer and Carol Franklin at the Department of Landscape Architecture, University of Pennsylvania, 1983

The houses in the French Village vary in their relationship to the street. The houses on Gate Lane are pressed right up against the roadway with little or no front yard. The houses on Elbow Lane are often on large properties with deep setbacks. The French Village is so special, partly because of the unexpected variety within a consistent texture, color and design vocabulary.

1. Christopher Gray, "The French Village," *House and Garden*, December, 1983, 82-86.

Gate House at the entrance to Gate Lane from Elbow Lane.
Source: *House and Garden*, July, 1929. CHHS

Site plan of the French Village, showing Wissahickon Park along the Cresheim Valley, coming up to the backyards.
Source: Drawings by Neil Kirkwood for an "Independent Study" with Leslie Sauer and Carol Franklin at the Department of Landscape Architecture, University of Pennsylvania, 1983

The French Village | Gate Lane

This incredibly compact row of houses, with almost "zero lot lines," borrows the park at the back to give a spaciousness to these otherwise small, individual houses on half-acre lots. House, garden, garage and communal parking areas are connected by walls that create a sense of a small village and a very private enclave. The houses are one room deep and step down into the steep valley. The use of local stone and the intimate, multi-leveled gardens demonstrate the principles of the Wissahickon style on a modest scale.

The "Gate House" at the entrance to Gate Lane, in the French Village.
Source: *House and Garden*, July, 1929. CHHS

In an article written for *The Survey* magazine in 1920, George Woodward promised that he would not raise rents as long as the same tenants stayed in a house. The only exception would be when the City of Philadelphia raised real estate taxes. In this case, the tax increase would be passed along in order to make the tenants tax-conscious voters in municipal elections.[14] While these arrangements with tenants could be criticized as paternalistic and controlling, Woodward was a friendly, outgoing man, who managed landlord-tenant relations with a light touch.

Following the class and racial prejudices of the time, Woodward rented almost exclusively to professionals or businessmen who were white Anglo-Saxon Protestants. Both he and Gertrude favored interesting people who could contribute to community life, letting houses to a number of prominent Philadelphia artists. They provided a studio on St. George's Road for Brandywine school painter Violet Oakley, a house on the lower part of St. Martin's Lane for Leopold Stokowski, the legendary director of the Philadelphia Orchestra, and attracted the Willet's Stained Glass Studio from Pittsburgh, renting them a renovated icehouse at the corner of Springfield Avenue and Lincoln Drive.[15]

The success of the Woodward neighborhoods resulted from the high quality of construction, the wide variety of housing types, the care with which they chose their architects and the family's great wealth, which enabled them to control large pieces of property. Unlike sprawling post-World War II suburbia, the density and physical layout of their clustered housing contributed to the cohesiveness of the community. Neighbors lived cheek-to-jowl and shared common spaces—walkways, alleys, parking courts and the "green" in front of the houses. At a larger scale, Woodward tenants could take advantage of the semi-public open spaces around community institutions—the church, the cricket club, the school, the railroad corridor and the historic commercial spine along the ridge road (Germantown Avenue).

The Wissahickon Style

A serendipitous convergence of many factors—architects, craftsmen, nurserymen, and enlightened developers—came together in an era of prosperity when new ways of living were being explored. The new development blended with earlier patterns to create a legacy of a livable community with a strong, local character. Without the riparian park, with its tributary fingers penetrating into the residential neighborhoods, there could not have been this sensitive response in the built fabric, expressed as a series of transitions from the most urban areas of the community to the most natural.

The multiple lessons of Mt. Airy and Chestnut Hill are essential to appreciate, understand and preserve the best of the Wissahickon Style—when nature and community formed a "sympathetic bond."[16] Beyond local applications, these lessons can be adapted to create new, more organic and more environmentally sound communities, where the natural world is fused imaginatively into the overall design.

Notes

The notes and index for all four volumes of this work are found in Volume IV, pages 845-901. In addition, in a nod to reader friendliness, the notes for the first three volumes are repeated on un-numbered pages at the end of each of those volumes.

Chapter 6: Making the Park (1850-1890)

1. On the Victorian age in the United States, see Daniel Walker Howe ed., *Victorian America* (Philadelphia, 1976), and Thomas J. Schlereth, *Victorian America: Transformations in Everyday Life* (New York, 1991). On the Victorian Age in Great Britain and in the British Empire see John M. MacKenzie ed., *The Victorian Vision* (London, 2001). For Victorian attitudes, see particularly Walter E. Houghton, *The Victorian Frame of Mind* (New Haven, Conn. 1957).

2. On Brown and Repton, see Tom Williamson, *Polite Landscapes: Gardens and Society in Eighteenth-Century England* (Phoenix Mill, U.K., 1995), 77-99, 141-159;Thomas Hinde, *Capability Brown: The Story of a Master Gardener* (New York, 1986); Roger Turner, *Capability Brown and the Eighteen-Century English Landscape* (New York, 1985); Elizabeth Barlow Rogers, *Landscape Design: A cultural and Architectural History* (New York, 2001) 250-256.

3. Galen Cranz, *The Politics of Park Design: A History of Urban Parks in America* (Cambridge, Mass., 1982), 3-59. This book also gives a good analysis and description of the urban pleasure park of the second half of the 19th century. See also Raymond M. Weinstein, "Amusement Parks," in Neil Larry Shumsky ed., Encyclopedia of Urban America (Santa Barbara, Ca., 1998), 22, and Judith A. Adams, *The American Amusement Park Industry: A History of Technology and Thrills* (Boston, 1991).

4. Fielder, *Love and Death*, xxvii-xxxiv.

5. See Stuart McConnell, *Glorious Contentment: The Grand Army of the Republic, 1865-1900* (Chapel Hill, N. C., 1992), 175-79.

6. On consolidation see Michael McCarthy, "The Philadelphia Consolidation Act of 1854: A Reappraisal," *Pennsylvania Magazine of History and Biography* (PMHB), October 1982, 531-84; Eli Kirk Price, *The History of the Consolidation of the City of Philadelphia* (Philadelphia, 1873); Elizabeth M. Geffin, "Industrial Development and Social Crisis," in *A 300-Year History*, 307-62; and Russel R. Weigley, "The Border City in the Civil War," in Ibid., 363-76.

   Before consolidation, Germantown had become an independent borough within Philadelphia County. Many of its residents were angry over what they saw as a legislative *coup d'etat*, fearing that their taxes would increase as a result of the merger, or that they would lose their sense of community identity. An editorial in the *Germantown Telegraph* for February 12, 1851, was typical of these sentiments: "From every quarter of the county, we hear but one sentiment relative to the villainous scheme to unite the rural parts of the county with the city. Meetings are being held, and remonstrances are being signed, representing this scheme in its true light. We have no doubt these representations will be heeded. . . ."

   Despite protests from the northwestern communities, the consolidation act passed three years later. In future years these sentiments would resurface in proposals to secede by communities adjacent to the Wissahickon or in refusals to admit that their communities were part of Philadelphia, listing their addresses as Germantown, Chestnut Hill, or Roxborough, Pennsylvania. David R. Contosta, *Suburb in the City: Chestnut Hill, Philadelphia* (Columbus Oh., 1992), 157-58.

7. Gary B. Nash, *First City: Philadelphia and the Forging of Historical Memory* (Philadelphia, 2002), 144. Nash has called this period "the most violent era of the city's history."

8. See the *Germantown Telegraph*, January 4, February 12, February 19, and September 24, 1851.

9. The best and most recent brief account of the origins of Fairmount Park is an article by Elizabeth Milroy, "Assembling Fairmount Park," in Katherine Martinez and Page Talbott (eds.) *Philadelphia's Cultural Landscape: The Sartain Family Legacy* (Philadelphia, 2000). Milroy is currently working on a new book on the origins of Fairmount Park. See also FPC, *Annual Report*, 1868, 10. A very thorough account of the early development of the park system can be found in the Fairmount Park Commission's first *Annual Report* in 1868, 5-13.

10. Quoted in Milroy, "Assembling Fairmount Park," 81

11. Thomas P. Cope, *Philadelphia Merchant: The Diary of Thomas P. Cope*, 1800-1851 (South Bend, Ind., 1978), 411-18.

12. Milroy, "Assembling Fairmount Park," 78-79.

13. Fairmount Park Commission (FPC), *Annual Report*, 1868, 9.

14. Lecture, Elizabeth Milroy to the Friends of the Wissahickon, March 21, 2002.

15. Milroy, "Assembling Fairmount Park," 76.

16. Public Law 547, Commonwealth of Pennsylvania, March 26, 1867.

17. Dennis Bechara, "Eminent Doman and the Rule of Law," *The Freeman*, May 1985.

18. Charles S. Keyser, *Fairmount Park: Sketches of its Scenery, Waters, and History* (Philadelphia, 1872), 92. Keyser was one of a number of Philadelphians instrumental in establishing Fairmount Park.

19. Ibid., 10.

20. FPC, *Annual Report*, 1870, 42.

21. Ibid., 41-42.

22. Ibid., 41.

23. Ibid. 41-42.

24. FPC, *Annual Report* 1871, 49.

25. FPC, *Annual Report*, 1878, 67. This report was the first issued since 1871.

26. Ibid., 89-90.

27. Ibid., 32-33.

28. Ibid., 33.

29. FPC, *Annual Report*, 1899, 7.

Chapter 7:
Preserving the Middle Valley (1900-1935)

1. Macfarlane, *Early Chestnut Hill*, 40.

2. Ibid, 128; Contosta, *Suburb in the City*, 30.

3. There are two histories of Chestnut Hill College: Sister Mary Helen Kashuba, *Tradition and Risk* (Philadelphia, 1999) and John Lukacs, *A Sketch of the History of Chestnut Hill College, 1924-1974* (Philadelphia, 1975).

4. Contosta, *Suburb in the City*, 74.

5. Morris Arboretum Staff, *Firmly Planted: The Story of the Morris Arboretum* (Philadelphia, 2001), 6-7.

6. John Morris, quoted in Ibid., 7.

7. Quoted in *Seasons*, the newsletter of the Morris Arboretum, (Spring 2003), 3.

8. Quoted in Ibid.

9. *Firmly Planted*, 6-7.

10. Ibid., 9.

11. Hocker, "Along the Wissahickon: Erdenheim."

12. Widener: Website:www.connections.smsd.org/titanic/widener.htm

13. Scrapbook 91 and 131, at the Historical Society of Montgomery County. This acreage includes the 117.33 acres that George Widener deeded to the Natural Lands Trust in 1972. Information from Curt Bish, Montgomery County Planning Commission. The total acreage of Erdenheim Farm is from the Whitemarsh Township Department of Building and Zoning.

14. The figure of 98 acres in 2001 comes from the Carson Valley School, courtesy of Clare Strenger, Director of Development.

15. Contosta, *Suburb in the City*, 154; Contosta, *Philadelphia's Progressive Orphanage: The Carson Valley School* (University Park, Pa., 1997), 10, 12, 93.

16. Board Minutes, Carson College for Orphan Girls, May 15, 1925.

17. Campbell, Scrapbooks, 6: 26; *The News* (a Germantown weekly newspaper), May 87, 1908; Whitemarsh Township, Department of Building and Zoning.

18. On golf course design see James M. Mayo, *The American Country Club: Its Origins and Development* (New Brunswick, N.J., 1998), 72, 128-129.

19. Contosta, *Suburb in the City*, 153-154; Campbell, Scrapbooks, 44: 72; David R. Contosta, *The Philadelphia Cricket Club* (Philadelphia, 2004), 34-39.

20. Plan of Philadelphia Cricket Club's Flourtown Golf Course, October 5, 1923, Philadelphia Cricket Club Collection, CHHS Archives; George V. Strong to Provident Mutual Life Insurance Company, August 18, 1953, Cricket Club Collection, CHHS; Whitemarsh Township, Department of Building and Zoning.

21. Fundraising letter from Wissahickon Park Extension Committee, undated, but probably written sometime in 1913, Morris Arboretum Archives, courtesy Robert Gutowski; Campbell, Scrapbooks, 33: 166.

22. *Philadelphia Bulletin*, April 9, 1927.

23. Theresa Stuhlman, archivist, Fairmount Park Commission, Memorandum to Fort Washington Park file, September 8, 1999, Fairmount Park Archives.

24. FPC *Annual Report*, 1929, 5; 1930, 6,7.

Chapter 8:
Coming of Age in a New Century (1890-1910)

1. Henry Adams to Brooks Adams, February 7, 1900, in J.C. Levenson et al. eds.*The Letters of Henry Adams*, (Cambridge, Mass., 1988), 87. Henry Adams was the great-grandson of John Adams, a signer of the Declaration of Independence, second president of the United States, and the grandson of John Quincy Adams, the sixth president of the United States. On Adams's mixed emotions about the United States at the beginning of the 20th century, see David R. Contosta, *Henry Adams and the American Experiment* (Boston, 1980), 91-107.

2. Jellett, Scrapbooks, 1: 29.

3. Lincoln Steffens, "Philadelphia, Corrupt and Contented," *McClure's Magazine* (July 1903), 249.

4. David Browlee, *Building the City Beautiful: The Benjamin Franklin Parkway and the Philadelphia Museum of Art* (Philadelphia, 1989), 20-27.

5. Ibid., 14-21.

6. Ibid., 21.

7. City Parks Association, Fairmount Park Art Association "A Special Report on the City Plan," Philadelphia, 1902.

8. These figures are taken from the FPC *Annual Report*, 1912, 5; 1938, 3. There were no annual reports between 1899 and 1912. It is only in the 1912 report that expansion figures are given, going back to 1888.

9. Wallace Roberts and Todd, *Fairmount Park Master Plan Summary*, 1983, 2.

10. On Goodman and this association see Contosta, *Suburb in the City*, 165-67.

11. Ibid.

12. *Public Ledger*, September 26, 1895.

13. *Evening Telegraph*, May 2, 1900.

14. Campbell, Scrapbooks, 9: 183; 16: 48; 21: 48; 22: 7.

15. Jellett, Scrapbooks, 1: 29.

16. Witold Rybczynski, *A Clearing in the Distance: Frederick Law Olmsted and America in the 19th Century*, (New York, 1999), 288.

17. Jellett, Scrapbooks, 1: 29.

18. Jellett, Scrapbooks, 4: 64; FPC, *Annual Report*, 1899, 7-9.

19. *Telegraph*, October 30, 1903; Jellett, Scrapbooks, 5: 81.

20. Cranz, *Politics of Park Design*, 49.

21. *Philadelphia Record*, Spring 1900.

21. Jellett, Scrapbooks, 1: 29.

23. *Philadelphia Evening Bulletin*, November 23, 1901.

24. Jellett, Scrapbooks, 1: 28, 2: 85.

25. Ibid., 2: 91; West, *The Wissahickon*, 60.

26. Cranz, *Politics of Park Design*, 49.

27. Jellett, Scrapbooks, 4: 125; *West, The Wissahickon*, 68.

28. *Philadelphia Record*, January 12, 1902.

29. Quoted in Michael Kammen, *Mystic Chords of Memory: The Transformation of Tradition in American Culture* (New York, 1993), 262.

Chapter 9:
Conservation and Civic Activism (1910-1940)

1. Website: Library of Congress, *American Memory: The Evolution of the Conservation Movement, 1850-1920*, Preface: "The Early Conservation Movement in Context." http://memory.loc.gov/ammem/index.html.

2. William T. Hornaday, *Our Vanishing Wildlife; Its Extermination and Preservation* (1913; reprint, New York, 1970), ix.

3. Alexis de Tocqueville, *Democracy in America* (1835; reprint, New York, 1956), 198.

4. Robert D. Putnam, *Bowling Alone* (New York, 2000), 19.

5. Ibid., 23-24.

6. Walter Sargent, "The Passing of the Old Red Schoolhouse," *New England Magazine* (December, 1900), 422.

7. Jellett, Scrapbooks, 5: 111.

8. West, *The Wissahickon*, 70, 80.

9. *Philadelphia Record*, November 25, 1901.

10. Jellett, Scrapbooks, 4: 80.

11. FPC, *Annual Report*, 1912, 13; FPC Minutes, June 8, 1900, January 13, 1915. On the demolition of the Old Log Cabin in 1872, see Jellett, Scrapbooks 2: 60.

12. *Independent-Gazette*, September 23, 1909, September 9, 1910, May 31, 1912; Campbell, Scrapbooks, 10: 98; 14: 28; 19: 8; 17: 6.

13. Jellett, Scrapbooks, 5: 73; 7: 62-63; Eunice Story Ullman, Valley Green Inn, unpublished typescript, dated May 26, 1970, 6, Wissahickon Collection, CHHS.

14. *Germantown Guide*, August 4, 1900; Campbell, Scrapbooks, 10: 38; FPC Minutes, December 28 and June 8, 1900, April 12, 1901.

15. Clipping from the *North American*, 1901, in Jellett, Scrapbooks, 7: 63.

16. See also *FOW Newsletter*, Spring, 1994. A pamphlet passed out at the Valley Green Inn during the 1960s not only claimed that Washington and Lafayette had dined there, but that the inn had been founded in 1683 and was frequented by Pastorius and other early settlers in the area, CHHS.

17. Ullman, Valley Green Inn, CHHS.

18. Jellett, Scrapbooks, 7: 54, 66 and 67; 9: 3.

19. Campbell, Scrapbooks, 10: 38; Jellett, Scrapbooks, 7: 62.

20. For these arguments see Campbell Scrapbooks, 21: 123; 24: 61. Unidentified newspaper clipping in Campbell Scrapbooks, 24: 61.

21. *Philadelphia Evening Bulletin*, November 29, 1909.

22. FPC, *Annual Report*, 1912, 7; 1914, 12.

23. Campbell, Scrapbooks, 28: 49; 29: 159, 202 and 204; *Germantown Guide*, December 4, 1915. Campbell, Scrapbooks, 28: 201.

24. *Philadelphia Evening Bulletin*, March 31, 1921, March 28, 1922, April 10, 1926, July 28, 1927, December 5, 1930.

25 Jellett, Scrapbooks, 1: 44; Campbell, Scrapbooks, 4: 6; 5: 204.

26. Pennsylvania State Game Commission Website: http://www.pgc.state.pa.us/.

27. Ibid.

28. Ibid.

29. *Independent-Gazette*, July 28, 1911.

30. On the origins of the name Chestnut Hill, see Contosta, *Suburb in the City*, 12-13.

31. The chestnut blight spread approximately 50 miles a year. Website: American Chestnut Society www.acf.org/.

32. Charles E. Little, *The Dying of the Trees: The Pandemic in America's Forests* (New York, 1995), 176.

33. Cornelius Weygandt, *The Wissahickon Hills: Memories of Leisure Hours Out of Doors in an Old Countryside* (Philadelphia, 1930), 237.

34. Jellett, Scrapbooks, 6: 91.

35. Ibid., 7: 70.

36. FOW "Newsletter," September 1928.

37. Quoted in Ibid., 5.

38. Livingston E. Jones, treasurer, to the Friends of the Wissahickon, December 11, 1926, in Jellett, Scrapbooks, 7: 70.

39. Tom Keels, "The Friends of the Wissahickon Celebrate 75th Anniversary," *Chestnut Hill Local*, September 30, 1999.

40. FPC, *Annual Report*, 1927, 5-6, 1928, 4-5, 1930, 6.

41. FOW Board Minutes, October 1, 1926. See also minutes of October 21, 1927.

42. A list of trees planted by the FOW between 1926-1932, compiled from FOW Board minutes, committee reports, and annual reports, 1926-1932.

Non-natives like the Japanese honeysuckle became a major problem in the valley while forsythia has simply died out. Note: some common and scientific names used here have changed over time.

hemlock (*Tsuga canadensis*)
witch hazel (*Hamamalis virginiana*)
pitch pine (*Pinus rigida*) out of region
catalpa (*Catalpa bignoniodes*) out of region
white pine (*Pinus strobus*)
shadbush (*Amelanchier arborea*)
red pine (*Pinus resinosa*) out of region
red bud (*Cercis candensis*)
rhododendron (*Rhododendron maximum*) out of region
black walnut (*Juglans nigra*)
hawthorne (*Crataegus crus-galli*) non native
red birch (*Betula nigra*)
paper birch (*Betula papyrifera*) out of biome
scarlet oak (*Quercus coccinea*)
dogwood (*Cornus florida*)
locust (*Robinia pseudoacacia*) out of region
magnolia (*Magnolia glauca*)
viburnum (*Viburnum*)
honeysuckle (*Lonicera japonica*) non native, invasive exotic
white birch (*Betula populifolia*) out of biome
mountain laurel (*Kalmia latifolia*)
beech (*Fagus*)
forsythia (*Forsythia*) non native
white spruce (*Picea glauca*) out of biome

43. FOW Board Minutes, May 28, 1929. September 29, 1931; Francis R. Strawbridge, president, FOW to "Dear Friend," June 25, 1935, letter found among FOW board minutes of the period.

44. Ibid., *FOW Newsletter* (June, 1936).

45. FPC, *Annual Report*, 1933, 1.

46. FPC, *Annual Report*, 1936, 43; 1937, 36. Copies of some of the WPA "work orders" may be found in the FOW archives. A good summary of the relief work undertaken by the FOW and then by various New Deal agencies appears in the FOW Newsletter for May, 1938.

47. FPC *Annual Report*, 1931,1937.

48. Report of Anna Blakiston Day, FOW board secretary, May 2, 1931.

49. Benjamin Kline, *First along the River: A Brief History of the U. S. Environmental Movement*, (Lanham, Md., 2000), 64-7.

50. Campbell, Scrapbooks, 23: 63; Jellett, Scrapbooks, 5: 12. According to the *Germantown Independent-Gazette* in May 1900, the golf club was organized by residents of Germantown and Chestnut Hill. The Fairmount Park Commission gave the club permission to use the Monastery, or old Gorgas Mansion, as a clubhouse. See Jellett, Scrapbooks 5: 25 FPC *Annual Report.*, 1940.

51. Albert Howard Weir ed., *Parks: A Manual of Municipal and County Parks* (New York, 1928), xix and endorsement letter of President Coolidge.

52. Ibid., xxi.

53. Katherine E. Cowing, "WPA Outbuildings in the Wissahickon" (University of Pennsylvania master's thesis, 1997), 12-13.

54. *Philadelphia Inquirer*, November 19, 1935, December 15, 1935.

55. *Philadelphia Evening Bulletin* November 6, 1937.

56. Thomas Goode and John F Bauman, *People, Poverty and Politics: Pennsylvanians During the Great Depression* (Lewisburg, Pa., 1981).

57. Priscilla Ferguson Clement, "The Works Progress Administration in Pennsylvania, 1935-1940," *PMHB* (April 1971), 244-60.

58. Kline, *First along the River*, (Lanham, Md., 2000), 64-7.

59. *Philadelphia Evening Bulletin*, May 2, 1936, November 1, 12, 15, and 16, 1937; *Germantown Courier*, December 8, 1937.

60. *Philadelphia Inquirer*, November 11, 1937.

61. *Philadelphia Evening Bulletin* November 1, 1937.

62. Cowing, "WPA Outbuildings in the Wissahickon," 1, 28.

63. Albert H. Good, *Park Structures and Facilities* (Washington, D. C., 1935). This book was later expanded into a three volume work, *Park and Recreation Structures* (Washington, D. C., 1938).

64. Quoted in Cowing, "WPA Outbuildings in the Wissahickon," 15.

65. Ibid., 2.

66. *The Beehive*, June 1939; Jellett, Scrapbooks, 8, 148; *FOW Newsletter* (Spring 1994); FPC Minutes, March 10, 1937.

67. A copy of this first trail map, issued in 1940, can be found among the map collections at the CHHS.

68. Website: Library of Congress, *American Memory: The Evolution of the Conservation Movement, 1850-1920*, Preface: "The Early Conservation Movement in Context." http://memory.loc.gov/ammem/index.html.

Chapter 10:
Five Wissahickon Communities (1900-1920)

1. Harold E. Spaulding, "Germantown," in *Workshop of the World* (Wallingford, Pa., 1990), 3-3 to 3-5.

2. Harry M. Tinkcom et al., *Historic Germantown From the Founding to the Early Part of the Nineteenth Century* (Philadelphia, 1955), 86-87.

3. Ibid.

4. Initial letter of invitation, Germantown and Chestnut Hill Improvement Association, December 1900, Community Improvement Association files, GHS.

5. These attitudes of Germantown's residents are expressed in a number of papers read before the Site and Relic Society of Germantown, collected and published as *Germantown History* (Philadelphia, 1915).

6. Duffin, interview by authors, April 5, 2007.

7. On the early history of Roxborough see Joseph Starne Miles and William H. Cooper, *A Historical Sketch of Roxborough, Manayunk, Wissahickon* (Philadelphia, 1940).

8. See John C. Manton, *Victorian Roxborough: An Architectural History* (Philadelphia, 1983).

9. The concept of parkways in the United States was largely the creation of Frederick Law Olmsted, who, according to Olmsted biographer Witold Rybcznski, wanted to bring "trees and greenery into the congested grid of city streets." Rybczynski, *A Clearing in the Distance*, 289.

10. On the early suburbanization of Chestnut Hill, see Contosta, *Suburb in the City*, 36-77.

11. The first of these two rail lines was the Chestnut Hill Railroad, opened in 1854, which connected at Germantown with the Philadelphia, Germantown and Norristown Railroad. Later, the Reading Railroad bought out both of these companies. The Chestnut Hill Railroad ran just east of Germantown Avenue (the ridge road), and opened up that side of the community to development in the mid-19th century.

12. On the development of Wissahickon Heights, see Contosta, *Suburb in the City*, 78-99 and David R. Contosta, *A Philadelphia Family: The Houstons and Woodwards of Chestnut Hill* (Philadelphia, 1988), 23-32.

13 Planned cities, towns, and neighborhoods had existed since the colonial era. William Penn and his surveyor, Thomas Holme, carefully laid out the original two-square-mile Philadelphia grid to be a rational and livable city. In the second half of the 19th century, there were a number of planned suburbs: Short Hills, New Jersey, designed by Alexander Jackson Davis; and Riverside, Illinois (near Chicago) and Druid Hills (outside Atlanta, Georgia), both designed by Frederick Law Olmsted. See Charles Beveridge, Paul Rocheleau and David Larkin, *Frederick Law Olmsted: Designing the American Landscape* (New York, 1998), 99-107; Robert Fishman, *Bourgeois Utopias: The Rise and Fall of Suburbia* (New York, 1987), 125-33.

Chapter 11: The Wissahickon Style (1920-1935)

1. See Walter C. Kidney, *The Architecture of Choice: Eclecticism in America, 1880-1930* (New York, 1974), 43-48; G.H. Edgell, *The American Architecture of Today* (New York, 1928), 98-101; and Thomas E. Tallmadge, *The Story of Architecture in America* (New York, 1936), 267-70.

2. Gwendolyn Wright, *Building the Dream: A Social History of Housing in America* (New York, 1981), 168-69. See also Hans Krabbendam, "Model Merion: Attempts to Create a Community in a Small Wealthy Philadelphia Suburb," in Hans Bertens and Theo d'Haen, eds., *The Small Town in America* (Amsterdam, 1995), p. 165.

3. Matlack Price, "The House of Robert T. McCracken, Esq., Germantown," *The Architectural Record* (1921), 49: 57.

4. Eileen Boris, *Art and Labor: Ruskin, Morris, and the Craftsman Ideal in America* (Philadelphia, 1986); R. J. Clark, ed., *The Arts and Crafts Movement in America, 1876-1916* (Princeton, 1972); and Paul Thompson, *The Works of William Morris* (New York, 1993).

5. Daniel Wilson Randle, in the preface to a reprint of *A Monograph of the Works of Mellor, Meigs and Howe*, (Boulder, Colorado, 1991), n.p.

6. On these Italian stonemasons and the local quarries, see Mike Yanni and F. Marcoe Rivinus, *The Quarries and Stone Masons of Chestnut Hill* (Philadelphia, 2004).

7. There were quarries on the northeast corner of Germantown Avenue and Cresheim Valley Road, another diagonally across the street on the southwest corner of Germantown Avenue and Mermaid Lane and, a third, south of Cresheim Creek on the east side of Germantown Avenue. Other quarries were located on Mermaid Lane between Ardleigh Street and Winston Road and in the 200 block of East Willow Grove Avenue, with several others clustered near Waverly Road and Cheltenham Avenue.

8. Andres Duany, *Smartcode: A Comprehensive Form-based Planning Ordinance* (Spring, 2005), 2.

9. A technique employed in redesign of Japanese gardens. The "borrowed landscape" incorporates views beyond the garden so that the landscape seems to extend beyond its boundaries.

10. George Woodward, *Memoirs of a Mediocre Man* (Philadelphia, 1935), 107.

11. See Contosta, *A Philadelphia Family*, 66-67. See also George Woodward, "Another Aspect of the Quadruple House," *Architectural Record* (July 1913), 51-55 and Matlack Price, "Architecture and the Housing Problem: Recent Work of Durhing, Oakie, and Ziegler," *Architectural Record*, (September, 1913), 24-247.

12. Woodward, *Memoirs*, 109.

13. Ibid., 107. The Woodwards may have also kept the rents low as a demonstration that wealthy families could afford to build modest but attractive residences and still make a small profit—a concept then known as "limited dividend" housing. George Woodward, president of Philadelphia's Octavia Hill Association for many years, probably borrowed this idea from the practices of this organization. A private real estate group, the Octavia Hill Association, purchased run-down houses in the city, repaired them, and rented them to working-class families for affordable rates, but rates that would also allow some return on the initial investment and provide enough capital to acquire new properties. This idea had been pioneered in England by the art critic and social reformer John Ruskin who provided funds to Octavia Hill to establish the first housing association that rehabilitated and rented housing to the poor in London.

14. George Woodward, "Landlord and Tenant," *The Survey*, December 11, 1920.

15. Contosta, *A Philadelphia Family*, 72.

16. The phrase "sympathetic bond' is taken from an article by Arthur I. Meigs, "Garth: House of Robert T. McCracken,Esq., Germantown, Philadelphia," *Architectural Record* (November, 1928).